# The Maniac in the Cellar

# The
# Maniac in the Cellar

Sensation Novels of the 1860s

**Winifred Hughes**

Princeton University Press
Princeton, New Jersey

To Fred

# Contents

But think of the shifts and perplexities of a wife with eight husbands, being not only mysteriously married like Aurora Floyd to her noble husband's horse-trainer, but . . . also to the Emperor of China . . . ; also, under peculiar circumstances, to the giant of a show that is coming to be set up at a fair in the neighborhood; also to a maniac whom she keeps in the cellar.

*Examiner*, 1863

. . . she gave me the Moonstone to read that was the first I read of Wilkie Collins East Lynne I read and the shadow of Ashlydyat Mrs. Henry Wood Henry Dunbar by that other woman I lent him afterwards. . . .

Molly Bloom in *Ulysses*

# Preface

**T**his study began with Dickens, but it was not long before he wrote himself out of it—or rather, was written out of it by the likes of his contemporary rivals Wilkie
Collins, Charles Reade, and M. E. Braddon. Like Dickens,
the sensation novelists insinuated elements of crime and
mystery into the lives of ordinary, respectable middle-
class characters. Like Dickens, they shamelessly exploited the familiar stereotypes of popular melodrama, in
particular the central confrontation between heroine and
villain, which tended to focus all the implications of the
universal moral conflict between good and evil on the
single issue of the heroine's chastity. Unlike Dickens,
however, the sensation novelists revised the traditional
significance of this confrontation, replacing the original
moral certainty with moral ambiguity. The aspects of the
sensation novel that began to emerge in the course of my
research as the most interesting and the most definitive
were precisely those aspects that separated it from the
works of Dickens. The plight of Lady Dedlock, a subplot
in Dickens' *Bleak House*, becomes the mainspring of the
typical sensation novel; Dickens' vision of the violated
hearth begins to take over. His description of the "cold
sunshine" striking Lady Dedlock's portrait over the man-
tle at Chesney Wold might serve as an epigraph for the
entire genre: "Athwart the picture of my Lady, over the
great chimneypiece, it throws a broad bend-sinister of
light that strikes down crookedly into the hearth, and
seems to rend it." Although Dickens sympathizes with
the fallen woman, although he permits Sir Leicester Dedlock to forgive his errant wife, he still exacts the traditional penalty of stage melodrama: Lady Dedlock's death
for her sin. If Braddon or Collins had written *Bleak*

*House*, Lady Dedlock would not only have become the central character, she would probably have married her original lover, committed bigamy, and then patched things up with Sir Leicester. Or else she would have been an out-and-out villainess, doing away with both lover and blackmailer before she got caught. The values of Esther Summerson's vine-covered cottage in the country, which Dickens feels obliged to affirm in the end, are vitiated in the sensation novel; while the cottage itself is frequently enough supplied, its inhabitants are likely to be the former bigamists, adventuresses, and even prostitutes (see Collins' *New Magdalen*) whom Dickens could not have pardoned.

For advice and encouragement at various stages of this project, I would like to thank Mark Spilka, George P. Landow, Samuel Hynes, and A. Walton Litz. I would also like to thank Robert Scholes, who gave me both inspiration and employment while I was writing and who suggested the title. My greatest debt is to Roger B. Henkle, more friend than dissertation advisor at Brown University, who not only suggested the topic but kept me laughing and in graduate school. Karen Steele, Susan Geary, Fred Spar, Hildred H. Crill, Josephine N. Hughes, and Riley Hughes also contributed both research assistance and moral support. Sharon Coppa, Marilyn Walden, and Pat Onofri helped immeasurably with the typing of successive versions of the manuscript. Finally, without the generous support of Marjorie Sherwood of Princeton University Press and the eagle-eyed copyediting of Tam Curry, the maniac might have remained in the cellar.

*8 November 1979*                              *W. H.*

# The Maniac in the Cellar

# 1

## The Sensation Paradox

### I.

"I wants to make your flesh creep."
The Fat Boy in Dickens' *Pickwick Papers*

In 1863 the irrepressible Mr. Punch carried this mock advertisement for a new journal to be entitled "The Sensation Times, and Chronicle of Excitement":

This Journal will be devoted chiefly to the following objects; namely, Harrowing the Mind, Making the Flesh Creep, Causing the Hair to Stand on End, Giving Shocks to the Nervous System, Destroying Conventional Moralities, and generally Unfitting the Public for the Prosaic Avocations of Life.

Among the regular highlights were to be numbered "Some extraordinary revelations of the habits and actions of exceedingly Low Life," a selection of "Arsenical Literature," "Confidential communications of a terrific, sanguinary, or vicious description . . . addressed to the Editors," and "the most graphic accounts of all Crimes with Violence, merciless Corporal Punishments (especially in the case of children), Revolting Cruelties to Animals, and other interesting matters." But the central attraction, surpassing even the "carefully selected Horrors of every kind, from the English and Foreign newspapers," turned out to be nothing less than "A Sensation Novel itself," containing "atrocities hitherto undreamed of, even by the most fashionable fictionists of Paris," the whole to be concocted by "an eminent sensation novelist, who will shortly be at liberty under a ticket-of-leave."[1]

Any unfortunate reader who may have missed the

latest issue of "The Sensation Times" at any point during the decade of the 1860s need not have despaired, however, or have quelled his appetite for the perverse and the horrific. The same years that fostered the publication of *Framley Parsonage, Silas Marner, Wives and Daughters*, and other equally tame fare also produced *Foul Play, The Woman in White, Aurora Floyd,* and *The Shadow of Ashlydyat*. Any patron of Mudie's Library, plagued by all the wholesome vignettes of homely existence in town or cottage, had only to order a copy of the most recent sensation novel to find himself plunged into a turbulent universe far removed from mid-Victorian stodginess and respectability.

The typical sensation plots, more than a hundred years later, are still guaranteed to make the flesh creep and the hair stand on end, for one reason if not another. In *Lady Audley's Secret* by M. E. Braddon, the fragile, childish wife of Sir Michael Audley is gradually revealed as a secret bigamist who has unceremoniously disposed of her superfluous husband by pushing him down an abandoned well. In Charles Reade's *Griffith Gaunt*, the hero himself commits bigamy under complicated and murky circumstances that lead up to a grand confrontation between his two wives—the first on trial for his apparent murder, the second arriving only at the last moment to volunteer the evidence that acquits her rival. In *East Lynne* by Mrs. Henry Wood, the "sensation scenes" include the arrest of a corpse for debt and the return of a runaway adulteress, disguised and disfigured, as the hired governess to her own children. And *Armadale* by Wilkie Collins achieves a kind of apotheosis of the genre in its nightmarish configurations of such favorite devices as the murderer's deathbed confession, the prophetic dream, the fatal adventuress, the unscrupulous private eye, and the shady physician's scientific methods of poisoning. One beleaguered reviewer, reporting on the sensation novel for *Fraser's Magazine* at the height of the vogue, was forced to conclude that "a book without a murder, a divorce, a seduction, or a bigamy, is not apparently considered worth either writing or reading; and a mystery and a secret are the chief qualifications of the modern novel."[2]

This half-horrified, half-jocular assessment, with its catalogue of lurid ingredients, actually serves as a working definition of an English best seller in the 1860s. Proclaiming Dickens as their prototype, the sensation novelists instantly monopolized the popular fancy of a decade, while provoking a substantial outcry from critics and moralists alike. The new sensationalism, judged more pernicious than its gothic and romantic ancestors, grafted a progressive approach to the Victorian bêtes noires of sex and violence onto the primitive and even childish formulas of stage melodrama, already tattered and threadbare. Although the results of this popular experiment, the novels themselves, are sufficiently chaotic, they succeeded in providing a racy alternative vision, which struck at the roots of Victorian anxieties and otherwise unacknowledged concerns. In the sensation novel's unlikely combination of elemental imaginative power and barren literary stereotype, of license and convention, there is evidence of a paradox worth investigating.

## II.

The Pantomime was succeeded by a Melo-Drama. . . . I was pleased to observe Virtue quite as triumphant as she usually is out of doors, and indeed I thought rather more so. We all agreed (for the time) that honesty was the best policy, and we were as hard as iron upon Vice, and we wouldn't hear of Villainy getting on in the world—no, not on any consideration whatever.
Charles Dickens, *The Uncommercial Traveller*

When the sensation novel exploded onto the literary scene at the start of the 1860s, it did so, predictably enough, in the character of a phenomenon, something in the nature of a traveling-circus exhibition—prodigious, exciting, and agreeably grotesque. In the first place it created a genuine publishing bonanza, as the most practical result of a national state of mind known as "Sensational Mania."[3] Even in the absence of complete statistics, this fact becomes obvious from the frequency and vehemence of the reviews in the higher-brow journals, for the most part sounding a note of alarm that very likely contributed to the popular stampede it decried. Not one of the sensation novel's numerous critics attempted to deny its hold over the expanding market for prose fiction; in fact, its popularity was cited as its single most alarming characteristic. Everyone from the lady of the manor to the lowest scullery maid was reading these "feverish productions"[4] with feverish voracity, buying out number after number, edition after edition of *East Lynne, Lady Audley's Secret, The Woman in White*, and *Great Expectations*.[5] Here, for the first time in an age of increasing literacy, was an undisputed example of "democratic art,"[6] not only being read by all classes of society but having its origins in the less-than-respectable quarters of lower-class literature.

Along with its popularity, the sensation mode appeared equally remarkable for its novelty, its recognizable status as an authentically new fictional form.[7] The trend toward conventional realism, dominant if never exclusive in the English novel from the time of its eighteenth-century beginnings, had culminated in the 1850s with the ascendancy of the domestic novel, which centered on the familiar events and social interactions of everyday life. The last comparable vogue was that of the Newgate novel, literature of the gallows and the prisons, which flourished during the 1830s and 1840s. The new genre had no perceptible infancy; its greatest triumph, as well as its masterpieces, coincided with its initial appearance. It sprang full-blown, nearly simultaneously, from the minds of Wilkie Collins, Mrs. Henry Wood, and M. E. Braddon; the minor efforts came afterwards in countless imitations, some by the original authors, of Lady Audley, Anne Catherick, and Lady Isabel Carlyle. As long as it occupied the limelight, the sensation novel—brash, vulgar, and subversive—was viewed with undeniable justice as something of a literary upstart.

All the commentators on the sensation novel—whether

scathing or tolerant, obstinate or perceptive, contemporary or later—have seized unerringly on its single definitive feature: its introduction into fiction of "those most mysterious of mysteries, the mysteries which are at our own doors."[8] Although sensationalism in the broad sense of the term was already an established tradition in the backwaters of the English novel, it had generally been relegated to the realm of romance, distanced from ordinary experience. During the 1860s there seems to have been a concerted attempt, often for reasons of morality, to distinguish this latest outbreak of sensational mania from its more respectable antecedents. Obviously it shares a general affinity with the eighteenth-century gothicism of Ann Radcliffe and "Monk" Lewis, the historical romance of Sir Walter Scott, the oriental tales of Byron, as well as with the more recent and somewhat more suspect performances of the Newgate novelists. What all of these diverse literary traditions have in common, along with their interest in the marvelous or the unusual, is a certain remoteness of setting, wildly exotic and thus ultimately comfortable in relation to their ordinary, middle-class audience. The accepted stage for the gothic orgies of crime and lust is the ruined castle with its crazed aristocrats and fiendish monks, operating in conjunction with the ghostly agents of the supernatural; the essential device of terror is a vague suggestiveness and imprecision, effective after its fashion.[9] The more disturbing elements of these romantic projections are deliberately converted into fantasy and stylized into convention, always at a convenient remove from the identifiable situations of everyday life. On another level, even the much criticized Newgate novel of Bulwer, Dickens, and Ainsworth deals in the unfamiliar materials of low life and the criminal classes, originally in the form of serious protest against the current criminal laws and social injustice.[10] The threat to middle-class security, however fearsome and unmistakable, is at least external and clearly defined, a matter for legislative reform rather than self-doubt or self-recognition.

In spite of the need for fantasy, an efficient literary vehicle for both escapism and self-protection on the part of the reader, even avowed romance demonstrated an increasing tendency to incorporate elements of realism as the nineteenth century progressed. As early as the 1790s, Ann Radcliffe showed an incipient ambivalence, an impulse to have her gothicism both ways, by tempering its outrageous mysteries with last-minute rational explanations.[11] Two decades later, Scott's historical novels reconstructed the life of previous ages in graphic detail; *Ivanhoe* in particular "made a perfect transition from the old world of fiction to the new. It used the themes of popular romance, and rationalized them."[12] The Waverly novels as well, with their separate and antithetical worlds of the Scottish highlands and lowlands, deftly exploited the area of tension between the mundane and the extraordinary. Still later, in the 1820s and 1830s, came the *Blackwood's* tale of terror, a minor but seminal influence on the young Dickens, which aimed at "realistic terror through precision of descriptive detail."[13] This represents the beginning of a new kind of sensationalist appeal—an appeal not to the terror of the unknown, of the vaguely suggested and barely imagined, but to the even more terrifying terror of the familiar.

Out of the welter of early sensationalist literature— gothic, romantic, Newgate—it is possible to distinguish at least two direct ancestors of the sensation novel: *Eugene Aram* (1832) by Edward Bulwer-Lytton and *Jane Eyre* (1847) by Charlotte Brontë. Although *Eugene Aram* was one of the original Newgate novels, it deviates from the more usual pattern, not only in its evocation of the gothic but also in its portrayal of a middle-class criminal-hero, a gentle and reclusive scholar who has long ago committed premeditated murder for the utilitarian motive of freeing himself from poverty in order to devote himself to the benefit of mankind. Such apparent respectability of the criminal, achieved through the preservation of a dark secret from the past, was later to become the hallmark of the sensation novel; it is clearly quite a different matter from the less equivocal stereotypes of the gallant highwayman in the Dick Turpin mold or the underworld rascal of the Jack Sheppard school, as popularized in the fiction of Harrison Ainsworth. Bulwer-Lytton himself eventually recanted with the revised edition of 1849, softening Aram's theoretical position and changing his crime to that of a mere accomplice in robbery and accidental murder.[14] In the sensation novel of the 1860s, the emphasis on violent crime was combined with the romantic and sexual motifs of Brontë's *Jane Eyre*. There followed an inordinate proliferation of domestic secrets and maniacs under lock and key. But in the authentic sensation novel, as we shall see, Jane no longer runs away from the would-be bigamist; she is much more likely to dabble in a little bigamy of her own.

Along with these relatively highbrow predecessors, the sensation novel also had its roots in the subliterary world of the penny dreadfuls and other working-class entertainments, noted for their paradoxical "combination of fierce melodrama and meek domestic sentiment."[15] In fact, there is a direct link with this popular fiction in the energetic person of M. E. Braddon, who continued to churn out anonymous serials well after the mainstream success of *Lady Audley's Secret*. With characteristic irreverence, Braddon describes her saleable merchandise as "most piratical stuff": "The amount of crime, treachery, murder, slow poisoning, and general infamy required by the Halfpenny reader is something terrible. I am just going to do a little parricide for this week's supply."[16] The sensation novel, like Braddon herself, borrowed freely from the popular formula, which hinged on the violent collision between the opposing realms of romance and domesticity, bringing them together chiefly through the seduction or violation of the heroine at the hands of the villain.

The popular taste in fiction closely paralleled and interacted with the theatrical convention of the period. Like the penny press, the nineteenth-century theater belonged to the masses, to the "mechanics, dock-labourers, coster-mongers, petty tradesmen, small clerks, milliners, stay-makers, shoe-binders, slop workers, poor workers in a hundred highways and by-ways,"[17] who were its patrons. This long interlude, in fact, particularly the first fifty years of it, represents "the only time since the Middle Ages that [the English theater] has been dominated by neither the aristocracy nor the middle class."[18] The staple was melodrama (originally more music than text), legally forced on the minor or unlicensed theaters by the royal patents, granted in 1737 and revoked only in 1843, which limited the production of "legitimate" drama to Drury Lane and Covent Garden. While literary tragedy languished in this hothouse atmosphere, degenerating into mere servile imitation of Elizabethan models, "there was compensation in the bustling high spirits and rough energy of the new melodrama,"[19] which was written expressly for the working classes and which kept in touch, in its own backhanded way, with their lives and their dreams, with the currents of social and technological change.[20] Financial instability, too, encouraged this popular bent. No writer of genuine talent or much education would long submit to the prevailing system of poor pay, harrowing deadlines, and nonexistent copyright protection, all of which contributed in turn to the customary dependence on plagiarism, adaptation of foreign works, and stock formulas. The basic pattern of Victorian stage melodrama, already set by 1800,[21] was rigid and uncomplicated, faithfully reflecting a world view of similar quality based on certainties and absolute moral distinctions. All of the fashionable variations—gothic, nautical, equestrian, domestic—followed the same general outline of external conflict between good and evil, embodied in heroine and villain, and final resolution of that conflict according to the most rudimentary principles of poetic justice. This is what the public wanted and what it got, for the better part of a century. When the villain began to develop a conscience, in later domestic melodrama, it spelled the end of his primitive vitality and foreshadowed the eventual decline of the melodramatic form itself.[22]

Again in the drama, as in the penny serials, there emerged that strange and paradoxical mixture of real and unreal, the same "realistic raw material processed into an end product of fantasy . . . a dream world disguised as a true one."[23] Whatever the difficulties of this, in the matter of artistic integrity, it seems to have produced a formidable effect on its unsophisticated audience: "The power of melodrama came from the tension it suggested between a threatening common reality and the perfect structure it upheld as a morally necessary transcendent reality."[24] The same process was at work in stagecraft as well. Mid-nineteenth-century acting technique, like the scripts themselves, remained inflated and exaggerated, often to the point of frenzy, with heavy reliance on gesture and tableau. At the same time, the mechanics of staging became increasingly efficient, the illusions increasingly elaborate. By the time the sensation drama appeared, theatrical technicians were capable of furnishing the required spectacle—fires, earthquakes and cataracts, naval battles in real water, detailed reconstructions of pubs or railway stations, horses and other live animals, even real hansom cabs driven across the stage. Thus the most extravagant and incredible excesses of melodrama could be effectively combined with a literal exactness in physical setting. When the first villain tied the first victim to the railroad tracks in a sensation drama of 1867, that victim was rescued in the nick of time from being run over by an actual train.[25]

The structural dynamics of melodrama, generally analyzed in connection with theater, are equally worth exploring for their relevance to sensational fiction. The fundamental distinction between melodrama and tragedy, the theatrical mode it most resembles, has been incisively drawn by Camus, in his lecture "On the Future of Tragedy":

This is what seems to me the difference: the forces confronting each other in tragedy are equally legitimate, equally justified. . . . In other words, tragedy is ambiguous and [melo]drama single-minded. In the former, each force is at the same time both good and bad. In the latter, one is good and the other evil.[26]

The particular appeal of melodrama is in the clear-cut dichotomy between good and evil and in the sense of personal wholeness, real or illusory, that results when there is no inner conflict.[27] The opposing powers are always outside the self—villains, social orders, natural disasters. Strife or division is entirely projected into the exterior world, the world of action, which becomes hostile and menacing.[28] If the pathological extreme of tragedy would be schizophrenia, that of melodrama would be paranoia.[29] In its purest form, melodrama tends toward the abstract and the allegorical, often toward superficial personifications of Good and Evil, which still make their appearance in a relatively sophisticated novel like *No Name* by Wilkie Collins. Both good and evil, heroes and villains, remain unexamined and unexplained, dramatized in terms of their visible results rather than their motives or origins. What melodrama provides uniquely, at its lowest common denominator, are "the simple pleasures of conventional or straightforward conflict, decked out in the various excitements of threats, surprises, risks, rival lovers, disguises, and physical combat, all this against a background of ideas and emotions widely accepted at the time."[30] The sensation novel preserves intact the form of popular stage melodrama—the ritual confrontation between heroine and villain—but at the same time, as we shall see, radically alters its meaning. The ideas and emotions evoked by such writers as Collins and Braddon were often very far from acceptable to the average reader or critic of the 1860s.

In technique, if not always in content, the sensation novel deliberately takes over certain aspects of the melodramatic vision that should not be automatically dismissed. Even at its most naive, melodrama functions as a projection of irrational human fears, a duplication of the phase of childhood magic and of dreams. In Eric Bentley's phrase, "melodrama is the Naturalism of the dream life." Its appropriate, indeed essential, technique is exaggeration, a heightening to the point of caricature: "Like farce, this genre may be said, not to tumble into absurdity by accident, but to revel in it on purpose. To question the absurd in it is to challenge, not the conclusion but the premise."[31] This notion of the absurd in melodrama opens up significant possibilities for approaching the sensation novelists, and even Dickens as well. Perhaps it might be added here that in an age of preoccupation with rationality and with explanations, both social and psychological, the sensation novel helped to keep alive an alternative set of values: the idea of mystery, of the imponderables of human existence. This is the special province of melodrama, as opposed to mere naturalism: "Something has been gained when a person who has seen the world in monochrome and in miniature suddenly glimpses the lurid and the gigantic."[32] These values of melodrama are, after all, essential traits of the artistic imagination, traits then in danger of being lost. It is better, surely, to preserve them, even in the debased form in which mystery has degenerated into *a* mystery, a Sherlock Holmes conundrum, until some future time when they can be revitalized.

No less an observer than T. S. Eliot has recognized "that melodrama is perennial and that the craving for it is perennial and must be satisfied."[33] Still, it is tempting to speculate on its particular association with the nineteenth century. Partly, of course, it began to replace tragedy, which was made problematic in modern life and art by the increasing complexity of social pressures and the decline of the heroic individual. Wylie Sypher has also argued, rather ingeniously, that melodrama is the single characteristic mode of nineteenth-century thought and art, that the Victorians perceived their situation in terms of extreme polarities and expressed it by means of overstatement and emphatic instances. This manner of perception reflects the nineteenth-century dilemma: "Melodrama cannot admit exceptions, for they would immediately involve the action too deeply within the context of actuality and trammel the gesture. The types must behave with a decorum of extremes; the resolution must be vividly schematic. The tensions must concentrate toward a last overwhelming tableau, a final stasis beyond which one must not think. The aesthetic values of melodrama are the values of crisis, the event accepted as consummation."[34] Faced with unprecedented change, the Victorians were looking for solutions; ambiguity did not have the same attraction for them as it has for us in the twentieth century.

With this general tradition of melodrama as common property, theater and fiction became more specifically interconnected during the 1860s. The term "sensation drama," which may actually have predated its counterpart "sensation novel,"[35] began to be applied to the craze for elaborate stage spectaculars, in which everything else, including plot, was subordinated to technical display and the thrills it induced. Along with the obligatory "sensation scene," the later Victorian melodrama tends to feature heroines who die of sin, suave West End villains, unrepentant adventuresses, detectives, and an emphasis on crime. But in spite of the new possibilities offered by evil or fallen central characters, in spite of the undertones of naturalism, the theatrical audience of the period still demanded a conventional happy ending for the sinless heroines. One play of Boucicault's was forced to reverse its final act in mid-production after a hostile reception; and Charles Reade translated the horrors of Zola into something more than a different language, rescuing Gervaise from her grim fate in his dramatized version of *L'Assommoir*.[36]

Frequently the two sensation genres actually coincided, as the same works passed from one to the other with all the ease of routine. *The New Magdalen* and *It Is Never Too Late To Mend* started out as plays, while *East Lynne* and *Lady Audley's Secret* not only reappeared as long-running hits and eventual repertory chestnuts but also inspired countless theatrical replicas of Mrs. Wood's suffering adulteress and Miss Braddon's golden-haired impostor. Dickens, Reade, and Collins all acted and wrote for the stage (in fact, Reade began his career as a less-than-flourishing dramatist), and none of them ever scrupled to import histrionic effects into his fiction. The analogy between the two forms—"one is a drama narrated, as the other is a drama acted"[37]—became a theoretical commonplace as well as a favorite defense of sensational methods and content. In practice, too, there were ostentatious if superficial borrowings. *No Thoroughfare*, a Christmas collaboration between Dickens and Collins, is divided into an overture and four acts, with chapter titles such as "The Curtain Rises," "Enter the House-keeper," "New Characters on the Scene," "Exit Wilding." And the seafaring episodes of *Hard Cash*—that incongruous jumble of shipwrecks, pirates, and sailor's hornpipes—make sense only in the once familiar context of nautical melodrama. The link with the drama proper was a matter of deliberate emphasis and considerable satisfaction for the major sensation novelists. They aspired, grandly if somewhat rashly, to the art of Shakespeare, to the portrayal of "the tragedy of existence" in "its sterner, its wilder, and its vaster aspects; adventures, crimes, agonies; hot rage and tumult of passions; terror, and bewilderment, and despair."[38] The products of this aspiration, not surprisingly, were enmeshed in the contingencies of their more immediate surroundings, quasi-Shakespearean perhaps, but closer to the stage melodrama of their own century.

### III.

The Secret! Ha!
The Secret! Ho!
*Punch*, 1863

The essence of the sensation novel—and the basis of its claim to recognition as a separate genre—is captured in Charles Reade's standard subtitle, "A Matter-of-Fact

Romance." What distinguishes the true sensation genre, as it appeared in its prime during the 1860s, is the violent yoking of romance and realism, traditionally the two contradictory modes of literary perception. Although remarkably few examples of modern prose fiction can be characterized as "pure" romance or "pure" realism,[39] one vision or the other normally dominates. The sensation novel, however, deliberately strains both modes to the limit, disrupting the accepted balance between them. The subject matter of the sensationalists is at once outrageous and carefully documented, "wild yet domestic,"[40] extraordinary in intensity and yet confined to the experience of ordinary people operating in familiar settings. The narrative technique combines a melodramatic tendency to abstraction with the precise detail of detective fiction, an unlimited use of suspense and coincidence with an almost scientific concern for accuracy and authenticity. The aim of all this, similarly paradoxical, appears to have been a kind of civilized melodrama, modernized and domesticated—not only an everyday gothic, minus the supernatural and aristocratic trappings, but also a middle-class Newgate, featuring spectacular crime unconnected with the usual criminal classes. The chosen territory of the sensation novelists lies somewhere between the possible and the improbable, ideally at their point of intersection.

This fundamental sensation paradox turns up again and again in the brief theoretical pronouncements of Reade and Collins, who borrowed their theory from Dickens, claimed him as their model, and in practice went far beyond anything he sanctioned. "I have purposely dwelt upon the romantic side of familiar things," remarks Dickens himself in the preface to *Bleak House*, but only after he has gone to ridiculous, even Readean, lengths in documenting parallel instances to support Mr. Krook's death by Spontaneous Combustion.[41] Like Dickens here, the lesser apologists for sensationalism typically find themselves torn in contradictory directions, at the same time demanding the freedom of romance or tragedy and falling back on the safer authority of literal fact. Reade, of course, offers the most extreme case of ambivalence; for him the literary art must be founded on a two-fold "basis of imagination and drudgery" and carried out according to a "severe system" of his own devising. His confirmed distrust of fiction is complicated by a view of fact as something even more implausible: "I feign probabilities; I record improbabilities: the former are conjectures, the latter truths: mixed they make a thing not so true as gospel nor so false as history; viz. fiction."[42]

In the preface to *Basil*, Wilkie Collins contributes a more rational and less eccentric analysis of this same process of artistic transformation: "My idea was that the more of the Actual I could garner up as a text to speak from, the more certain I might feel of the genuineness and value of the Ideal which was sure to spring out of it." Although he admits that "the noblest poetry of prose fiction [is] the poetry of every-day truth," he proposes to extend the range of what is true in art beyond the accepted limits of average, predictable experience: "I have not thought it either politic or necessary, while adhering to realities, to adhere to every-day realities only. . . . Those extraordinary accidents and events which happen to few men seemed to me to be as legitimate materials for fiction to work with—when there was a good object in using them—as the ordinary accidents and events which may, and do, happen to us all."[43] It might be said of any sensation novelist, as it has been of Wilkie Collins, that "he exults indeed in the improbable and in the fringes of actuality, but lavishes his pains and skill in attempting to prove them otherwise."[44] It is the mixture of different "realities," the startling contrast between the event and its mundane surroundings, that gives the sensation novel its special pungency and produces its undeniable effect.

The exact nature of that effect, if not its power, is a matter of some dispute between the sensational theorists and their contemporary critics. For one anonymous observer in the *Westminster Review*, the chief annoyance comes from Collins' practical bent, his scrupulous footnotes on technical questions of law, medicine or chemistry: "It is not artistic to tell this to the reader. The process of watching our dinner being cooked takes away our appetite." The *Quarterly*, on the other hand, finds the more obvious result of this foundation in the Actual anything but tedious or unappetizing to the multitude of readers:

> The sensation novel, be it mere trash or something worse, is usually a tale of our own times. Proximity is, indeed, one great element of sensation. It is necessary to be near a mine to be blown up by its explosion; and a tale which aims at electrifying the nerves of the reader is never thoroughly effective unless the scene be laid in our own days and among the people we are in the habit of meeting.

The combination of propinquity and explosiveness ensures the same popular appeal as that of broadside journalism. In fact, there is a whole sensational subgenre, with its origins in actual criminal reports, appropriately identified as "the Newspaper Novel."[45] Although this epithet was originally meant in derision, Collins and Reade ought to have been flattered by their own contrary interpretation of its significance. While Reade flaunts his unrivaled collection of newspaper clippings as a ballast to the dangers of the imagination, Collins looks in the same direction for a solution to the prosaic quality of modern existence: "I know a great many excellent people who reason against plain experience . . . who read the newspapers in the morning, and deny in the evening that there is any romance for writers or painters to work upon in modern life."[46] The "matter-of-fact romance" of these sensation novelists is by its very nature paradoxical and open to paradox; not surprisingly, it embodies some of the hidden strain and ambivalence present in mid-Victorian society as well as the underlying dialectical process in the literary form of the novel itself.

To its original audience in the 1860s, the sensation novel appeared blatantly recognizable as well as ubiquitous, hardly in need of official critical definition. Its typical features—both content and narrative technique—are grandiose and inflated, glorious targets for parody. First of all, plot and incident predominate. In Reade's opinion, "fertile situations are the true cream of fiction; these once supplied, any professional writer can find words"[47] to contain them. The sensation novelists prize action and complication for their own sake, whether the total structure of the tale is episodic or tightly patterned. The first approach is Reade's favorite; with only the most general sort of outline, he specializes in extreme situations, carrying each as far as he dares, introducing any twists or turns that spontaneously occur to him, piling on the shocks and catastrophes until his lopsided construct collapses of its own weight. In his full-length triple-deckers, there is invariably more than one plot line and usually more than one setting, with two groups of interrelated characters widely separated from one another by expanses of ocean and fallible mails. Although he considers suspense as "the soul of narrative,"[48] Reade seldom musters the patience for a protracted build-up of anticipation, preferring instead a constant succession of climaxes that maintains the emotional intensity at its highest endurable pitch. Even his cases of murder are rapidly solved.[49] The difficulty with this, of course, is that climax becomes the routine, subjecting the reader to an endless roller-coaster effect that eventually loses its thrill.

Collins, on the other hand, makes the most of suspense, of drawn-out mystification or impending menace, in unraveling his ingenious constructions through all their interlocking segments. The representative Collins production has been aptly described in a *Spectator* review as "a kind of literary centipede of a hundred different joints, each separately alive, and each popping out of the one that preceded it."[50] In spite of the length and complexity of his major works, Collins never lets go of the central mystery, never gets sidetracked by subplots or burgeoning scenarios. During the serialized progress of *No Name*, Wilkie's most expansive and most Dickensian of novels, Dickens still saw fit to warn him that "great care is

needed not to tell the story too severely. In exact proportion as you play around it here and there, and mitigate
the severity of your own sticking to it, you will enhance
and intensify the power with which Magdalen holds on to
her purpose."[51] For Collins, unlike Reade, the beauty is in
the design, not in its parts, whatever their inherent melodramatic potential. Still, from their opposite perspectives, both writers, like all genuine sensationalists, place
their highest value on plot, on what will happen next if
not what has happened already. On the largest scale, this
preference leads to elaborate construction, which in its
extreme form leads to mystery; the "purest type" of the
sensation genre is the "novel-with-a-secret," or more
likely, a secret-within-a-secret.[52] On a smaller, more local
scale, it produces "sensation scenes" of the most immod-
erate description, with their torrents of passion and their
astonishing "curtains," which in Reade and Collins
shamelessly coincide with the close of a serial installment.

The plot devices of the sensation novel, however bizarre
and multiform they may at first appear, can actually be
reduced to the generic principle of doubling; in essence
they are all "double-edged," as *Temple Bar* says of bigamy
and *le mort vivant*, two of the most prominent among
them.[53] The favorite expedient, universal in Victorian
melodrama, is mistaken identity, caused by crime, accident, illegitimacy, or deliberate impersonation. Innocent
characters may simply look like each other, as in *The
Woman in White* or *Griffith Gaunt*, or bear identical
names, as in *Armadale*, while adventuresses of every
sort, from the redeemable Magdalen Vanstone to the de-
praved Lydia Gwilt, can be expected to act out the false
roles dictated by their motives of crime or revenge. Under
the general category of mistaken identity are found the
more particular cases of bigamy and the return of the
dead alive. The first became so popular after the distinguished precedent set by Lady Audley, that a new subgenre proliferated, known as the "Bigamy Novels."[54] Just
as the most childish of heroines is likely to have a dis-

carded husband or two in the background, so the most
carefully certified of corpses is apt to revive at an interesting juncture or turn out to have been the horrible result of
a planned or chance substitution. The concealments
necessary for these continual shocks and surprises suffered by the characters in sensation novels depend on the
elaborate stage contrivances of missing letters, reported
accidents, blackmail attempts, and trips to Australia or
America. Mistakes of this kind conveniently furnish the
dramatic scenes of confrontation and recognition that
take place between parted lovers, former husbands and
wives, victims and would-be murderers. Perhaps the
single most indelible image from all the sensational literature of the 1860s is that of Laura, Lady Glyde, the
heroine of *The Woman in White*, solemnly lifting her veil
beside her own tombstone inscription. The novels reveal a
recurrent preoccupation with the loss or duplication of
identity: Lady Isabel Carlyle in *East Lynne* living as a
stranger in her previous home, watching her husband
caress another woman; Griffith Gaunt, in a state of bewilderment, confronted by his two equally virtuous
wives; Franklin Blake in *The Moonstone* staring at the
paint-stained nightgown that proclaims him a thief. Although the implications of this motif may be carried further than mere surface resemblances, like those re-
counted in Reade's "Doubles,"[55] the most common use of
it, except in Dickens, is simply as a melodramatic coup, a
supreme occasion for the orgies of passion or surprise.
Everywhere in the lesser sensation novels the unwitting
protagonists experience their strange encounters with
the empty form of the *doppelgänger*.

Incident as well as character is subject to the principle
of duality. Sensation plots are typically structured
around a recurrence of similar or identical situations, not
infrequently in the shape of dreams or omens and their
ultimate fulfillment. The profusion of secrets, as well as
sheer ignorance, brings on all sorts of complications, lend-
ing various misleading appearances to a single action or
event. So much of the trouble in melodrama is entirely il-

lusory, so much of the emotion wasted, and all because someone has neglected to write a letter or provide an explanation, or because the newspapers have printed an erroneous report. There is always something going on beneath the surface, some apparent catastrophe, some hidden layer of motive or intrigue. The universe of the sensation novel, which encompasses all the variations of these curious phenomena, is ruled by coincidence rather than logic; accident alone can always be counted on to reunite any pair of long-lost friends or enemies, to uncover a calamitous secret, to create or salvage a desperate situation. Behind these coincidences, to mitigate their arbitrary character, emerges the hand of Destiny, arcane and vaguely supernatural, transcending probability or doubt.

The only artistic technique that could possibly accommodate all these outrageous contrivances is exaggeration, the instinctive realm of melodrama. Villainy, disasters, emotions—everything in a sensation novel is larger than life; intensified, distorted, prodigious; invested with the quality of nightmare. Humanity is seen *in extremis*, perpetually at the point of crisis. Under these conditions, rhetoric begins to flourish, whether establishing an eerie atmosphere or conveying hysterical dialogue or lashing emotion into frenzy. Reade's notorious capitals—"HE IS NOT YOUR SON"—are meant as more than mere embellishments; they become typographical signals of extremity. At its best, generally with Reade, the sensation novel verges on surrealism; at its worst, there is hardly any limit to pretension and bombast, hardly any depth of tastelessness left unsounded. To the mid-Victorian critics, however, there is no point in making distinctions between effectiveness and failure in this particular mode: "All exaggeration, it has been said, is weakness, and grotesqueness is the resource of feeble artists."[56] Even when they did succeed, the sensationalists were bucking the critical tide.

It was a rare critic indeed who would echo the lament in *Fraser's* that "the fault of many novels of the day is lack of incident and over-abundance of dialogue."[57] That was in 1860, and so was presumably canceled by the immediate onslaught of sensationalism. The nearly unanimous objection to the novel of incident, as practiced during the sensation decade, takes either of two related forms: aversion to the "plotting novel," even in theory, or ridicule of its particular excrescences. The most obvious deficiency, played up by gloating reviewers, is the neglect of character delineation:

> A sensation novel, as a matter of course, abounds in incident. Indeed, as a general rule, it consists of nothing else. . . . The human actors in the piece are, for the most part, but so many lay-figures on which to exhibit a drapery of incident. Allowing for the necessary division of all characters of a tale into male and female, old and young, virtuous and vicious, there is hardly anything said or done by any one specimen of a class which might not with equal fitness be said or done by any other specimen of the same class. Each game is played with the same pieces, differing only in the moves.[58]

More tolerant critics, willing to accept the premise of melodrama, question the "moves" on their own terms and still find them wanting. In the matter of the sleepwalking episode in *The Moonstone*, for example, "the confiding temper of the reader has, in vulgar parlance, been made a fool of"; while in the case of *Lady Audley's Secret*, "when the explanations of these mysteries are given, it is true that they turn out absurdly incredible; but by that time you have finished the book."[59]

*Punch* seizes unerringly on the meaninglessness behind much of the superficial cloak-and-dagger excitement in sensation literature: "Do you know that you remind me of a sensation novel; when the secret's out there's nothing in it?"[60] The rambunctious serial parody entitled "Mokeanna; Or, The White Witness: A Tale of the Times" fairly wallows in storms, clues, secrets, and bigamous marriages. A sleepwalking donkey in the title role leads the way to "The Secret Truss," a bundle of hay lost in the "Dungeon Keep" (and obviously meant to be confused with the Secret Trust in Collins' *No Name*). The main import of its contents, particularly an "illegible codicil in the *habendum* of a closely-written Deed," is to reveal the nonexistence (rather than the scandalous existence) of complex relationships: "See here!" says the Baronet to the farm girl, "You are not my wife. I never saw you before."[61] According to G. H. Lewes, a more formidable opponent than *Punch*, sensation novels depend on "breathless rapidity of movement; whether the movement be absurd or not matters little, the essential thing is to keep moving." One final, less common reaction, voiced in R. H. Hutton's *Spectator*, deplores the "artificial" concentration on technique as such, characteristic of skillful tales of mystery or suspense, which exhibit "a sort of disinterested delight in the technical machinery of novels quite apart from the human interests which that machinery used to subserve."[62] However alien the sensation content appears to sophisticated readers of the twentieth century, the "delight in form" looks familiar—and more acceptable to us than it was to its own contemporaries.

In keeping with their love for the stage, the sensation novelists evolved an original "dramatic" method of narration,[63] not to be confused with the Henry James technique of the same title. Although Collins' belief "that the Novel and the Play are twin-sisters in the family of Fiction" could easily have passed for critical dogma at the time,[64] the sensationalist practice, as usual, diverges radically from the established norm. Where Lewes or Bagehot would base narrative construction and unity on the formal regulations of the drama, the sensationalists focus instead on the primacy of action and dialogue in spinning a tale. Theoretically at least, the fictional characters should "play out the play" on their own account without authorial interference, since, in Dickens' phrase, "it is, as it were, their business to do it, and not mine."[65] The author should dramatize his story rather than himself, abandoning the role of omniscient puppeteer favored by Thackeray and Trollope. Not only should the narrator refrain from comment in his own voice or discursive di-

gressions in the manner of Fielding, he should also avoid
explicit dissection and analysis of character, as practiced
preeminently by George Eliot. Even the direct representation of a character's thoughts, an obvious convention of
narrative, is frowned upon as an intrusion beyond the
narrator's sphere as well as an interruption in the flow of
events. In the middle of his novels, disruptively enough,
Reade becomes at once belligerent and apologetic
whenever his characters might be expected to indulge in
reflection:

> But, not to fall into the error of writers who underrate
> their readers' curiosity and intelligence, and so deluge
> them with comments and explanations, we will now
> simply relate what Wylie did, leaving you to glean his
> motives as this tale advances.

> Her mind was in a whirl; and, were I to imitate those
> writers who undertake to dissect and analyze the heart
> at such moments, and put the exact result on paper, I
> should be apt to sacrifice truth to precision; I must stick
> to my old plan, and tell you what she did: that will
> surely be some index to her mind, especially with my
> female readers.

In typically Readean fashion, he blasts those writers of
psychological fiction who "keep putting their heads from
behind the show, and openly analyzing their pale creations, and dissecting them, and eking them out with
comments, and microscoping their poodles into lions."[66]
The dramatic method of Reade and the other sensation
novelists is partly a result of inadequacy; partly also, I
think, a defense mechanism necessitated by their choice
of shocking or offensive material. If Kate Gaunt, in
Reade's novel, were to open her mind during the course of
her near seduction, its contents might be too hot for any
Victorian to handle. In any case, when the aim is sensation, scene is everything, a *raison d'être* in itself.

This dramatic theory of characterization encourages
the practice of individualizing by means of externals—

through dress, mannerisms, and physical peculiarities. Not even Dickens, who originally patented the tag-line character, escapes censure on this question, and of course his lesser imitators are regularly castigated for their flashy pasteboard figures. The reviewer in *Temple Bar* distinguishes rather scathingly between "character" and "characteristics," denouncing the sensation "trick of substituting characteristics for character, and palming off the one for the other." Henry James diagnoses Lady Audley as "a non-entity, without a heart, a soul, a reason. But what we may call the small change for these facts—her eyes, her hair, her mouth, her dresses, her bedroom furniture, her little words and deeds—are so lavishly bestowed that she successfully maintains a kind of half illusion."[67] It is true that speech, action, and external appearance must bear the weight of character portrayal in a genre that is specifically—insistently—concerned with extreme passions and intricate emotional states. Hatred, jealousy, murder, fear, illicit love are all exhibited under a glaring spotlight and worked for maximum effect, without the benefit of any revelations of their internal processes. Often the secret itself prevents full disclosure of motivation to the reader; even a central character like Braddon's Aurora Floyd can be allowed to perform her histrionics for a couple of volumes without our knowing why, what is at the root of them, or becoming in any way involved. Not surprisingly, the sensation novels are populated with hulking idiots, hunchbacks, and deformed villains as well as doll-like murderers and preternaturally beautiful adventuresses. More than one contemporary reviewer has remarked on the amazing prominence of hair, and to a lesser extent eyes, as dramatic or symbolic devices, especially in Braddon and Ouida. Henry James lists the alternating hues of Aurora Floyd's tresses—"blue-black, purple-black, and dead-black"—while Margaret Oliphant concludes that "hair, indeed, in general, has become one of the leading properties in fiction."[68]

There remains one final element of sensational writing that again takes much-criticized precedence over characterization. This is setting, which assists or controls the mood and provides the background for violence and tempestuous passion. Although the action is firmly anchored in the mundane realities of city streets, railways, and telegraph offices, there is still room for Braddon's crumbling country mansions with their disused wells or Collins' eerie Norfolk Broads and Shivering Sand, not to mention the various contributions of storms, fires, and midnight darkness. Collins in particular is a brilliant creator of atmosphere; some of his most effective prose is devoted to the painting of remarkable landscapes, as in this passage from *The Moonstone*:

> The last of the evening light was fading away; and over all the desolate place there hung a still and awful calm. The heave of the main ocean on the great sandbank out in the bay, was a heave that made no sound. The inner sea lay lost and dim, without a breath of wind to stir it. Patches of nasty ooze floated, yellow-white, on the dead surface of the water. Scum and slime shone faintly in certain places, where the last of the light still caught them on the two great spits of rock jutting out, north and south, into the sea. It was now the time of the turn of the tide: and even as I stood there waiting, the broad brown face of the quicksand began to dimple and quiver—the only moving thing in all the horrid place.[69]

What the sensation novel adds to melodrama, as a kind of counterweight, is the same solidity of physical detail characteristic of nineteenth-century realism.

### IV.

There is nothing half so interesting to the great mass of mankind as a mysterious murder in a street cab, or a full-blown adultery made patent in court.
                    E. S. Dallas, *The Gay Science*

The "ordinary domestic relations . . . are the legitimate province of novels," intoned the *Edinburgh Review* in 1857,[70] echoing a sentiment by no means uncommon during the period. It was left to the sensation novelists, a disreputable lot, to stage the rebellion against the domestic monopoly, heaping scorn on its Trollopian "chronicles of small beer"[71] and ostentatiously overstepping its narrow bounds. The ensuing debate over the appropriate subject matter for fiction, with skirmishes on both moral and aesthetic grounds, still carried persistent overtones of the novel's presumed inferiority to the forms of serious art, along with the usual dose of Victorian sanctimony.

In this context, the sensationalists invoke the unassailable precedent of stage tragedy, from the Greeks to Shakespeare, asserting that the novelist "is privileged to excite" in equal measure "all the strong and deep emotions" that traditionally belong to the playwright.[72] Perhaps the most eloquent statement of their position appears in Dickens' *All the Year Round* in an unsigned article entitled "The Sensational Williams." The article begins with a protest against the critical cant of the day: "If any one writes a novel, a play, or a poem, which relates anything out of the ordinary experiences of the most ordinary people—some tragedy of love or revenge, some strange (though not impossible) combination of events, or some romance of guilt and misery—he is straightway met with a loud exclamation of 'Sensational!' " Although admittedly "the difference between an artist who can look into the psychology of crime and terror, and the botcher who can do nothing more than lay on the carmine with a liberal brush, is so great as to be essential," this vulgar abuse of sensationalism should not be allowed to obscure its fundamental validity as an artistic technique: "life itself is similarly sensational in many of its aspects, and Nature is similarly sensational in many of her forms, and art is always sensational when it is tragic." The themes of great art can hardly be restricted to "the amenities of respectable, easy-going men and women": "The mystery of evil is as interesting to us now as it was in the time of Shakespeare; and it is downright affectation or effeminacy to say that we are never to glance into that abyss."[73]

This protest is followed by a mock review of *Macbeth* as it would have been written by the "anti-sensational critics," who would offer the opinion that a certain Mr. Shakespeare "has no idea of tragedy apart from the

merest horrors of melodrama." These fastidious observers
find themselves revolted by the succession of ghosts,
carnage, and indelicate language in nearly all of the
plays: "There is something so homicidal and Newgate-
Calendarish about Mr. Shakespeare's mind"; "nothing is
too nasty for Mr. Shakespeare's Muse"; Lady Macbeth is
"perhaps the most unnatural character that even Mr.
Shakespeare's lurid and unhealthy imagination has ever
conceived."[74] Silly as it looks now, "The Sensational Williams" mimics all too accurately the tone affected in
many of the enlightened periodicals. If few of the pure
sensation writers could stand up to the criterion of
tragedy, nevertheless the more responsible among
them—certainly Reade and Collins—ought to be considered as pioneers in new territories of the imagination,
territories that even the realists of the 1860s could no
longer pretend to ignore.[75]

Among the nonordinary realities appropriate to tragic
art, most of the sensationalists include sexual passion in
all its irregular aspects, typically surrounded by an air of
moral ambiguity that Dickens, their supposed leader,
found disturbing if not downright revolting. In a genuine
sensation novel it becomes in effect an obligation to incorporate a liberal amount of seduction, bigamy, or even
prostitution, preferably in connection with the heroine.
From Aurora Floyd, the unwitting bigamist, to Lady
Isabel, the foolish adulteress, to Mercy Merrick, the penitent woman of the streets, any number of heroines fall, or
almost fall, on their way to worldly or other-worldly sal-
vation. At the same time, the villainess assumes an
equally prominent role in the charming and dangerous
person of Lady Audley, Mrs. Archbold, or Lydia Gwilt. Of
course the reviewers profess themselves scandalized by
the general threat to morality, but the main objection can
be narrowed down to a distaste for female passion and
sexuality, most explicitly stated in one of Mrs. Oliphant's
articles for *Blackwood's*:

What is held up to us as the story of the feminine soul
as it really exists underneath its conventional cover-

ings, is a very fleshly and unlovely record. . . . Now it is no knight of romance riding down the forest glades, ready for the defence and succour of all the oppressed, for whom the dreaming maiden waits. She waits now for flesh and muscles, for strong arms that seize her, and warm breath that thrills her through, and a host of other physical attractions, which she indicates to the world with a charming frankness. . . . were the sketch made from the man's point of view, its openness would at least be less repulsive. The peculiarity of it in England is . . . that this intense appreciation of flesh and blood, this eagerness of physical sensation, is represented as the natural sentiment of English girls, and is offered to them not only as the portrait of their own state of mind, but as their amusement and mental food.[76]

Even the sensation novels written by men focus on the feminine point of view; both Reade and Collins draw effortless portraits of mature, sophisticated, sexually aroused women, heroines as well as adventuresses.

Anticipating the violated sensibilities of Mrs. Grundy, the sensation novelists came up with a variety of ingenious solutions to the problem of Victorian censorship. There is always the old dodge of pious moralizing, much indulged in by Mrs. Henry Wood whenever one of her heroines oversteps the mark. Then there is the new dodge, practiced by Wilkie Collins, of crusading for reformed prostitutes in the name of humanity and Christian charity. As in popular stage melodrama, a failure of chastity seems to have become more palatable in the case of thoroughly evil adventuresses who receive their just deserts or wretched penitents who die before the end. By this logic, Lady Audley, a fiend in human form if there ever was one, is more acceptable than Aurora Floyd or Magdalen Vanstone, mixed characters whose transgressions have mitigating circumstances. What rankles most with the critics is the happy ending, and restored character, bestowed on these heroines in defiance of melodramatic convention: Magdalen pursues "a career of vulgar and

aimless trickery and wickedness, . . . from all the pollu-
tions of which . . . she emerges, at the cheap cost of a fever,
as pure, as high-minded, and as spotless as the most dazzling white of heroines"; "Lady Audley is meant to be de-
tested, while Aurora Floyd is meant to be admired. The
one ends her days in a madhouse; the other becomes the
wife of an honest man, and the curtain falls upon her
'bending over the cradle of her first-born.' "[77] It should
also be mentioned here that the predilection for bigamy,
that essentially English and middle-class crime, helps in
its own way to keep lust within bounds, as Mrs. Oliphant
ironically notes:

> [Braddon] has brought in the reign of bigamy as an in-
> teresting and fashionable crime, which no doubt shows
> a certain deference to the British relish for law and or-
> der. It goes against the seventh commandment, no
> doubt, but does it in a legitimate sort of way, and is an
> invention which could only have been possible to an
> Englishwoman knowing the attraction of impropriety,
> and yet loving the shelter of the law.[78]

Bigamy thus has the advantage of making sexual offense
into an actual crime, something for which the offender
might theoretically be arrested and sent to jail.

In the sensation genre as a whole, illicit sex is generally accompanied, sometimes even eclipsed, by violent
crime, preeminently murder: "no novel in the present day
can be reckoned complete without one."[79] In spite of the
routine objection that any criminal romance, whether
Balzac or a penny dreadful, "leaves an unpleasant and
unwholesome flavour behind,"[80] even the stuffiest reviewers are apt to betray something of the axiomatic Victorian fondness for murder. As early as 1827, De Quincey
had begun to analyze "the tendency to a critical or aesthetic valuation of fires and murders" as a "universal"
phenomenon, one of the "spontaneous tendencies of the
human mind when left to itself." Although few commentators would admit to sharing such a cool attitude toward
the "aesthetics of murder,"[81] they do point out the Eng-

lish novelist's "preference of crime to vice," actually permitting a backhanded endorsement of it as "perhaps an advantageous circumstance, so far as vulgar morality is concerned."[82] Murder acquires a certain legitimacy, even wholesomeness, in comparison with the vaguer, weaker, less legally punishable sins of the flesh:

> We think that the "Lady Audley" style is more national, more our own. A good sound, brutal murder, with plenty of blood in it, chimes in better with our patriotic feelings: it is not un-English. . . . If there must be sin and crime to give flavour to English fictions, we vote for murder.[83]

But if crime is less objectionable than vice, there still seems to be an essential connection between them, a connection that cannot be explained away as a simple preference for one over the other. "All the passions tend to murder," observes Reade in his private Notebooks, and it may be that sexual repression finds a convenient outlet in violence. Reade's modern biographer cites the murder of Jane Hardie in *Hard Cash* as a skittish denial of her already dramatized sexuality: "In this manner sex is replaced with blood, according to the approved moral pattern of Sensation fiction."[84] The pattern is not always so blatant as in *Hard Cash*, where the openly sensual heroine becomes the direct victim of murder, but it does seem to work as a sort of general principle for the sensation novel. Too much sex begets murder, often with the offender as the criminal, as in *Armadale* or *Lady Audley's Secret*. And of course murder may function as a diversion, for both author and audience, a more socially acceptable channel for energy that might otherwise be sexual.

Once the "tragic" material of violent crime has been established as a proper domain of fiction, there remains the question of the practical use of it in the sensation novels. As part of their juxtaposition of realistic and romantic elements, the sensationalists of the 1860s not only raise crime from its recent Newgate origins, but also remove it from the traditional realm of kings and chieftains and grandiose villains. A delightful critique in *Blackwood's* looks back wistfully to the days of Sir Walter Scott, whose buccaneers are "presentable in respectable society" and whose "crime is all above-board."[85] In "The Decay of Murder," Leslie Stephen offers a more perceptive analysis of the same trend toward "prosaic," scientific crime as yet another indication of the modern decline of the hero and receding of "ancient energy." Not entirely in jest, Stephen attributes the current shortage of great crimes to the "tyranny of the majority," which leaves the art of murder in the "inferior hands" of the less intelligent classes because everyone else has become too conscious of the "average standard" to attempt anything, such as murder, that might provoke notice. The strained performance of "our sensation novels" is interpreted as "a symptom of this decline of vigour": "They are unnatural because any one who would introduce the play of strong passions into the milk-and-water commonplace of modern society is forced to be unnatural."[86] In other words, by definition they are attempting the impossible. This disappearance of tragedy in modern sensational literature, lamented in aesthetic terms by Leslie Stephen, elicits a more fundamental moral objection from Henry James:

> Crime, indeed, has always been a theme for dramatic poets; but with the old poets its dramatic interest lay in the fact that it compromised the criminal's moral repose. Whence else is the interest of *Orestes* and *Macbeth*? With Mr. Collins and Miss Braddon (our modern Euripides and Shakespeare) the interest of the crime is in the fact that it compromises the criminal's personal safety.[87]

All too often in these novels, crime becomes mere excitement, an effort to wring as much "sensation" as possible out of unpromising circumstances. The hysteria and superficiality at once reflect and rebel against an age in which the "fashion of vice, like that of dress, is colourless and monotonous."[88]

In typically paradoxical fashion, the sensationalists

justify their choice of subject matter on one other serious basis besides the conventions of tragedy. Whatever their value as escapism, the higher forms of the sensation novel, particularly the works of Reade and Collins, are also in the business of propaganda, of crusading for social or political reform. More often than not, however, this reformist aim is swamped by the lurid details it evokes; few twentieth-century readers would guess that *The Woman in White* has anything to do with abuses in private lunatic asylums. Even Reade's major novels-with-a-purpose, *Hard Cash* and *It Is Never Too Late To Mend*, go off on feverish tangents, which betray the author's eccentric obsessions rather than illuminate his cause. Still, this further pretension of the sensation novel provides one more opening for critical attack. While the *Edinburgh Review* would deny any novelist, necessarily operating in the sphere of imagination, a license to treat of "subjects which properly belong to the intellect," the *Quarterly* denounces even Dickens as "a grievous offender in this line," who "never sinks so nearly to the level of the ordinary sensation-novelist as when he is writing 'with a purpose.' "[89] For the sensationalists, as for the earlier writers of utilitarian romance, the legitimate moral purpose offers sufficient justification for their documentary method. In the sensation novel, the most outlandish fantasy meets up with the hard detail of protonaturalism.[90]

## V.

Murder had a part in their imaginative lives that was far out of proportion to its actual incidence.
Richard Altick, *Victorian Studies in Scarlet*

The conspicuous appeal of sensationalism for the proper Victorians of the 1860s represents a complex of factors that together created a market unprecedented in the short history of the English novel up to that time. It is not enough to blame the commercial exploitation of "periodicals, circulating libraries, and railway bookstalls"[91] or the newly, and often barely, literate popular audience, which demanded strong and instant entertainment in return for its shilling. Although the reading habits of the lower middle and even working classes did exert a considerable influence on the conventions of the sensation novel, everyone else read Wilkie Collins and M. E. Braddon with apparently equal satisfaction. Most contemporaries interpret the sensation vogue as a morbid or unhealthy symptom, whether or not they identify it as a side-effect of the more wholesome official outlook of the Victorian period. E. S. Dallas sees "the craving which exists among us for sensation" as "but the reaction from over-wrought thinking," merely the frivolous leisure of a genuine "age of thought."[92] Ruskin, in an unsympathetic essay on "Fiction, Fair and Foul," at least recognizes the crucial role played by the drab monotony of urban life, which may produce an unnatural appetite for excitement. However reluctantly, he also acknowledges the process by which the "hot fermentation and unwholesome secrecy of the population crowded into large cities" has already created a new subject matter for literature in creating novel "modes of mental ruin and distress . . . in a certain sense, worth study in their monstrosity." What modern fiction does, in its "fouler" incarnation, is to anatomize these hideous new forms of moral disease, "purporting thus to illustrate the modern theology that the appointed destiny of a large average of our population is to die like rats in a drain, either by trap or poison." "Normal evil," as Ruskin calls it, traditionally dependent on physical vigor, has been replaced by urban "decrepitude," by "aberration, palsy, or plague."[93] The *Quarterly* takes similar offense at the so-called Newspaper Novel, even if it is written "with a purpose": "There is something unspeakably disgusting in this ravenous appetite for carrion, this vulture-like instinct which smells out the newest mass of social corruption, and hurries to devour the loathsome dainty before the scent has evaporated."[94] Many of the reviewers express this same sort of distaste, directed not at the underlying social causes, but at the messengers who bring the bad news of them by simply dramatizing their effects. Not all of the sensation novelists were trustworthy or artistically skilled, but obviously there were serious reasons for studying social corruption as well as a natural interest in the material provided by modern situations. It becomes easier to understand and to sympathize with the excesses and the hysteria of mid-century sensationalism when they are seen in the actual context of smothering respectability and fastidiousness. The extremes of the sensation novel are in one sense a sign of desperation and dissent. A rare defense in the *Westminster Review* is based on this same rebellious impulse: "We are so thoroughly impressed with the conviction that art and morals alike suffer by the prudish conventionalities of our present English style, that we are inclined to welcome rebellion against it merely because it is rebellion."[95]

For its readers, the sensation novel filled a specific need by supplying the antidote to a surfeit of prosaic respectability. The primitive "emotion-hunger of the people,"[96] given voice in the cheaper serials, had its equivalent at higher levels of sophistication. An unfavorable notice in the *Westminster*, dismissing the question with a breezy "there is no accounting for tastes," cites without comment an intriguing and suggestive instance: "When Richardson, the showman, went about with his menagerie he had a big black baboon, whose habits were so filthy, and whose behaviour was so disgusting, that respectable people constantly remonstrated with him for exhibiting such an animal. Richardson's answer invariably was, 'Bless you, if it wasn't for that big black baboon I should be ruined; it attracts all the young girls in the country.' "[97] The sensation novelists, too, were dealers in big black baboons; their audience found a perverse attraction in their horrific wares. M. E. Braddon, often considered a brazen practitioner in perversity, seems to have understood the nature of her own brand of art. In a passage from *Eleanor's Victory*, she describes the popularity of a "sensation" picture called "The Earl's Death":

Although the picture was ugly, there was a strange weird attraction in it, and people went to see it again and again, and liked, and hankered after it, and talked of it perpetually all that season, one faction declaring that the lucifer-match effect was the most delicious moonlight, and the murderess of the Earl the most lovely of womankind, till the faction who thought the very reverse of this became afraid to declare their opinions, and thus everybody was satisfied.[98]

Beyond this desire for the perverse, undoubtedly aggravated by Victorian prudery, there is a more fundamental void left by the contracted and stultifying world view of materialism, modern science, and strictly domestic fiction. Even the opponents of sensationalism occasionally recognize this, while endeavoring to account for the whole unfortunate phenomenon, whose motivating force can be understood as a kind of "hectic rebellion against nature—frantic attempts by any kind of black art or mad psychology to get some grandeur and sacredness restored to life—or if not sacredness and grandeur, at least horror and mystery."[99] In a self-styled "age of analysis and criticism,"[100] of rational and scientific explanation, the missing dimension of transcendence was liable to take on strange and twisted forms. If the sensation novel was often merely a vulgarization of loftier tendencies, still it did penetrate to something essential in the Victorian psyche, to vital elements otherwise unaccounted for. Its primitive, troublesome vision collided sharply with that of the reigning domestic novel—which was never quite the same again.

# 2

## The Sensation Novel and Victorian Theories of Fiction

### I.

"I hate all mysteries. . . . And as for secrets, I consider them to be one of the forms of ill-breeding."
Lady Janet in Collins' *The New Magdalen*

---

**A**lthough the sensation novel has since been consigned to oblivion, from the viewpoint of alarmed contemporaries, its lurid manifestations presided over a "literary reign of terror," which transformed the moral and cultural landscape of a decade. The fad appeared to be omnipresent during the 1860s, indiscriminately swallowing up the various modes of narration: "Everything must now be sensational. Professor Kingsley sensationalizes History, and Mr. Wilkie Collins daily life. One set of writers wear the sensational buskin, another the sensational sock."[1] Its popular and commercial predominance was undisputed, a recognized if deplorable fact of the day. At the same time, more surprisingly, the sensation novel left its mark in the realm of literary theory, even if mostly in the form of reactions against it; the critics never felt safe in simply ignoring it. When Trollope was writing his *Autobiography* in the mid-1870s, the sensation novel still seemed prominent enough to be considered one of the two poles in current fiction, with the sensational method itself as the main basis of distinction:

Among English novels of the present day, and among English novelists, a great division is made. There are sensational novels and anti-sensational, sensational novelists and anti-sensational, sensational readers and anti-sensational. The novelists who are considered to be anti-sensational are generally called realistic.[2]

Curiously—some critics thought ominously—the rise of the sensation genre coincided with the height of the novelist's newly won prestige, his new presence as a social and ethical force. After decades on the fringes of respectability and artistic significance, the novelist had become acknowledged as "now our most influential writer. If he be a man of genius his power over the community he addresses is far beyond that of any other author."[3] It is no wonder that the sensation vogue appeared all the more formidable at a time when prose fiction could no longer be disregarded, when it had finally established its right to be taken seriously.

Of course, the loudest alarm was sounded by the moralists, led by no less a figure than the archbishop of York, who disapproved of sensation novels and preached a sermon against them.[4] For the more conservative Victorian reviewers, the period between Scott and the 1860s was already to be looked upon with nostalgia as a golden age when English novels were "family reading," noted throughout the novel-producing world for "a certain sanity, wholesomeness, and cleanliness unknown to other literature of the same class." This wholesome state of affairs was endorsed on the practical level because the novel provided the chief amusement of youth, invalids, and women,[5] and on a somewhat more elevated plane because its legitimate office was to express "good and noble thought": otherwise "the art is prostituted," and human nature itself maligned, by "pictures of life which would make us all a set of crawling worms unfit to be suffered to exist, much less to be made subjects of a work of art. If men be all mean and interested and worldly-minded, then it is no more proper to make them subjects of fiction than wasps, toads, and maggots."[6]

Not only do the sensation novelists haunt the "sinks and sewers of society" in their minute portrayal of "the obscene birds of night";[7] they also begin to sympathize with their own abominable creations, or to make light of their ingenious crimes. Here M. E. Braddon is judged the particular offender: "The moral of the story [*Eleanor's Victory*] seems to be, that to cheat an old man at cards and to forge a will are no impediments to attaining distinction in the world, and, indeed, are rather venial offenses"; "Few other novelists could have invented anything so diabolical as the murder [in *Henry Dunbar*], or have depicted with seeming complacency the after-life of the criminal. The impression made is, that the murderer was a clever man, and was very hardly used." Worse even than this is the false sense of proportion—moral no less than aesthetic—engendered by her exclusive preoccupation with a certain kind of human activity:

> According to Miss Braddon, crime is not an accident, but it is the business of life. She would lead us to conclude that the chief end of man is to commit a murder, and his highest merit to escape punishment; that women are born to attempt to commit murders, and to succeed in committing bigamy.[8]

When crime is represented as routine, not to mention universal, the critics start to bridle in self-defense. This is the "taint" that "clings" to the most inoffensive readers of criminal romance, who at the least have been keeping disreputable company: "we feel as if we had been conniving at their guilt, if not actually accomplices in it."[9]

In the Victorian period, as these and endless similar examples prove, there was no need for the casual reviewer to apologize for assuming the role of moralist; Mrs. Oliphant, indeed, speaks of the "conclusion to our sermon,"[10] as though that were a perfectly ordinary designation for a critical essay. Novels, too, are routinely evaluated as three-volume sermons, according to the principle that "art provides the most powerful, though the least obtrusive, means by which the standard of morality is affected." The category of "light literature" is no longer exempt from such sober-minded moral scrutiny. On the contrary, "this literature is effective by reason of its very lightness: it spreads, penetrates, and permeates, where weightier matter would lie merely on the outside of the mind. . . . We are by no means sure that . . . prose works of fiction do not constitute precisely that branch of the intellectual activity of a nation which a far-seeing moralist would watch with the most vigilant concern, and supervise with the most anxious and unceasing care."[11] Reade and Collins, as the most reputable of the sensationalists, counter this sort of argument with claims of their own to transcend "the clap-trap morality of the present day" with "the Christian morality which is of all time."[12] Still, the clap-trap morality rankles; they feel a need to defend themselves against it. Under the guise of a "Romantic Old Gentleman" and novel-reader, Collins lodges this half-humorous protest against the dreary champions of respectability:

> If the dull people of our district were told tomorrow that my wife, daughters, and nieces had all eloped in different directions, leaving just one point of the compass open as a runaway outlet for me and the cook, I feel firmly persuaded that not one of them would be inclined to discredit the report. "This is what comes of novel-reading!" they would say.[13]

Closely allied with these moral objections—and undoubtedly lurking behind most of them—are the inveterate social antagonisms, given a redefined focus by the urban situation and increased working-class literacy. Critics looking for damning evidence against the sensation novel have only to cite its origins in the cheap publications for the masses; these are correctly identified as "the original germ, the primitive monad, to which all the varieties of sensational literature may be referred, as to their source." The imagery of disease becomes prominent as critics of sensationalism describe the unnerving progression by which this "virus is spreading in all directions, from the penny journal to the shilling magazine, and from the shilling magazine to the thirty shillings volume."[14] Despite their successful infiltration of the mainstream market, the basic plot lines of these fashionable novels are considered to be all too often indistinguishable from those of the crudest broadsides: "But (as many of our readers will know)," says the reviewer in *Temple Bar*, "we have not been speaking of a serial story of 'Reynolds's Miscellany' or the 'London Journal,' but of a novel, 'large numbers' of which, it was advertized on its appearance, would be 'taken' by the circulating libraries, where well-appointed carriages most do congregate."[15]

The threat to literary standards is only exceeded by the threat to social distinctions. Reading sensation novels becomes a subversive pursuit because it brings the middle and lower classes together over the same printed page: "[M. E. Braddon] may boast, without fear of contradiction, of having temporarily succeeded in making the literature of the Kitchen the favourite reading of the Drawing-room"; "Unhappily, the sensational novel is that one touch of anything but nature that makes the kitchen and the drawing-room kin."[16] It is hard to imagine that the critics would have raised such a vociferous outcry if the fashion had spread in the opposite direction—from the middle class downward. As it was, neither the original impetus toward sensationalism nor the particular conventions of the sensation novel had been developed under middle-class control. The content and implications of the genre, far more than those of the popular domestic romance on which it was based, tended to diverge from or even attack the most cherished of middle-class values.

The blurring of social distinctions, remarked in actual life in the mild form of a shared literary taste, becomes more flagrant and more disquieting in the world of the novels themselves. Not only do the middle- or upper-class characters mingle a little too freely with their inferiors, they begin to imitate lower-class behavior, most strikingly in such matters as irregular morals or "domestic relations of an exceedingly peculiar character."[17] In *No Name*, for example, the youthful Magdalen Vanstone discovers that her parents' happy and conventional home life has been carried on for decades without benefit of legal marriage. After she has been disinherited because of this, Magdalen herself takes to the stage, assumes an alias, participates in an elaborate deception masterminded by a professional con man, and ends up utterly cast away in the public streets. Her own marriage—legal and socially advantageous—is worse than prostitution, a deliberate mockery of the domestic ideal. Miss Braddon's notorious Aurora Floyd, daughter of a wealthy banker, is much given to the language and society of the stables; she elopes to the continent with her father's groom at the age of seventeen and then conceals this abortive marriage from her second husband, a solid, good-natured country squire. The scene in which she horse-whips a half-witted servant draws particular fire from the reviewers: "We are certain that, except in this novel, no lady possessing the education and occupying the position of Aurora Floyd could have acted as she is represented to have done."

Even more intolerable, perhaps, than the spectacle of a well-born lady behaving like "a very low type of female character"[18] is the reverse of this—a woman of the streets behaving like a lady. In *The New Magdalen* by Wilkie Collins, a reformed prostitute successfully impersonates a colonel's daughter and marries a gentleman. In *Armadale*, an unreformed murderer, once a lady's maid, passes for a respectable governess: "She is described as a beautiful, accomplished, plausible lady, approaching middle age, who, after having passed her life in kennels and gambling houses and casinos and jails, shows no trace in her demeanour of such associations. . . . [But] the criminal dock, the prison, the companionship with a procuress, must tell even on an educated woman who had sunk to such infamy."[19]

It is axiomatic in the sensation novel that crime, evil, and violent or illicit passion have already found their way into ordinary middle-class surroundings. The result is perceived as nothing less than a direct, full-scale invasion of the middle-class domestic paradise:

> It is on our domestic hearths that we are taught to look for the incredible. A mystery sleeps in our cradles; fearful errors lurk in our nuptial couches; fiends sit down with us at table; our innocent-looking garden walks hold the secret of treacherous murders; and our servants take £20 a year from us for the sake of having us at their mercy.[20]

The key to this invasion is the sensation novel's assault on the heroine, invariably the moral and emotional center of traditional melodrama. It might be said that her sole function on the nineteenth-century stage is to defend her honor against the violence or blandishments of the villain: the core of the dramatic action lies in the conflict between them. What the sensation novel does is to disturb this balance; the aesthetic structure remains the same, but the issue is no longer so simple. Although she is still the central figure, the sensational heroine begins to represent a moral ambivalence rather than a moral certainty. Although the reader is still expected to feel for her, if anything even more intensely, she is no longer invulnerable, but likely to emerge as weak, foolish, impetuous, or vengeful. Even if she is guiltless in intention, like Aurora Floyd, she can no longer be considered the untarnished symbol of the middle-class ideal—the angel of the hearth, the embodiment of chastity. "It is easier, in fact," warns the *Christian Remembrancer*, "to turn nun, hospital nurse, or sister of mercy, to take up and carry through the professed vocation of a saint, than to work out the English ideal of wife, mother, and presiding spirit of the house, after any wide departure from custom and decorum."[21]

For whatever reasons, the heroine of the sensation novel has become enmeshed in a sordid tangle of crime, blackmail, and seduction; she has become a participant, however unwilling, as well as merely a victim. When Aurora Floyd secretly pays off her lower-class husband to keep out of the way, her action signals the beginning of a radical change in the meaning of the heroine and thus in the meaning of melodrama itself.

At the same time, in sensation novels of the *Lady Audley* tradition, the heroine's rightful place is usurped altogether by the villainess, the golden-haired impostor who masquerades as a conventional wife while plotting murder on the side. Not even a man of the character and position of Sir Michael Audley is able to guarantee the sanctity of his home against the intrusion of crime and madness. The implications of this are devastating: the outward semblance of the domestic ideal may prove worse than empty; the angel of the hearth may turn out to be an incubus. With the followers of Dickens, and with their followers at a further remove, the middle-class retreat—Rose Maylie's cottage in *Oliver Twist*—can no longer be taken for granted. Social and moral chaos has spread even to the inner sanctum, infecting the emblem of domesticity. The one island of security and certitude remaining in a tumultuous age has been invaded and despoiled.

Whether heroine or villainess, it is always a woman who demands the spotlight in the typical sensation novel. This in turn leads to a conflict between the aesthetic requirements of plot and the conventional social role assigned to women. Because, ideally, "the life of women cannot well be described as a life of action," their fictional prominence can only bring about a distortion of the accepted social order. E. S. Dallas has examined this process at some length in *The Gay Science*:

When women are thus put forward to lead the action of a plot, they must be urged into a false position. To get vigorous action they are described as rushing into crime, and doing masculine deeds. Thus they come forward in the worst light, and the novelist finds that to make an effect he has to give up his heroine to bigamy, to murder, to child-bearing by stealth in the Tyrol, and to all sorts of adventures which can only signify her fall. . . . It is not wrong to make a sensation; but if the novelist depends for his sensation upon the action of a woman, the chances are that he will attain his end by unnatural means.

Both Dallas and Mrs. Oliphant remark on the fact that women novelists are themselves the culprits, that "one of the earliest results of an increased feminine influence in our literature [has been] a display of what in women is most unfeminine."[22] Once again it is M. E. Braddon who transgresses most blatantly, betraying her familiarity with the least reputable strata of London life: "She knows much that ladies are not accustomed to know, but that they are apparently very glad to learn. The names of drinks, the technicalities of the faro-table, the lingo of the turf, the talk natural to a crowd of fast men at supper, when there are no ladies present but Miss Braddon, the way one gentleman knocks another down—all these things—the exact local coloring of Bohemia—our sisters and daughters may learn from these works."[23] The ultimate source of all these objections, unhesitatingly identified by Mrs. Oliphant, is woman's "one duty of invaluable importance to her country and her race which cannot be overestimated—and that is the duty of being pure. There is perhaps nothing of such vital consequence to a nation." If the ideal middle-class society is founded on the cornerstone of womanly purity, then it is quite understandable to find the "equivocal heroines"[24] of the sensation novel condemned as a threat to the entire social and moral fabric of Victorian England.

## II.

In these times, when the tendency is to be frightfully literal and catalogue-like—to make the thing, in short, a sort of sum in reduction that any miserable creature can do in that way—I have an idea (really founded on the love of what I profess), that the very holding of popular literature through a kind of popular dark age, may depend on such fanciful treatment.

Charles Dickens, Letter (1859)

If the sensation vogue undeniably provoked the worst literary criticism of the period—the rampant Grundyism, the sweeping misjudgments of the artistic function—it also inspired some of the liveliest and most incisive debate. The mere existence of the sensation novel, at the height of the trend toward realism, raised fundamental critical problems for contemporary observers. Its tremendous popularity alone challenged the critics to defend and, in the process, to rethink their own most basic assumptions about the role of fiction: its relation to life and to fact, its nonmimetic aspects, its appropriate aesthetic structures. And, Jamesians to the contrary, they did just that, with articles in all the most prestigious journals, from *Blackwood's* to the *Quarterly* to the *Contemporary*. Of course, much of the criticism is naive, narrow-minded, or prejudicial; but the best of it reveals an initial groping toward concepts, a forming of critical vocabulary, in order to begin discussing the novel as a distinct form of literary art.

The contribution of the sensation novelists themselves to this critical debate is somewhat problematical, to say the least. The extent of the "literary fraternalism" among the so-called Dickensians—Dickens, Collins, and Reade—is certainly questionable, and their common observance of any coherent "literary creed"[25] even more so. Reade is notoriously eccentric and unreliable in his attempts at literary analysis; Collins seems to have remained unaware of the contradictions between his theory and practice; and Dickens' own comments, for the most part, are scattered and fragmentary. As we have seen already, in the previous chapter, the sensation novelists' conflicting impulses to fact and fantasy most often result in an unresolved ambivalence, at least on the theoretical level. Perhaps their most durable offering has been Wilkie Collins' unabashed formula, "Make 'em laugh, make 'em cry, make 'em wait." To credit their "literary dogma" as the motivating force behind their choice of sensationalism[26] is at once to ignore the operation of other, less calculable factors and to overestimate the role of explicit literary theory in the creation of their brand of fiction. With critics and novelists alike, most of the relevant "dogma" takes the form of outrage or apology after the fact.

The accepted critical context for all these skirmishes is that of "Realism," in its original, nineteenth-century definition. That original sense, already showing signs of wear by the end of the 1850s,[27] may seem irrecoverable at this point, but certain basic preconceptions can still be delineated. In the first place, there is a general consensus, with G. H. Lewes, that "Art always aims at the representation of Reality, i.e. of Truth";[28] no aura of doubt or dissatisfaction yet adheres to these terms. Since there are two kinds of truth, or at least two different ways of perceiving truth,[29] it is possible to distinguish between two principal schools of art based on truth—Realism and Idealism. The former, in David Masson's phrase, paints "life as it is actually and historically," while the latter depends on "some suggestion snatched from nature, in one or other of her uttermost moments, and then carried away and developed in the void."[30] Although the Victorian concept of Idealism is always susceptible to tinges of utopianism or even simple escapism,[31] its main impetus is toward artistic generalization, toward the portrayal of "types" and universal passions.[32] Similarly, in the name of genuine Realism, Lewes objects to the popular heresy of "detailism," which "confounds truth with familiarity, and predominance of unessential details. There are other truths besides coats and waistcoats, pots and pans, drawing-rooms and suburban villas." As both Lewes and Masson recognize, the opposition between Realism and Idealism is in itself misleading, for "Realism is . . . the basis of all Art, and its antithesis is not Idealism, but *Falsism*."[33] With twentieth-century hindsight, it is clear that these notions of Realism and Idealism have the same basis—that they are two sides of the same world view, that one logically implies the other. Their use as critical terms reflects a state of general agreement about what life is really like, about what constitutes verisimilitude

and what constitutes exaggeration. Not even the sensation novelists question the premises that make the distinction possible between the two modes; they use the
same terminology in their own defense, claiming, like the
realists, the "nearest and truest view" that they can
achieve "of the one model, Nature."[34] But the critics think
otherwise, and in fact the out-and-out sensationalists
(Dickens being generally classified as a successful or unsuccessful Idealist) have neglected rather blatantly to
play the game according to the prevailing rules.

The mimetic standard, unsurprisingly, is the one most
often invoked against the sensation novelists, as opposing
reviewers echo the universal refrain of "unnatural," "artificial," "false," "grotesque." Whenever characterization
is discussed, always as the glory of Victorian fiction, even
the most rigorous critics start to betray their fundamental allegiance to a naive form of verisimilitude. It becomes the highest tribute to a novelist's skill to think of
his characters as "real, living, breathing" men and
women, with whom the reader feels "intimately ac-
quainted."[35] Without this intimacy and this quality of
lifelikeness, the characters fail, and with them the novels
they populate. Again and again M. E. Braddon's startling
creations are cited as evidence of "her entire ignorance of
human nature and mental processes"; Olivia Marchmont,
of *John Marchmont's Legacy*, is "but a creature of Miss
Braddon's imagination . . . unreal as a hobgoblin," while
Lady Audley herself is "scarcely a human being," "though
she may be a fine conception."[36] The villain, like his
female counterpart, is no longer to be considered exempt
from the ordinary laws of probability: "When a man acts
as a villain, he does not, as Miss Braddon seems to think,
cease to be a man." In short, "when the characters in a
novel cease to be true to nature, they lose their chief interest"[37] for readers who want familiar companions
rather than imaginary constructs.

Not even G. H. Lewes, erstwhile opponent of "coat-
and-waistcoat realism,"[38] entirely escapes falling into the
terminology and frame of reference associated with the

most naive of his contemporaries. According to his analysis, even Dickens' unforgettable figures are discovered to be "merely masks,—not characters, but personified characteristics, caricatures and distortions of human nature." The popular success of these "wooden horses" derives from their irresistible operation on the reader's own fund of personal experience: "Universal experiences became individualized in these types; an image and a name were given, and the image was so suggestive that it seemed to *express* all that it was found to *recall*, and Dickens was held to have depicted what his readers supplied." For Lewes, this phenomenon, far from constituting a legitimate process of art, simply conceals the underlying "falsity" of characters like Pecksniff, Gamp, and Micawber.[39] R. H. Hutton, another eminent critic of the day, considers Mrs. Gamp "a great humorist's creation *on a hint* from human life, and not human life itself" and labels Dickens a transparent illusionist, almost a charlatan, finishing him off with this cryptic dismissal: "A realist as regards *human* nature he never was at all."[40]

No sooner have the realists established the antiromantic criterion of "truth-to-life" in the novel than they find their position under siege from the opposite direction. The sensational fiction of the 1860s launches its attack on the realist center from both extremes at once, appealing to the validity of both fantasy and fact. Reade and Collins, in particular, profess to challenge the realists on their own ground and to surpass them according to their own standards. What, after all, could be more "real" than literal fact? When the sensationalists begin to brandish their documentation and their expert testimony, it is time for the critics, perforce, to clarify their own concept of verisimilitude. While "real" and "living" characters remain much in demand, the use of actual circumstances, especially of the bizarre variety favored by the sensation novelists, is justifiably viewed as a subversion of the essential spirit of Victorian realism. At stake here is the preservation of the fictional illusion, so dear to the realist's heart: "In real life we accept such facts because they *are* facts; but in reading a novel, the whole groundwork is so necessarily make-believe, that the facts must seem very natural to make us forget their unreality."[41] As Mrs. Oliphant remarks of an incident in *Hard Cash*, "Such a thing might happen in fact; but fiction is bound as fact is not . . . and must consider *vraisemblance* as well as absolute truth." Or again: "Facts are of all things in the world the most false to nature, the most opposed to experience, the most contradictory of all the grand laws of existence. . . . for us truth and fact are two different things."[42]

This, of course, presupposes the actual operation of such "grand laws"; indeed all nineteenth-century realism is dependent on an instinctive belief in the order and significance of the universe and of "life-as-it-is."[43] The realist vision is essentially a moral one; the issues are moral ones in this kind of universe, where "reality" itself is moral. Mrs. Oliphant's attitude is not at all atypical; it is only a logical extreme of the common realist perspective. For the Victorians, unlike their twentieth-century successors, "truth" and "human nature" are constants; not only do they have an objective existence that can be observed and imitated by the artist, they obey certain innate laws, predictable and immutable. Within this context of belief, generally valid for the nineteenth-century realist novel, Mrs. Oliphant, with her usual dogmatism, narrows the moral focus to her own conventional formulas of right and wrong: "It is noway necessary for the production of these strong effects that the worse should be made to appear the better cause, or that it should be represented as possible that certain qualities of mind or amiabilities of temper are sufficient to bring a character safely through all kinds of actual and positive wrongdoing without fatal or even serious damage. This is a great mistake in art, as well as falsehood to nature."[44] The violation of Mrs. Oliphant's narrow code is not finally important, but the larger violation is: the unmistakable tendency of the sensation novel to undermine the prevailing

Victorian world view, to alter the perception of "reality" and to revise its traditional meaning. In a universe that mingles the implications of fact and fantasy, the "grand laws of existence," taken for granted by the realists, are no longer functional; they have been replaced by a new set of assumptions, about to become dominant in its turn.

The sensation novels, then, are neither realist nor idealist—"neither exact nor exalting," as the reviewer in *Temple Bar* puts it; they "represent life neither as it is nor as it ought to be."[45] Although the champions of realism and idealism certainly quarreled with each other, the sensationalists should more properly be considered the adversaries of both. The two great modes, in their mid-Victorian incarnation, coexist without difficulty because they express complementary aspects of the same view of reality. It is sensationalism, however, that disrupts this comfortable outlook; in mingling elements of both realism and idealism, the sensation novelists create something that belongs to neither. In fact, it is this mixture itself, this disregard of fundamental categories of art, that becomes the focus of the aesthetic objections to the sensation novel.

These basic philosophical premises leave their mark on the specifics of form in the Victorian novel. According to the realist code, the principles governing formal aesthetic structure are generally considered to be based on probability, on a direct correspondence, that is, between such literary conventions as plot or incident and the patterns of ordinary (middle-class) life. The "proprieties of art," as Hutton calls them, are infringed in the sensation novel by too much emphasis on the extremes of human experience, by too much repetition of a single, specialized device: "To heap together startling and exceptional incidents in defiance of all probability is the obvious resource of inferior artists. Such incidents do doubtless occur in modern life, nor is there any reason why they should not be introduced . . . in the novels which undertake to represent it. But our sense of the fitness of things is offended by the continual recurrence of what ought to be most sparingly employed to bring about a catastrophe or to disentangle a plot."[46] The result is a distortion of reality, "an entire society swarming with thieves, murderers, adulterers, and bigamists,"[47] in which the strange or the unusual has become the commonplace, in which the exceptional has displaced the rule.

Amid the rush of events in *Hard Cash*, Reade pauses to quarrel with some anonymous practitioner of "Criticism," who has complained that novelists routinely "suppress the small intermediate matters which in real life come by the score between each brilliant event, and so present the ordinary and the extraordinary parts of life in false proportions." Reade's answer to this is "that epics, dramas, novels, histories, chronicles, reports of trials at law, in a word, all narratives, true or fictitious, except those which, true or fictitious, nobody reads, abridge the uninteresting facts as nature never did, and dwell as nature never did on the interesting ones"; it is up to the reader's own common sense to redress "that just balance of the 'sensational' and the 'soporific,' which all writers, that have readers, disturb."[48] Of course, all this is transparently self-serving and only calls attention to Reade's most flagrant inadequacies; but still there is a valid basis to his argument, as well as a hint of the future in it. The sensation novel, however rude in execution, at least recognizes heightening, exaggeration, and foreshortening as legitimate narrative techniques; it scorns the realist values of apparent artlessness and unobtrusive manipulation of effect. Once again, the dispute over aesthetic proportion shows how inevitably form is tied to world view, how inescapably the sensationalist rebellion against the approved literary conventions implies equal rebellion against the premises they support. The methodical, predictable "reality" of the Victorian consciousness breaks down under the new order of the sensation novel, with its unsettling distortions and juxtapositions of material that is all too recognizably drawn from the context of modern urban experience.

For Thackeray, the archrealist, the province of the

novel, as distinguished from drama or poetry, is inherently restricted to the "drawing-room"—to the levels of reality where "a coat is a coat and a poker a poker; and must be nothing else according to my ethics, not an embroidered tunic, nor a great red-hot instrument like the Pantomime weapon."[49] Although the more astute critics avoid this extreme viewpoint, most of them would undoubtedly agree with G. H. Lewes that the two fictional realms of fantasy and social realism ought to be kept duly separated from one another: "We are by no means rigorous in expecting that the story is to move along the highway of everyday life . . . [but] if we are to travel into fairy-land, it must be in a fairy equipage, not a Hansom's cab."[50] But the sensation novelists are particularly fond of cabs and continually hire them for even the most romantic occasions. For the reviewer in *Temple Bar*, this cavalier defiance of literary decorum undermines the author's credibility, which itself remains unquestioned as a virtue in fiction, and an indispensable virtue at that: "One would have thought that when something exceptionally terrible and mysterious had to be made credible, the more distant and unknown the locality, the more easily would the wonder-telling author be believed"; but it is characteristic of the sensation novelists to "despise that distance which not only lends enchantment to the view, but which justifies both writer and reader for accepting as likely the grossly improbable."[51]

The *Spectator* elaborates on this attitude, investing it with only the most practical and literal of implications: "No one would call Scott's great romance [*Ivanhoe*] 'sensational.' The remoteness of the time protects it from the charge; we know generally that the age of Richard I was an age of violent deeds; . . . we do not know instinctively, and the softening effect of distance makes us careless to inquire, whether this or that incident is probable." Even the tragedy of Oedipus is here seen to revert, on the same principle, to an already ancient mythology: "No Greek audience would have endured such a story, had the scene been laid in the Athens or Thebes of their own age. . . .

Men who would rebel against the notion of a fate which governed their own lives, would accept it without difficulty of the shadowy personages of a far distant past."[52]

In other words, the terrible or the improbable is something that happens to somebody else in some other era. To let it happen to oneself, or to one's peers or contemporaries, is simply unthinkable. It is interesting to find this instinct of self-preservation solidified into aesthetic theory; all the reviewers, except the avowed moralists, claim to analyze the sensation novel in terms of its "artistic fault."[53] "The contempt of the probable," as *Temple Bar* has it, is what makes the sensation novel a totally unprecedented phenomenon, what distinguishes it, in the worst possible way, from all its venerable antecedents in the long history of romance:

> When before did it ever enter the head of the writer of romance to find a field for the exercise of his more awful powers just at his own door or round the corner? With a due sense of the fitness of things, rather did he travel far afield, and seek, in remote and somewhat obscure regions, for a reasonable arena wherein to make men and women act outrageously. Outrageous their actions did not seem, happening in places where personal experience had not gone before, and set the boundaries of the probable and the improbable.[54]

Those boundaries, it appears, are essential to the Victorian equanimity; without them the premise of a rational, moral, orderly universe begins to crumble. The very concepts of probability and its opposite, as defined by the Victorian critics, are inextricably linked with a particular view of what is "real," of what goes on in modern, civilized, middle-class society. The *Christian Remembrancer*, in warning against the sensation novel, compares its "exceptional outrages of morality and custom" with the more obviously stunning breach of physical laws in ghost stories and other supernatural fiction: bigamy, for example, "is sensational as fully, though in a lower field, as are ghosts and portents; it disturbs in the same way the reader's sense of the stability of things, and opens a new, untried vista of what may be."[55] And these moral and social apparitions, as the critics are well aware, prove far more difficult to exorcise.

Since realism is almost exclusively identified with character—with the minute portrayal of "speaking, moving, living, human creatures"[56]—the other elements of narrative, notably plot, are slighted, even discredited, in both novels and reviews of the period. Plot, as separable from or opposed to the working out of character, had become distinctly old-fashioned by mid-century, a throwback to conventional melodrama.[57] The sensation novelists are routinely berated for action that overrides character, rather than illuminating or growing out of it. E. S. Dallas, in *The Gay Science*, a somewhat eccentric mid-Victorian anatomy of criticism, makes a rare attempt to analyze the novel of incident on its own merits and to defend its philosophical validity:

> Not only does Thackeray thus insist upon a theory of character which implies in the sense of the poet the withering of the individual; we see precisely the same tendency in the school of fiction, which is the right opposite of his—what is called the sensation school. In that school the first consideration is given to the plot; and the characters must succumb to the exigencies of the plot. . . . The difference between the two lies solely in the relation of the characters pourtrayed to the actions described. In the novel of character man appears moulding circumstances to his will, directing the action for himself, supreme over incident and plot. In the opposite class of novel man is represented as made and ruled by circumstance; he is the victim of change and the puppet of intrigue. Is either of these views of life wholly true or wholly false? We may like the one better than the other. We may like to see men generally represented as possessed of decided character, masters of their destiny, and superior to circumstance; but is this view of life a whit more true than that which pictures

the mass of men as endowed with faint characters, and as tossed hither and thither by the accidents of life, which we sometimes call fate and sometimes fortune? The art of fiction, which makes characters succumb to the exigencies of plot, is just as defensible as that which breaks down incident before the weight of character.[58]

Here both kinds of novel, contradictions and all, are fitted into Dallas' own favorite scheme of the "withering" of the hero. This is not just an arbitrary distortion, however convenient it may at first appear. Both the realists and the sensationalists are trying to come to grips with the same overwhelming experience of urban, technological society; both reflect the newly diminished stature of the individual amid the crowding and the complexities of modern existence. The fictional characters who "mould circumstances," no less than those who capitulate, are thoroughly ordinary, even petty; they are the puppets of *Vanity Fair*. When the sensation novelists undertake to restore the exceptional to human life—the terrible, the mysterious, the intense—they find it impossible to do so in terms of character. Instead they rely on external circumstance, which must be stupendous enough in itself to elevate the most commonplace of dramatis personae, to ignite aspects of their being that would otherwise remain dormant. In the sensation novel, character does not resist plot or create it, but is plunged headlong into its turbulent depths. Heroes and villains alike are at the mercy of accident, of external caprice. Although specific plots more often than not are primitive and cumbersome, the underlying substance of all of them points to naturalism and beyond, to a new view of human character as a shifting and uncertain quantity, played upon by forces outside its control. Among the critics of the 1860s, Dallas is alone in recognizing this larger import of the sensation novel. Once he has filtered out the particular flaws of execution, which in his opinion mar "the plotting novels, as they are now written," he is prepared to concede their fundamental point: "To show man as the sport of circumstance may be a depressing view of human nature; but it is not fair to regard it as immoral or to denounce it as utterly untrue."[59]

Neither is it fair to pass over the characters in the novel of incident as mere automata, as a sort of collective artistic mistake. Subordinate they may be, at times interchangeable, but they are not wholly devoid of interest. If nothing else, assuming that the typical sensation novelist starts out with bizarre situations—with crimes, secrets, illicit passions—he is then automatically forced to account for them on the level of characterization by creating individual men and women who are somehow capable of sustaining and acting out such improbable deeds. Approached from this angle, admittedly a backhanded one, human nature reveals itself in unexpected ways. Because they are ruled by circumstance, the characters in a sensation novel tend to be weak, vacillating, and inconsistent; they lack wholeness; they lack an integrating central core. This causes obvious problems of coherence—and the least effective figures dissolve into irreconcilable fragments—but it also opens up new possibilities. In order to provide some justification for the erratic behavior of their murderers, bigamists, and adulteresses, the sensation novelists are driven to exploit the irrational elements of the psyche, the obscure and unreasonable motivations that in the twentieth century are associated with the subconscious. Inner forces, as powerful and uncontrollable as fate, claim equal numbers of victims. Evil or antisocial action is no longer the direct result and expression of evil character, as in conventional melodrama, but derives from combinations of circumstance, weakness, insanity, impulse, "sensation" at its most basic. As one reviewer complains of M. E. Braddon, "nerves, feeling, excitement, will, and inclination are the sole motive powers of every character she cares for."[60]

Most of the time the actual portraits fall short because the writers have not yet acquired the techniques for dramatizing the subconscious and because they are generally satisfied with superficiality; but at least the idea itself is new—the relativity of human character as well as of human standards of morality. Again, this indicates a substantial change in the bearings of popular literature, which traditionally requires the strictest adherence to duty on the part of the individual: "He was master of his own destiny," so the message goes; "we can control ourselves and master our own feelings and desires if we want to."[61] In the sensation novel, even the heroine, without ceasing to be heroine, is permitted to indulge in such indiscretions as eloping with horse trainers or fleecing near relatives under false pretenses, while the blame ultimately rests with vague inner compulsions, accidental rather than essential in relation to character.

Within the limits of their genre, the sensation novelists come up with various provisional solutions to the problem of character motivation. One of these, suggested by Dallas in precisely this connection, is the unusual prevalence of idiots: "There is always, in a sensation novel, one, or it may be two, half-witted creatures. The utility of these crazy beings is beyond belief."[62] Straight idiocy, which afflicts such major characters as Anne Catherick in *The Woman in White* or Steeve Hargraves in *Aurora Floyd*, proves invaluable as a source of mystification and incomprehensible clues. The next best thing is insanity, most often temporary or intermittent, which regularly supplies the complications for Reade and Braddon. Lady Audley's much-touted "secret," dangerously anticlimactic when it is finally revealed, turns out to be a case of hereditary insanity, which has incited her to bigamy and murder. The lessons of Lady Audley's fate are then recklessly applied to the hero and through him to human nature in general: "There is nothing so delicate, so fragile, as that invisible balance upon which the mind is always trembling. Mad to-day and sane to-morrow. . . . Who has not been, or is not to be mad in some lonely hour of life? Who is quite safe from the trembling of the balance?"[63]

As *Fraser's* hastens to point out, this attitude effectively absolves Miss Braddon's characters from any moral responsibility for their own actions. At the same time, it also absolves them of logic or internal consistency. Again and again, the reviewers deplore the self-contradictions of one character or another, the fact that he or she "does not resemble a rational being."[64] Absurd as it looks now, this touch of madness differentiates the new Braddon prototype from the uniform and predictable stock figures of popular melodrama, whose dominant feature is a self-righteous sense of personal wholeness. However vulgarized the form, this irreverent approach to characterization both reflects and encourages a new perspective on the springs of human conduct, even in ordinary, middle-class characters.

Along with his numerous sketches of half-wits and maniacs, Reade, like Braddon, also experiments with the irrational impulses of normal, basically virtuous characters who entangle themselves in farfetched predicaments. The experimental nature of even his best writing reveals itself most glaringly in *Griffith Gaunt*, which mixes two antithetical kinds of characterization in the same love triangle. While the heroine and her priestly advisor are convincingly portrayed from within, the hero is permitted no internal psychology at all. With Kate Gaunt and Brother Leonard, whose spiritual involvement very nearly leads to an adulterous affair, Reade attains a surprisingly modern representation of two "self-deceivers"[65] and their subconscious motives. Not only does he break his own rules about authorial analysis, pointedly if sparingly, but he also seeks out the perfect narrative emblems for his heroine's inner confusion—as when Kate, at a crucial juncture in her infatuation, falls on the stairs and orders an invalid's bed, leaving her husband "as good as a widower." Griffith himself, the hero turned bigamist, is a strange, transitional figure, revealingly misplaced in the same novel. Probably because Kate escapes with her innocence, however artificially, Reade permits himself considerable latitude in developing the stages of her near seduction. Griffith, however, is actually and knowingly guilty of contracting an illegal marriage with his second wife. His ruling passion of jealousy, by definition subjective, assumes a tangible, external form, descending on him suddenly, often provoking a fit of brain fever or epilepsy: "That terrible passion had transformed its victim in a moment: the ruddy, genial, kindly Griffith, with his soft brown eye, was gone; and in his place lowered a face, older, and discolored, and convulsed, and almost demoniacal." Instead of facing up to this ambivalent combination of "hero, and now malefactor," Reade simply reverts to the classical notion of frenzy imposed from without: "Well said the ancients that anger is a short madness." But Griffith's emotion has none of the grandeur of Achilles' wrath; he is only a dull, ordinary country squire who suspects his wife of infidelity. The method here is incongruous and inept; the result is violent schizophrenia, which divides Griffith Gaunt into two separate and unrelated personae. Still, it shows that Reade, like the other sensationalists, is concerned with the relationship between inner and outer forces, both irrational, which combine to reduce individual characters to ambiguity and inconsistency.

Although the conventional hero has undergone a universal decline, a withering or eclipse, in the fiction of the period, his paltry successors find themselves occupying radically different positions in the opposing worlds of realism and sensationalism. In the realist novel, character may be diminished but it is still central. Even a loser like Amos Barton, in George Eliot's *Scenes of Clerical Life*, dominates the brief tale in which he appears. Even though he is distinguished only as "superlatively middling, the quintessential extract of mediocrity,"[66] to whom nothing at all remarkable happens, the entire point of narrating his "sad fortunes" in the first place depends on a thoroughgoing study of his character, on a sympathetic appreciation of the disparity between his own prosaic blundering and the more "glorious possibilities" of human nature as a whole. However uncompromising in their choice of insignificant characters, the realists are always willing to lavish their art and their concern on the average man in his average faults and

frustrations. The Amos Bartons of realist fiction, however
far removed from the center of their universe, still com-
mand the aesthetic and moral focus of the novels themselves; they matter in terms of the narrative structure, if
not in terms of the reality it proposes to represent.

That reality, solid and bristling with detail, is pervaded
by a sense of limitation on the scope and effectuality of
human actions; it is ultimately impervious to human will
and chicanery. But if the individual has no final control
over his own destiny, at least he cooperates in achieving
it. Even if there is no direct "moulding of circumstances,"
as Dallas would maintain, at least there is congruence between character and fate. The world portrayed in the
Novel of Social Reality, to borrow Masson's phrase,[67] is itself diminished, a fitting location for the diminished hero.
His reality may be circumscribed, even stifling in its
density, but at least it is determined, on a larger scale, by
the same rules that determine his character—the social
code of Thackeray and Trollope, the moral law of consequences in George Eliot. These rules, which are themselves "real" to the novelists who employ them, give
"shape and meaning" to the world[68] and thus, at least in-
directly, to the individual's experience of it. Most of all,
the rules are intelligible; they can be understood if not
controlled. Although the characters may be denied power
and triumph over the conditions of their world, they are
usually able, by the end of the novel, to reach some sort of
workable compromise.

A "novel without a hero," using Victorian terminology,
is hardly paradoxical; character and circumstance belong
to the same vision of reality—a reality that is limited but
not utterly meaningless. What the Victorian critics find
hard to accept, in the case of the sensation novel, is romance without a hero. It is strange and disquieting for
them to discover the ordinary, reduced, middle-class protagonist, at home in a place like Vanity Fair, suddenly
cast adrift in the universe of sensational romance—
tumultuous, improbable, unpredictable. Not only are its
workings beyond individual control, as in the realist

novel, they are equivocal and arbitrary. There are the same limits on human will and significance, but no limit at all on events, as long as they proceed by extremes. Events dwarf character without making any larger sense in themselves; the patterns may be intricate and astonishing, but they offer no clue to the fundamental pattern or meaning of existence. The "hand of Destiny," much overworked in Braddon, Collins, and Wood, beckons impartially to good and evil, decreeing seduction or unmerited death fully as often as it enforces poetic justice. Destiny, however piously invoked, has no moral content in the sensation novel. This fact again distinguishes the formulas of the new genre both from the conventional, moralistic standards of popular melodrama and from the more complex meanings and interconnections of classic realism. In the world of the sensation novel, where accident has been canonized in the place of system, anything can happen, while the characters have no chance of learning the rules, whether to play along with them or simply to comprehend.

In the sensation novel, the traditional dynamics of romance and melodrama have been substantially disrupted. Superficially, the paradigm looks familiar: the cataclysmic events, the intense passion and suffering of the principals, the resolution of conflict, in fulfillment or death, at the end. But the traditional order, the original source of this heightened and mysterious universe, requires an element of the supernatural or the superhuman, which enables the hero, by virtue of his own strength or divine intervention, to contend with the forces of his extravagant destiny. If there is no direct intervention of the supernatural, there must at least be a genuine, undiminished hero. Above all, there is significance in the total design, a local manifestation of ultimate truth. With the rise of the sensation novel, even romance has been demythologized. Although the sensation novelists consciously set out to recover its values, so painfully missing in their experience of modern society, they find it impossible to restore the old balance; the relation of nineteenth-century man to the mysterious, to the terrible and the passionate, has been knocked irrevocably askew. And although the sensation novelists insist upon meanings beyond the normally human, beyond the social and the commonplace, they have difficulty giving them substance—hence the pale and arbitrary figure of Destiny, hence the rule of accident. According to E. S. Dallas, the fairy tale, that popularized and democratic form of romance, has historically provided a context for the nonhero's encounter with the heroic:

> But in modern literature we have the same phenomenon—the weak and the foolish made much of, and treated as of equal account with heroes and demi-gods, while, at the same time, we hear no word of a supernatural grace—gift of a fairy, or favour of God—by which the weakness of man can be rendered of so much importance, and out of the mouth of a fool so much wisdom may proceed. And so throughout all the art of the day, and much of its thinking, we are troubled with a sense of disorder.[69]

In the sensation novel, where the universe has not been tailored to the limited expectations of the nonhero, that sense of disorder is particularly acute. The land of romance is no longer faraway and self-enclosed, like the highlands of Scott's Waverley novels, where an Edward Waverley or Frank Osbaldistone is only in temporary exile from civilization. On the contrary, the "withered," middle-class protagonist, the Victorian era's conception of itself, has been summarily abandoned, without any means of control or comprehension, in an ancient, hostile, and violent realm, which only a hero, or a divine fool, could presume to conquer or make sense of. Without the supernatural or heroic presence, which has receded in all nineteenth-century literature, there is no longer any inherent explanation for the patterns of romance; the heightened universe has become arbitrary and inexplicable, and the unheroic characters themselves, as a result of their contact with that universe, are becoming increasingly equivocal.

The "plotting" novelists, in their revolt against realism, assert the primacy of accident: "They and their audience, one suspects, often found the fortuitous more appalling than the logical."[70] And they use it not only as a means of harrowing their readers' nerves but also as a measure of a certain kind of experience that the realists prefer to overlook. All melodrama defies logic in favor of exaggeration and irrationality, arbitrary occurrences, the direct projection of fears and wishes in their least complicated form. All melodrama, in sharp contrast to tragedy, has an affinity with the absurd. Of course, to a sophisticated audience, the most primitive, straightforward versions may become absurd in the sense of ridiculous or laughable because their premises no longer seem valid. This is just at the point of happening to the old melodramatic formulations when the sensation novel, a relatively late development, begins to combine the absurdity of childish exaggeration with the less familiar absurdity of disorientation, the nonhero's loss of moorings in a universe where he does not belong. Because it is in touch with the deepest, subconscious anxieties of its age, in spite of its reliance on outworn convention, the sensation novel becomes absurd in a more sinister and disturbing way. If it had not been disturbing, if it had not undermined the most cherished of values, it would not have provoked such visceral outrage. Perhaps it is only fair to grant the sensation novelists, at least the best of them, some method in their madness, some intuitive awareness of what they were doing.

Northrop Frye has suggested an approach to Dickens' melodrama, the skeleton in the closet for most critics, through this notion of absurdity: "This disregard of plausibility is worth noticing, because everyone realizes that Dickens is a great genius of the absurd in his characterization, and it is possible that his plots are also absurd in the same sense, not from incompetence or bad taste, but from a genuinely creative instinct. If so, they are likely to be more relevant to the entire conception of the novel than is generally thought." Here Dickens parts company from the sensationalist rabble by providing a detailed representation of Victorian society—a society whose structures, "as structures, belong almost entirely to the absurd, obsessed, sinister aspect of it"; this, according to Frye, is what makes Dickens' social vision "anarchistic" and "revolutionary," in spite of its platitudes.[71] With the sensation novelists proper, the social background is assumed without being depicted; anarchy keeps breaking forth but it is free floating, attached neither to social institutions nor even to obsessed and demonic villains, of which there are remarkably few. This phenomenon in itself registers a new uncertainty about the sources of violence and passion, an uneasy feeling that they are close to home and no longer so easily accommodated by conventional morality and religion. Even M. E. Braddon, at her most commercial, knew what would scare people most effectively and she knew that it had nothing to do with monks in medieval castles. Much of the absurdity in the sensation novel—the arbitrary, the nightmarish, the uncontrollable—attempts to deal with the ongoing experience of a crisis in attitude. It may be that this represents a "vulgarization,"[72] or a popularizing, of tendencies observed elsewhere, but for that very reason its message is all the more unmistakable.

For the critics, the supreme absurdity of the sensation novel lies in its implausible mixture of the contrary modes of perception: romance and realism. According to their rules, fantasy should be labeled as such; it should stay comfortably remote from ordinary concerns; it should not be allowed to impinge on the "real" world, as the Victorians have defined it. As G. H. Lewes never tires of repeating, "in proportion as the story lies among scenes and characters of familiar experience, in proportion as the writer endeavours to engage our sympathy by pictures of concrete realities, and not by *abstractions* of passion and incident, the critic demands a closer adherence to truth and experience."[73] The sensation novelists, in trying to do both, are not playing fair; they make use of "illegitimate means to produce an effect upon the reader."[74] Even David Masson, the champion of Dickensian idealism, sees the two realms as distinct although they may occur in the same novel, the idealist characters only being "fitted for a world projected imaginatively beyond the real one, or inserted into the midst of the real one, and yet imaginatively moated round from it."[75] The juxtaposition of fantasy and realism, commonplace enough in twentieth-century fiction, results here from a sometimes frenzied attempt to penetrate the dense surface of the realist world, to release its hidden energies and exorcise its fears, to confront realities beyond the everyday. Whatever the failures and inadequacies of the sensation novel, that is an unusual ambition for a genre of popular literature.

## III.

But when we have the halt, and the maimed, and the blind for the magnates of our kingdom, when we make heroes of the sick, and pets of the stupid, when we chant the poor man's epic, and make a merit of the weak man's nothingness, we are like to find ourselves in an inverted world, and amid many confusions.

E. S. Dallas, *The Gay Science*

The most prodigious sensation of all, for the bemused observers of the 1860s, was the enormous success of the sensation novel; said Mrs. Oliphant of Miss Braddon: "She never invented any circumstance so extraordinary as this public faith and loyal adherence which she seems to have won."[76] Dean Mansel, writing in the *Quarterly*, felt obliged to put on record his belief "that, when the reading public wakes up from its present delusion, it will discover, with regard to some at least of the favourites of the day, that its affections have been bestowed upon an object not very different in kind from the animal of which Titania was enamoured"; still, in 1863, at the height of the vogue, "it must be confessed that there are as yet but few signs of its abating." Another reviewer, in that same year, preferred to express the opposite opinion, perhaps as a matter of wishful thinking: "serious hopes may be confidently entertained that the 'sensation' system is dying a natural death, and that a novel may soon become popular which contains only a moderate number of horrors and a mitigated amount of criminality."

Such predictions of imminent demise, in the case of the sensation novel, themselves became a critical cliché. In fact, *Blackwood's* was still hopefully echoing the same refrain as late as 1890: "But surely this sensational business must soon come to an end, or be suspended for half a generation or so. . . . there must surely come satiety at last."[77] While everyone was forced to admit the staggering popularity of Titania's ass, the *Westminster* alone detected an encouraging sign in the sheer numbers of publishable sensation novels: "Considering the facility with which novels are written, published, and read in our day, considering that a certain public is to be found for anything which issues in three volumes and calls itself a romance, it is really much to the credit of the age, and testifies highly to the progress of public education, that so many books of this class are produced which deserve to be read, and that so small a number, comparatively, are worthy only of utter contempt or positive condemnation."[78] It was certainly a time for minor novelists to flourish, and a rare opportunity for authentically popular fiction to make its influence felt in the higher reaches of major literature.

Meanwhile, of course, there was critical dissatisfaction with the spectacle of serious and talented novelists wasting their time on such popular trash. It is difficult to appreciate, at a distance of more than a hundred years, how prominent the issue of sensationalism was in literary circles and how fierce the opposition became between partisans of the two "schools." No doubt much of the rancor was owing to invidious comparisons and maneuvering for position "at the top of the tree"[79]—first between Thackeray and Dickens and, after their deaths, between Reade and Eliot. There is a peevish note, as well as genuine disagreement, in Thackeray's comment to one of the hosts on his second American tour: "Dickens doesn't like me; he knows that my books are a protest against his—that if the one set are true, the other must be false."[80] The most belligerent antagonism, typically enough, resulted from Reade's paranoid obsession with George Eliot. In reaction to an unfavorable notice in the *Galaxy*, Reade addressed the editors in this vein: "George Eliot is a writer of the second class. . . . adroit enough to disavow the sensational, yet to use it as far as her feeble powers would let her," adding gratuitously that "her greatest quality of all is living with an anonymous writer, who has bought the English press for a time and puffed her into a condition she cannot maintain."[81] Although this self-betraying diatribe was wisely left unpublished at the time, a later article on Charles Reade in *Once a Week*, part of a series on English men of letters, turns out to have been composed anonymously by the subject himself.[82] Not content merely with effusive self-flattery ("he is the greatest living English writer of fiction"; "By the million readers of the time to come, Reade, Dickens, and Thackeray will be handed down to fame together"; etc., etc.), Reade nervously devoted more than two-thirds of his essay to a comparison of his own works with those of George Eliot, intended to show her "borrowing" or "imitation" of his ideas. He cited lengthy parallel passages from *Hard Cash* (1863) and *Felix Holt* (1866), centering on the trial scenes, in which both heroines testify in behalf of their lovers; he contrasted *The Cloister and the Hearth* (1861) and *Romola* (1862-63) as fictional portraits of medieval Europe; he even detected plagiarism in a passing image of thundering wagon wheels. Still, behind Reade's overreaction, there was something of a contest between the two schools, which invariably worked to the disadvantage of the sensationalists in the highbrow periodicals.

In spite of its more ludicrous aspects, particularly where Reade is involved, this personal squabbling had its legitimate counterpart on the level of literary process.

Even in the mid-Victorian period, formal realism never existed in a vacuum but developed according to a "constant dialectic"[83] with conflicting notions of art. Pure idealism, as defined at mid-century, failed to provide a genuine antithesis because it depended on precisely the same concept of what was "real"; it actually reinforced the validity of realism by keeping the realms of novel and romance decently separated. The new sensationalism, however, posed an uncomfortable challenge to the underlying assumptions of both realism and idealism. The lowly sensation novel, the best-selling genre of the 1860s, was a force to be reckoned with, a gadfly to the dominant literary mode. In theory, sensationalism was routinely denounced; in practice, even Trollope and Eliot began to incorporate recognizably sensational elements into their own portrayals of everyday life. In its crude and chaotic fashion, the sensation genre offered something essential that realism lacked. There is intriguing evidence of this in the fact that Thomas Hardy, in his first published attempt at fiction, chose to write a sensation novel.

It should not be surprising that, while certain features were borrowed by everyone from the realists to the naturalists, the sensation novel failed to survive as an entity in itself. If the sensation novel was almost entirely restricted to one particular decade in literary history, that is because it represents a transitional model, at once anachronistic and prophetic. In their search for an alternative to realism, the sensation novelists turned back to the only nineteenth-century precedents they knew—stage melodrama and the remnants of popular romance. The penalty for this was severe: they were finally unable to detach themselves from the hoary conventions of an obsolescent mode, even though they were responding to a new situation for which they found realism inadequate. The old stereotypes, revived and decked out in modern, middle-class dress, could not quite contain the new meaning. Because of this tension between meaning and form, the sensation novel was discomfiting and controversial to the mid-Victorians. For the same reason, it showed a tendency to degenerate into a perplexing hybrid, which could not quite be taken seriously but at the same time could not safely be ignored. The sensation novel was fossilized in a state of transition; the writers were caught in the midst of the painful process of discarding the old forms and creating new ones. Because the conventional melodramatic structures still remained intact, the shift in their original meaning was all the more glaring and their bankruptcy all the more conspicuous.

The revolutionary implications of the sensation novel were recognized, regretfully, at the time: "In these days of fiction," mourns the reviewer in *Temple Bar*, "a change has really come over the spirit of our dreams."[84] By the 1860s, even popular romance—the genre of dreams, of wish fulfillment, of escapist diversion—has become tinged with nightmare, with the particular nightmares of modern, urban, middle-class man. With the rise of the sensation novel, melodrama has lost its innocence; the old black-and-white simplifications, ultimately so comforting, no longer seem relevant in the face of an altered experience. The strict conventional morality that supplied the dynamics of stage melodrama, the symbolic conflict between good and evil, is beginning to give way to a new ambivalence, a more devious line of action on the part of both heroine and villain. As the old certainties inevitably disintegrate, anxiety looms larger than wish fulfillment. The happy ending, when it is observed, is palpably arbitrary, blatantly manipulated; often it has no intrinsic connection with what has gone before, not even the conventional, moralistic value of "virtue rewarded." In many of the sensation novels, the resolution is severely qualified (by Jane Hardie's murder in *Hard Cash*, by Sir Michael Audley's betrayal in *Lady Audley's Secret*); in others (*Griffith Gaunt, The Woman in White*), the characters have suffered so much that the ending is less a rebirth than a mere survival. After all the rampant bigamy and murder, the loose ends of plot may be nearly impossible to tie up; an extreme example is Reade's *Griffith Gaunt*, with its contorted rearrangement of bigamous couples, its grim parody of the happy ending in marriage, so violently distasteful to Dickens.[85] Whether it has bestowed arbitrary suffering or arbitrary happiness, the sensation novel is moving toward an absurdist perspective, in which both the universe and human conduct are irrational and frequently determined by accident. For both heroes and villains, the final nightmare is a loss of control, not only over external events but even over their own actions.

Behind all of these changes in meaning there is a pervasive sense of doubt, the beginnings of a general decline in faith. Without the traditional consensus of belief, at its most basic in popular fiction and on the popular stage, melodrama itself becomes an impossibility: "melodrama must build on a firm foundation of absolute certainties and immoveable verities or crumble into dust"; "melodrama is ultimately dependent upon absolute faith and the unquestioning acceptance of dogma."[86] Once exceptions or ambiguities begin to creep in, the connection has already been severed between literary form and the vision that originally inspired it. From the testimony of the sensation novel, it seems clear that by the 1860s the old melodramatic vision was no longer valid, even on the popular level. The structures remain, and in some cases the perfunctory moralizing, but the spirit is gone. The *Christian Remembrancer*, predictably alarmist, is nevertheless prophetic in linking the sensation novel with a broader moral and social revolution: "The 'sensation novel' of our time, however extravagant and unnatural, yet is a sign of the times—the evidence of a certain turn of thought and action, of an impatience of old restraints, and a craving for some fundamental change in the working of society."[87] The sensation novel itself was to be swept away by these changes, of which it had served as a prelude.

# 3

## Charles Reade and the Breakdown of Melodrama

### I.

So good a heart, and so wrong a head, surely no novelist ever before had combined!

Anthony Trollope, *Autobiography*

---

**T**he Victorian period is already so well stocked with certified eccentrics that it seems almost gratuitous to dig up still another. It is a risk worth taking, however, in the case of "Mad Charles" Reade, as he was christened at Oxford, where he endured his undergraduate career in the 1830s, cutting lectures, dressing flamboyantly, and playing the fiddle.[1] The young Reade was a sensitive, egotistical loner, virtually friendless and absorbed in his own odd projects. He was victimized from the outset by the ambitions of an overbearing, puritanical mother, who disapproved of writing as a career, and by his own election at the age of twenty-one to a lifetime fellowship at Magdalen College, for which the only notable requirement was technical celibacy. Despite periodic attacks of depression and nervous exhaustion, Reade pursued an erratic course of passive resistance, taking mistresses when he was not allowed a wife and suffering through an arid fourteen-year apprenticeship during which he was unable to produce a single line for publication. Instead of abandoning his youthful crotchets after he had achieved belated fame as both playwright and novelist, he put them on public display in his undignified squabbles with his publishers, his naive self-trumpeting, and constant lawsuits. Trollope, with whom he carried on an extravagant feud for years, describes him in his *Autobiography* "as endowed almost with genius, but as one who has not been gifted by nature with ordinary powers of reasoning."[2] It is hardly surprising, given his reputation and brooding introspection, that Reade compulsively defended himself from the vague imputation of insanity, not neglecting to mention in print that he had on one occasion been declared officially sane by a specialist.[3] His most recent biographer, Wayne Burns, finds enough evidence to speculate that beneath his just indignation against contemporary lunacy statutes there lurked a personal obsession and unacknowledged fear of madness.[4]

The typically Readean combination of hidden self-doubt and clamorous self-aggrandizement is given free rein in the notorious Notebooks and Notecards, a voluminous pastiche of newspaper clippings, plot ideas, New Year's resolutions, and factual curios of human behavior, all meticulously labeled and ingeniously cross-indexed. Reade valued the Notebooks as "a steam engine for truth," as a systematic digest of Baconian logic and induction by means of which he attempted to "apply the modes of Physical investigation to letters." He prided himself on their rigorous organization and borrowing of methodology from the "science of sciences, statistic."[5] What this "severe system"[6] actually reveals is the colorful disarray of Reade's eccentric preoccupations, the wildest possible contents complacently recorded and solemnly classified. The favorite subjects, patiently analyzed by the two modern experts in Readiana, include every sort of crime and disaster, medical oddities, "Lunatica," examples of androgynism—highly seasoned nourishment for an unself-conscious "lust for blood and violence."[7] The most random survey turns up such bizarre phenomena as a mulatto girl who has been ordered 190 lashes by her "religious" mistress and sent home as a corpse on horseback, a female sailor with a sickly husband ("Mem! Find this one out photograph her and write her"), or "a man or woman suffocated by charcoal in a *very small* room and dried to a mummy. No odor. Skin like parchment, joints creak like a mannequin's, body light as a feather. This has twice appeared in Paris within the last seven years and been recorded in the journals."[8] With facts like these, who would pretend to rely on mere unaided imagination?

Reade's passion for documentation—almost a parody version of the methods of Zola—barely conceals his chronic doubt and ambivalence about both his own talent and the fictional process itself. Again and again, in prefaces, letters, or private Notebooks, he reiterates his scientific theory of fiction, "continually trying to justify" it even to himself according to his biographer,[9] and perhaps protesting a bit too much: "All fiction, worth a button, is founded on facts"; the "union of fact and imagination . . . a kind of intellectual copulation . . . has procreated the best fiction"; "*Hard Cash*, like *The Cloister and the Hearth*, is a matter-of-fact romance; that is, a fiction built on truths; and these truths have been gathered by long, severe, systematic labor."[10] In his diary this practical method is more explicitly linked with uncertainty about his own limited powers of invention:

> June 20, 1853—The plan I propose to myself in writing stories will, I see, cost me undeniable labor. I propose never to guess where I can know. . . . My story [*It Is Never Too Late To Mend*] must cross the water to Australia. . . . To be consistent with myself, I ought to cross-examine at the very least a dozen men that have farmed, dug, or robbed in that land. If I can get hold of two or three that have really been in it, I think I could win the public ear by these means. Failing these I must read books and letters, and do the best I can. Such is the mechanism of a novel by Charles Reade. . . . If I can work the above great system, there is enough of me to make one of the writers of the day; without it, No, No.[11]

In spite of his fondness for the "great system," in spite of his self-protective instinct "to supplant inner consciousness with outer facts,"[12] Reade is never entirely convinced of the validity of fiction. After all the insistence on "facts" and "truth," it is telling to find the eccentric novelist Mr. Rolfe, Reade's astonishingly accurate self-portrait in *A Terrible Temptation*, ironically disparaging his craft of "writing lies": "My business is lying, and I drudge at it; so to escape now and then to the playground of Truth and Justice is a great amusement and recreation to poor me. Besides, it gives me fresh vigor to replunge into mendacity; and that's the thing that pays." Torn between mendacity and truth, alternately defensive and suspicious of his own creations, Charles Reade consistently takes refuge in documentary evidence to absolve himself of any blame. Of course, the facts are still of his own choosing and "as violently colored as his own temperament."[13]

## II.

"With you facts are no longer stubborn things; you can twist them all your way."
Richard Bassett in Reade's *A Terrible Temptation*

Melodrama, in its popular manifestations in the penny press and on the nineteenth-century stage, offers a strikingly appropriate vehicle for the two conflicting impulses toward order and strangeness. Its paradoxical combination of formulaic stereotype and lurid subject matter neatly parallels Reade's own irregular oscillation between system and outrageous obsession. The whole appeal of popular melodrama depends on its harrowing or titillation with perfect safety. Any excess of emotion or terror is effectively contained within predetermined bounds; the danger is only temporary, if not perfunctory, and the ultimate triumph of right and justice is comfortably assured. The narrative and rhetorical structures, timeworn and familiar, commanded an instant response from the well-conditioned Victorian reader or audience. Reade, like the other sensation novelists, was both fascinated and dissatisfied with the ready-made scaffolding of stage melodrama. While he liked the safety of formula, with its implied pattern and conventional meaning, he also felt limited by it. Reade was obsessed with order because, ultimately, he was obsessed with chaos, with the ever-present threat of the protagonist's loss of control, whether over external circumstances or over his own internal processes.

*It Is Never Too Late To Mend*—hopeful and ironic title—marks an era in Reade's history, as the first "matter-of-fact romance" based on his scientific theory, the first full-length triple decker with pretentions to major literary importance, the first popular hit. Like his two previous attempts at fiction, the new novel, completed in 1856, was again derived from an original play, in this case, the abysmally unsuccessful *Gold*. In both versions of his story, Reade aspires naively to an "epic theme" in his treatment of the gold rush and rapid colonization of Australia at mid-century, "a theme broad and high, yet piquant and various as the dolphin and the rainbow."[14] His plot, as usual, provides simply the barest framework on which to attach as many fantastic Australian adventures as he can manage to invent or, even better, to lift bodily from current travelogues. The hero, George Fielding, and the heroine, Susan Merton, both plain, simple-hearted country folk, are separated because George fails to meet old Farmer Merton's requirement of £1,000 from any suitor for his daughter's hand. While George goes off amid plentiful tears to seek his fortune in Australia, Susan is left, unprotected and unsuspecting, at the mercy of John Meadows, a middle-aged financier who is in love with her and has secretly engineered the convenient debts of both the Fielding and the Merton families. Meadows proves to be a particularly adept melodramatic villain, pulling the various strings of his complicated transcontinental machinations—intercepting letters, hiring thieves to pursue George in the gold-mining camps, and finally bringing Susan to the point of reluctantly accepting his insistent proposals of marriage.

For all the vaunted documentation, Reade's epic theme succumbs without much of a struggle, and he seems willing to admit it. In a letter to his American publisher, he argues for changing the title from the projected *Susan*

*Merton*: "My new novel is an original and important work but both its originality and its importance moral and fictional are unconnected or slightly connected with Susan Merton. The scenes in which she figures are the stale and conventional part of the work."[15] In the novel itself, he feels compelled to apologize, rather lamely, for her lackluster performance: "My reader shall laugh at her: my unfriendly critic shall sneer at her. As a heroine of a novel she deserves it: but I hope for their own sakes neither will undervalue the original in their passage through life. These average women are not the spice of fiction, but they are the salt of real life." In the early chapters, before he has entirely given up on his conventional hero and heroine, Reade makes at least a modest effort to prop up his faltering subject with his own brand of florid, overblown rhetoric, trotted out as a replacement for the missing narrative substance. When George Fielding is uprooted from his country home and sent across the ocean, the narrator launches a Homeric simile:

> The oak of centuries yields to an impalpable antagonist, whose very name stands in proverbs for weakness and insignificance. This thin light trifle rendered impetuous by motion buffets the king of the forest, tears his roots with fury out of the earth, and lays his towering head in the dust; and even so circumstances, none of them singly irresistible, converging to one point, buffeted sore another oak pride of our fields, and for aught I know of our whole island—an honest English yeoman.

Later, when the scene shifts to Australia, Reade works himself up into pages of false rhetorical frenzy over his anti-Carlylean preference for topics of the present day:

> I say before heaven and earth that the man who could grasp the facts of this day and do an immortal writer's duty by them, i.e., so paint them as a later age will be content to engrave them, would be the greatest writer ever lived: such is the force, weight, and number of the grand topics that lie this day on the world's face. . . .

When we write a story or sing a poem of the great nineteenth century, there is but one fear—not that our theme will be beneath us, but we miles below it; that we shall lack the comprehensive vision a man must have from heaven to catch the historical, the poetic, the lasting features, of the Titan events that stride so swiftly past IN THIS GIGANTIC AGE.

In spite of the impressive capitals, this is another return to self-doubt and justification of his fictional method. He is forced to content himself with getting a little mileage out of describing what he is unable to do: "I cannot sing this song, because I am neither Lamartine nor Hugo nor Walter Scott. I cannot hum this song, because the severe conditions of my story forbid me even to make the adventurous attempt."

There is compensation, however, in the interpolated sequence that follows two otherwise minor characters, the parson Francis Eden and the thief Tom Robinson, into a Victorian jail. Reade's factual source is the Royal Commissioners' Report on Birmingham Borough Prison, compiled after one Edward Andrews, aged fifteen, had hanged himself on 28 April, 1853.[16] In this dry account of illegal punishment and laxity on the part of visiting magistrates, Reade found a humanitarian cause comparable to that of *Uncle Tom's Cabin* and admirably suited to his own fantasies. The resulting fictional exposé satisfied his personal ambition and seemed to justify his most extravagant claims for *It Is Never Too Late To Mend*: "The soul of it are the scenes in which a bad man is despaired of and tortured by fools, and afterward not despaired of by a wise and good man, but encouraged, softened, converted. These psychological scenes and the melodramatic scenes that follow, in which the thief's understanding is convinced as well as his heart, are the immortal part of the work."[17] Reade was quite correct in differentiating this "immortal part" from the rest of his novel, but as we shall see, he remained blissfully unaware of the actual nature of his own accomplishment.

In the prison scenes, for the first time, Reade has come

into his element. The unlucky prisoners in "——— Gaol"
are abandoned by their literary creator not only to the operation of the "separate and silent system," a disciplinary
experiment that Reade deplored, but also to the ingenious
tortures devised by the fiendish governor, Mr. Hawes. He
begins with illegal deprivation, not merely of conversation and human society but of adequate food, bed, gaslight, and medical care. Then there is the crank—intended for those sentenced to hard labor, but routinely
overweighted and misapplied. The crank in the fictional ——— Gaol, unlike the Birmingham original,[18] is
entirely purposeless; it is not used to turn a corn mill or
anything else but becomes in Reade's hands a diabolical
engine of nonproductivity, an absurdist "monster got by
folly upon science to degrade labour below theft; for theft
is immoral, but crank labour is immoral and idiotic too."
For the refractory (that is, the overtasked), Hawes' favorite penalties are the "dark cell" and the "punishment
jacket." The first is solitary confinement in what the narrator calls "the frightful darkness that chilled and
crushed the Egyptians, soul and body," a "terrible and
unnatural privation of all light." For Robinson, among
others, it carries the threat of insanity. The second
punishment, based on the straitjacket reserved for dangerous criminals according to the bylaws of Birmingham
Prison, is minutely detailed and just slightly exaggerated
in the novel:[19]

> They jammed him [Robinson] in the jacket, pinned him
> tight to the wall, and throttled him in the collar. This
> collar, by a refinement of cruelty, was made with un-
> bound edges, so that when the victim, exhausted with
> the cruel cramp that racked his aching bones in the
> fierce gripe of Hawes's infernal machine, sank his
> heavy head and drooped his chin, the jagged collar
> sawed him directly and lacerating the flesh drove him
> away from even this miserable approach to ease. . . .
> The next time they came into the yard they found him
> black in the face, his lips livid, insensible, throttled,
> and dying.

The prison chaplain adds to this description by giving it a name with extreme emotional connotations: "Don't you see that the torture before our eyes is crucifixion?" With these resources, it is no wonder that the jailors resort to an old-fashioned flogging only once in three hundred pages.

Reade's talent for sadism, latent in the Notebooks, surfaces here in scene after scene of torture, both protracted and repeated, in graphic and sickening detail. The narrative method is heavy-handed enough but effective for Reade's purposes; the reader is literally staggered by the multiplication of horrors and the unrelenting pace, finally brought to a pitch of intensity that is almost unbearable. Reade himself is every bit as inventive as Hawes and practices much the same system on his long-suffering public. What Reade is attempting—something that Dickens rarely tries and never succeeds in—is to re-create dramatically the gradual process of systematic degradation and brutalization that turns the happy-go-lucky thief Tom Robinson, elsewhere in the novel a kind of picaresque hero, into a sullen, intractible savage who "hated the human race," who "curled himself up like a snake and turned his back upon mankind, and his face to the wall." It is in the interest of realism, as well as reformist zeal, that we are spared nothing of this process, that we are compelled to witness the incessant agony of Robinson at the crank and in the pillory, the goading and gloating of Hawes, the complacent rebuffs of the nondescript first chaplain Mr. Jones, the distortion of time in the black cell, the small, recurring episodes that lead to numbness and despair. Although Reade cannot entirely resist overplaying his hand (see, for example, Robinson's melodramatic curse: "May your name be shame, may your life be pain, and your death loathsome! May your skin rot from your flesh, your flesh from your bones, your bones from your body, and your soul split for ever on the rock of damnation!"), still there is undeniable power in his portrayal of atrocity and depravity. At the least, Robinson's ultimate corruption cannot be dismissed as unmotivated or unprepared for.

The case of Edward Andrews, which prompted the Royal Commissioners' Report, is revived and embroidered in the story of Edward Josephs, a docile, miserable boy who has been caught stealing a piece of beef from a butcher's shop. Wherever possible, of course, Reade sentimentalizes the victim and exaggerates his ill-treatment. Relying on his usual device of repetition, he foreshadows the boy's end by having another prisoner named Gillies, this time only thirteen years old, assigned an impossible task at the crank, strapped into the jacket when he fails, deprived of dinner, bed, and gas, and finally driven to attempt suicide when he knows the warder will discover him in time. Whenever Reade's villain-ous governor is feeling fractious or irritated, he generally relieves his mind by taking it out on poor Josephs, so that during Mr. Eden's illness "Josephs suffered body and spirit without intermission. The result was that his flesh withered on his bones; his eyes were dim and seemed to lie at the bottom of two caverns; he crawled stiffly and slowly instead of walking." The onlooker is treated to every new suffering the "martyr" undergoes, until at the final "crucifixion" the reader himself is forced to partici-pate by imagining it along with the narrator:

Were you ever seized at night with a violent cramp? then you have instantly with a sort of wild and alarmed rapidity changed the posture which had cramped you. . . . As for existing cramped half an hour that you never thought possible. Imagine now the severest cramp you ever felt artificially prolonged for hours and hours. Imagine yourself cramped in a vice, no part of you moveable a hair's breadth, except your hair and your eye-lids. Imagine the fierce cramp growing and grow-ing, and rising like a tide of agony higher and higher above nature's endurance, and you will cease to wonder that a man always sunk under Hawes's manpress. Now then add to the cramp a high circular saw raking the throat, jacket straps cutting and burning the flesh of the back—add to this the freezing of the blood in the body deprived so long of all motion whatever. . . .

After constant abuse of this kind, Josephs at length contrives to escape by hanging himself from the prison win-
dow with his pocket handkerchief, but not without lingering on through a tortuous last night—during which the
narrator helpfully tolls the hours—complete with pa-
thetic reflections on the moon and sky, on sin and the
mercy of God, and assorted invocations to his mother. By
this time, it is a happy release for all concerned.

In the character of Hawes, the prison governor, Reade
tries for a satanic monster, a gigantic figure of unmitigated evil: "He was a much greater man than Jones [the
original chaplain]: he was like a torrent, to whose progress if you oppose a great stone, it brawls and struggles
past it and round it and over it with more vigor than before"; or again, "In short this little blockhead bade fair to
become one of Mr. Carlyle's great men. . . . Such a black
ray of the narrow, self-deceiving, stupid, bloody past was
earnest Hawes." What he ends up with instead is a psychological study of a petty sadist, not totally credible but
studded with flashes of remarkable insight. Reade seems
to understand his villain's sick dependence on the thrill of
violence and torture, his mindless need for his daily fix of
it: "Hawes loved to punish his prisoners, and indeed could
hardly get through the day without it"; "Barren of mental
resources, . . . [he] must still like his prisoners and the
rest of us have some excitement to keep him from going
dead. What more natural than that such a nature should
find its excitement in tormenting, and that by degrees
this excitement should become first a habit then a need?
. . . Gin grows on a man—charity grows on a man—
tobacco grows on a man—blood grows on a man."

When the performance is especially diverting, when for
instance a swooning prisoner in the jacket is doused with
a bucket of water, Hawes and his gloomy cohorts indulge
themselves in "an exulting chuckle." The governor's involvement in his duties provides something more than
amusement, however; his victims constantly provoke him
to furious rage, to shouted threats and curses and shaking
of his fist: "It shall last till I break you, you obstinate
whining dog. You are hardly used are you? Wait till to-

morrow, I'll show you that I have only been playing with
you as yet. But I have got a punishment in store for you
that will make you wish you were in hell." Not only does
he lose his composure over these incidents, he considers
himself locked in a personal contest with his hapless victims ("I never was beat by a prisoner yet, and I never
will"), which deprives him of any possible superiority or
grandeur in evil. Hawes' favorite satellite, a brutish
warder named Fry, who curses or chuckles on cue, adds a
sadistic twist of his own by being "an enthusiast in his
way" and keeping a blood-lust diary of prison events,
which may bear some resemblance to portions of Reade's
own Notebooks.

Hawes' antagonist, Francis Eden, is meant to be more
than an ordinary hero—in fact, a Christian saint: "Now
for a moment or two the sacred orator was more than
mortal; so high above earth was his theme, so great his
swelling words. He rose, he dilated to heroic size, he
flamed with sacred fire: his face shone like an angel's, and
no silver trumpet or deep-toned organ could compare with
his thundering, pealing, melting voice." Along with the
standard heroic qualities, however, the prison chaplain
reveals a curious affinity for his self-appointed task. On
his first afternoon in the jail, he tries out the dark cell "to
see what it is like" and later continues his research by
bribing a warden to strap him into the punishment jacket
and leave him there for half an hour. "Well, but I like
that!" comments the astonished governor; "that is entering into the system." Mr. Eden proves to be another sadistic collector like Reade and Fry, though in the service of
virtue of course, who shows engravings and photographs
of suffering to a moronic prisoner and vividly illustrates
his sermons: "Here he ransacked history, and gave them
some thirty remarkable instances of human cruelty." The
forms of retribution for the sin of cruelty are ghoulish or
excessive, in Eden's accounts; in one case a man tried for
cruelty to animals is killed in a freakish train accident,
while in another a pair of convicted murderers, who have
accompanied their unwitting victim over his destined

grave, are themselves forced to walk over their own open grave on their way to the gallows. Eden's methods are hardly distinguishable from those of the prison governor, though enlisted in the opposite cause: "I will proceed against him by the dogwhip of the criminal law, by the gibbet of the public press, and by every weapon that wit and honesty have ever found to scourge cruelty." When Hawes is finally expelled from his position, Mr. Eden forgets his own previous advice about mercy and blasts his defeated adversary with rhetorical fire and brimstone:

> Other homicides' hands are stained, but yours are steeped in blood. To your knees MAN-slayer! . . . The avenger of blood is behind you. . . . Cry mightily for help—cry humbly and groaning for the power to repent. Away! away! Wash those red hands and that black soul in years and years of charity, in tears and tears of penitence, and in our Redeemer's blood. Begone, and darken and trouble us here no more.

Here and in like passages of rant in Reade's own voice, Wayne Burns finds an indignation that is almost "psychopathic": "Eden's humanitarianism is but Hawes' sadism, plus moral sanctions, and the moral sanctions are in themselves rationalizations."[20] The good parson, like Reade himself, appears to be far more interested in the "thirty remarkable instances of human cruelty" than in the reasons for adducing them.

It should be clear by this time that in the prison sequence of *It Is Never Too Late To Mend*, Reade temporarily oversteps the bounds of convention to liberate a genuine source of energy, albeit a perverted one, within himself. This is strong stuff, a little too strong for the usual melodramatic formula; in fact, the torture scenes in the later stage version provoked a spontaneous outcry from a normally circumspect theatrical critic and nearly started a riot on opening night.[21] In the frame tale, the George-and-Susan sections of the same novel, Reade proves that he has learned how to manipulate the techniques of respectable melodrama—the superficial storm and bombast with nothing very menacing behind it. But in "the immortal part of the work," he consciously sets out to shock and disturb his readers, ostensibly for a reformist purpose, and unconsciously unleashes his own sadistic and violent preoccupations. The resulting intensity, not to say frenzy, at last begins to put a strain on the innocuous melodramatic form. Unintended, undoubtedly subconscious, meanings begin to take nightmarish shape amid the ruins of the supposedly conventional battle between light and darkness. The angel of goodness, the wishfully-named Parson Eden, is finally discovered to be wearing the same grotesque leer as his satanic counterpart. The problem is that Reade can neither admit what is happening nor channel it in any original direction. All he can do is repeat his effects to the breaking point, mounting a brutal physical assault against both characters and reader, and then let the inchoate energy thus generated peter out in the alternate plot. Even when he has obviously transcended the clichés of melodramatic content, he has no other means of expression at his disposal except the old stereotypes; these he pushes to the limit and beyond, truly shocking and disgusting the usual audience for soft-core titillation. He is left with excellent, if unsophisticated sadomasochistic fantasy, but distinctly problematical art.

### III.

"His features are softening," said Grace to herself, as she came upon him once fast asleep. "I trust it is no indication of the brain."

*Punch*, 1868

The next propaganda novel, following *The Cloister and the Hearth* and several potboilers, is *Hard Cash*, first serialized in 1863 in *All the Year Round* under Dickens' title *Very Hard Cash*. Reade had begun collecting materials for this new "matter-of-fact romance" as early as 1858, when he took on an essential role in the court case of one E. P. Fletcher, an apparently unstable and epileptic young man, heir to a substantial fortune from his father's business, who had been legally committed to an insane asylum by the firm in question.[22] Like one of his own fictional super-heroes, the now-famous novelist volunteered to keep Fletcher in hiding and guard him from forcible recapture. He managed to get him certified sane by two disinterested physicians, demanded a public trial under the lunacy statute, and conducted a simultaneous campaign in the newspapers, for as he asserted in one of a series of open letters, "These soldiers of Xerxes [the Commissioners in Lunacy] won't do their duty if they can help it; if they can't, they will. With them justice depends on Publicity, and Publicity on you. Up with the lash!!"[23] After numerous delays, the case was finally tried in July of 1859; Fletcher was completely vindicated and awarded damages. As usual, Reade got carried away on the swelling tide of his own righteous indignation and developed a positive mania for a subject that had always intrigued him. As he claims in the narrator's voice in *Hard Cash*, "I have accumulated during the last few years a large collection of letters from persons deranged in various degrees, and studied them minutely."[24] Off guard, Reade himself betrays a little of his fictional character Dr. Wycherly, a zealous amateur "collector of mad people."

Although the overall plot of *Hard Cash* shows distinct improvement over the loose meanderings of the frame tale in *It Is Never Too Late To Mend*, there is still the same hurried, crazy-quilt effect that comes with trying to cram in as many sensational occurrences as possible while suppressing the "small intermediate matters" that might put them into some more plausible perspective. Here Reade manages to touch all the conventional bases in high style, never looking back or pausing long enough for the reader to ask any questions. The novel opens with a pastoral undergraduate idyll—the story of the meeting between Julia Dodd and Alfred Hardie at the Oxford-Cambridge boat races and their subsequent courtship. The inevitable complications set in when their marriage is mysteriously forbidden by Alfred's hitherto affectionate father, Richard Hardie, a former suitor of Julia's mother and a presumably successful banker. Mrs. Dodd offers the hope that any opposition to their union will be dispelled by the return of her husband, Captain David Dodd, from China with a fortune of £ 14,000 in "hard cash" to be settled on his two children, Julia and Edward. Leaving things in this tantalizing state back home, the narrator digresses cavalierly for 150 pages of nautical melodrama, complete with hurricanes, pirates, and shipwrecks, in which the life of Captain Dodd and the safety of his cash are continually endangered and despaired of. When he reaches England at last, Captain Dodd takes the money immediately to Richard Hardie's bank although it is after regular business hours. The archvillain Mr. Hardie, desperately trying to stave off imminent bankruptcy, pockets the £ 14,000, throws away the receipt, and denies all knowledge of the transaction. This bold pretense, when Captain Dodd attempts to reclaim his own, causes the captain to fall down in a violent fit, after which he is carried home raving. Young Alfred Hardie, whose inheritance has also been embezzled by his enterprising father, suspects the truth, informs the Dodds, and determines to marry Julia in order to settle his fortune on her and her cheated family. It is at this point, on the very morning of the wedding, that Alfred is decoyed away and entrapped in a madhouse.

Of course, this is exactly where Reade wants him. The matter-of-fact novelist is off on another crusade, this time tilting against the gaping loopholes in the Victorian lunacy laws and the occasional evidence of malpractice in private asylums. As far as possible, Burns has pointed out, Reade intended to duplicate his previous masterstrokes from the excruciating prison scenes of *It Is Never Too Late To Mend*, in what is obviously a similar and promising situation. The only difficulty, again according to Burns, is that the issue remains less clear-cut in *Hard Cash* and the facts less gruesome: "Reade's first aim was to harrow his readers, just as he had harrowed them in his prison epic, and in making his asylum scenes 'less horrible' and . . . 'more lifelike,' he vitiated his purpose, and by modern standards, his art. For it was through his castigation of 'the infernal little disciples of Carlyle'—a castigation unchecked by 'literary tact'—that he now and again approximated the art of Carlyle and Dickens."[25] But this dismisses *Hard Cash* too easily. Although Reade has for the most part abandoned the crude, battering-ram techniques of his earlier novel, he has produced something more than a "vitiated" rerun. Once again, in *Hard Cash*, he indulges several of his pet obsessions and makes at least tentative approaches to his own deepest fears, anxieties, and fantasies.

The accepted pattern of sensation melodrama includes the removal of the hero, and often the heroine as well, from the safe and comfortable routine of ordinary life to a place of danger, where the normal social order and conventions no longer obtain. A typical example of this is the uninhabited South Sea island in Reade's *Foul Play*, where a convicted (though innocent) forger is marooned with a general's daughter who has already been formally betrothed to another man. In *Hard Cash*, however, the traditional island is replaced by a madhouse, and the implications begin to change. When Alfred Hardie walks boldly and voluntarily into Silverton Grove House, expecting to secure information about the missing £14,000, he finds himself suddenly imprisoned in a narrow, unfurnished room, equipped with an invisible spring-bolted entrance, a realistically painted iron bookcase with iron books, and most amazing of all, "a knob without a door," the door itself having been blocked up. At the first mention of the word "asylum," he tries wildly to escape, breaking through windows, leaping across ledges at great heights, dangling from tree branches, and ending up half-drowned in an enormous tank of cold water. While on the run in the asylum grounds, he cries out an appeal to any other sane man to fight with him for release and receives this horrible reply:

Instantly the open windows were filled with white faces, some grinning, some exulting, all greatly excited; and a hideous uproar shook the whole place—for the poor souls were all sane in their own opinion. . . . Several mild maniacs ran out in vast agitation, and to curry favor, offered to help catch him. Vast was their zeal. But when it came to the point, they only danced wildly about and cried, "Stop him! for God's sake stop him! he's ill, dreadfully ill; poor wretch! knock out his brains!" And, whenever he came near them, away they ran whining like kicked curs.

Poor Alfred has been dropped down a sinister rabbit hole, without any White Rabbit, where everything conspires to defeat logic and reason, where each new crisis is accompanied by the delirious chant of the lunatics and their anarchic tumult. The loss of rational control first releases physical violence and sadism. The lunatics themselves are as violent as their keepers; their suggested cure for Alfred's "dreadful illness" is to "knock out his brains." The attendants oblige him with the next best thing; he is promptly manacled and strapped down to his bed in a padded cell and left there without defense against the loathsome insects that crawl over his face until daybreak. Later he is enlivened with a dose of opium that causes fever, blindness, and nosebleed, followed by a blister applied to his shaven head. One of the more accomplished sadists has perfected "the art of breaking a man's ribs, or breastbone, or both, without bruising him externally" by walking up and down the patient on his knees. (This scene was much shortened and cleaned up in book form; in the serial version, the keeper knees Alfred in the face and is bitten through the cartilage in the middle of his nose for his trouble.)[26] In either version, this is vintage Reade, displaying again his sadomasochistic combination of fear and enjoyment at scenes of torture.

Worse than any physical torture is the agony of being imprisoned by legal order and being treated like a dangerous maniac. Alfred develops an aversion to the wretched creatures with whom he is confined, asking Mrs. Archbold, matron of the asylum, before dinner, "May I sit by you? There is something so repugnant in the very idea of mad people." Characteristically, Reade evades the authorial responsibility for examining his hero's interesting state of mind:

> For then rolled over that young head hours of mortal anguish that no tongue of man can utter, nor pen can shadow. Chained sane amongst the mad; on his wedding-day; expecting with tied hands the sinister acts of the soul-murderers who had the power to make their lie a truth! We can paint the body writhing vainly against its unjust bonds; but who can paint the loathing, agonized soul in a mental situation so ghastly? For my part I feel it in my heart of hearts; but am impotent to convey it to others; impotent, impotent.

Burns suggests that in this fevered passage Reade is "on the verge of self-recognition," of admitting his reluctance to venture into his own or his characters' "inner consciousness."[27] Surely there is also a suggestion of the failure of his artistic form, of the inadequacy he senses in his own rant and rhetoric. Whenever he becomes hysterical, as in the revealing cry of "impotent, impotent," there is likely to be an underlying tension between the melodramatic stereotype and some authentic emotion.

Here the emotion seems to be "that terror of a madhouse, which is natural to a sane man"—and even more natural to a man in doubt of his sanity. In all three consecutive asylums to which Alfred's villainous father has him removed, "the whole treatment of this ill-starred young gentleman gravitated towards insanity," for "what they wanted was to gnaw his reason away, and then who could disprove that he had always been mad?" The external conspiracy of classic paranoia threatens more than external peril; it attempts to operate on the inner being, to coincide with the internal source of anxiety. Both author and hero are afraid of more than unjust laws. Of course, Reade stops short of recognizing any predisposition of his own for which the physical madhouse may be a convenient projection; but he does identify with Alfred's plight—"I feel it in my heart of hearts"—and does occasionally betray a personal uneasiness by putting himself in where he need not belong: "These statistics have been long before the world, and . . . tell a dark tale to the reader of things; so dark, that I pray Heaven to protect me, and all other weak, inoffensive persons, from the protection of my lord chancellor in this kind."

Between the sensation scenes of chaos and torture, Reade intersperses episodes of Humpty-Dumpty logic and Kafkaesque bureaucracy. The doctors throughout prove far crazier than their patients; while some of them are simply hirelings, most appear to believe in their own cockeyed theories. Dr. Wycherly, who signs the certificate of insanity and runs the second of Alfred's three madhouses, prides himself on complex and incomprehensible diagnosis. It is he who first insinuates the possibility of "incipient disease of the cerebro-psychical organs" and proceeds to enumerate the symptoms of "incubation of insanity." For him, rather paradoxically, a confession of previous delusion is the surest test of a cure: "Indeed, this consciousness of insanity is the one diagnostic of sanity that never deceives me; and, on the other hand, an obstinate persistence in the hypothesis of perfect rationality demonstrates the fact that insanity yet lingers in the convolutions and recesses of the brain." Thus Alfred finds that he can be released as sane only if he admits to being mad. The great specialist carries the matter even further in the case of James Maxley, a working-class creditor of Mr. Hardie's, who has become deranged after the loss of his wife and his savings. When Maxley knocks at the door requesting an order to be committed to an asylum, the doctor exclaims, *"Now there is a sensible man."*

In Alfred's case, Wycherly considers the rational powers not lacking but too highly developed, evidently because they surpass his own; with his usual talent for obscure reasoning, he voices his doubt "whether anybody can be as clever as he is, without the presence of more or less abnormal excitement of the organs of intelligence." He and Alfred, his favorite maniac, study the classics together and spar on learned subjects. The proofs of Alfred's brilliance, however, are somewhat less than convincing, since they depend on Reade's own eccentric opinions about the Latin poets, the mixed metaphors of Shakespeare, and the inferiority of poetry to philosophy.

At the same time, no small part of the hero's frustration results from the bureaucratic red tape and legal technicalities in which his appeal for a public hearing becomes continually embroiled. Once he has crossed the threshold of the asylum, he belongs to an absurdist world, where no one in charge credits a straightforward statement and where "Mr. Baker could be punished for confining a madman in this house without an order and two certificates; but he couldn't for confining a sane person under an order and two certificates." In fact, one inmate of Drayton House, having signed himself in for treatment, is told that since the original signature was illegal, he cannot reverse it by so simple a procedure as signing himself out again. Reade's Lunacy Commission, although never developed in its full symbolic potential, still suggests at least something of the method, as well as the broader implications, of Dickens' Circumlocution Office.

Another danger in the breakdown of rational control is the release of unbridled sexuality. In Reade's lunatic asylums, the social conventions and institutions that serve to inhibit both violence and libido have entirely ceased to exist. In a society where mad people leer at the dinner table and steal the food from each other's plates, it is hardly surprising to discover an "erotic maniac," a deranged woman who must be returned in handcuffs from her regular forays into "the men's side." The mere maniac, however, is less dangerous than the matron and "keeperesses." An alarming reversal of the natural order seems to have taken place: all the desire and all the pursuers are female. The boyish hero finds himself in the position of a Joseph Andrews or a Tom Jones, panted after by lustful hordes but forcibly prevented from keeping faith with his true love on their wedding day. Nurse Hannah, otherwise known as "baby-face biceps," because she possesses "a pretty and rather babyish face, diversified by a thick biceps muscle in her arm that a blacksmith need not have blushed for," is physically intimidating and androgynous but, by contrast, ridiculously timid and tender-hearted in love. When Alfred persuades her to have pity on him and initiate an escape attempt, she requests her payment in kisses.

This innocent diversion provokes the wrath and jealousy of a far more formidable personage, Edith Archbold, the matron of the asylum—a dark, vigorous, sophisticated woman of thirty. Contrary to sensational tenets, Reade takes some pains to account for her raging emotions, to analyze Alfred's effect on her at their first meeting, when he "pierced at once to her depths" by arousing successively her terror, pity, admiration, and vanity in the course of his wild resistance and ultimate surrender to her protection. At first, she determines to check her inclination, but "a feeling hidden, and not suppressed, often grows fast in a vigorous nature. . . . it smouldered, and smouldered, till from a penchant it warmed to a fancy, from a fancy to a passion." Although she is a cunning adversary, who keeps Alfred in a state of bewilderment, Mrs. Archbold is ruled by her sexual desire. When she intervenes in Alfred's punishment, one of the keepers remarks crudely, "Of course, if you have fallen in love with him, my cake is burnt. 'Tisn't the first lunatic you have taken a fancy to." The object of her lecherous affection is hardly safe even locked in his room at night; on one occasion, Alfred is suddenly awakened from dreaming of Julia, but is "doubtful whether he was quite awake, for two velvet lips seemed to be still touching his. He stirred, and somebody was gone like the wind, with a rustle of flying petticoats, and his door shut in a moment." As for the "dastardly vision" herself, "she had sucked fresh poison from those honest lips, and filled her veins with molten fire. She tossed and turned the livelong night in a high fever of passion, nor were the cold chills wanting of shame and fear at what she had done." In the daytime, she alternates between insult and tearful supplication: "Morals apart, it was glorious love-making."

True-hearted Alfred is at first bemused, then annoyed by the complications: "The men had left off . . . bullying him; but his guardian angels, the women, were turning up their sleeves to pull caps over him, and plenty of the random scratches would fall on him. If anything could have made him pine more to be out of the horrid place, this voluptuous prospect would."

The game becomes more serious when Alfred is transferred to Drayton House and reencounters the fiery Mrs. Archbold. After saving him from a draught of morphia by means of an anonymous billet-doux, she conspires with the vicious Dr. Wolf to intercept his letters to the commissioners, intending to keep him under her benevolent sway, for "hers was hot love, but not true love like Julia's." At last she risks everything by telling Alfred that Julia is engaged to a clergyman and offering to free him from the asylum on her own terms:

> Passion, impatience, pity, and calculation, all drove her the same road, and led to an extraordinary scene, so impregnated with the genius of the madhouse—a place where the passions run out to the very end of their tether—that I feel little able to describe it; I will try and indicate it.

During this "extraordinary scene," Mrs. Archbold loses all control, "pour[ing] burning love in his ear" and pleading to be accepted as "your housekeeper, your servant, your slave": "O Alfred, my heart burns for you, bleeds for you, yearns for you, sickens for you, dies for you." When the righteous hero spurns her, she transforms lust into hate, vowing to degrade him, to make him "love me like a dog" by carrying out the ultimate and "fiendish" threat: "I'll drive you mad." The effect of all this, with the added information that Julia has visited her father at Drayton House during their tête-à-tête, is that "she had done what no man had as yet succeeded in; she had broken his spirit."

Meanwhile, Reade has endeavored, with some success of his own, to imagine "a place where the passions run out to the very end of their tether." By attributing the result to "the genius of the madhouse," although both Alfred and Mrs. Archbold are perfectly sane, he pretends to disapprove of Mrs. Archbold's conduct and contrives to duck any unacceptable implications of his work. Still, within these limits, he has given expression to a vivid fantasy of what might happen when all conventional restrictions are magically removed and libidinous irrationality rules. This association of sex with violence and insanity, as the sensation novel demonstrates, is generally Victorian as well as peculiarly Readean.

Once Mrs. Archbold has deserted Alfred, Dr. Wolf (and Reade) tighten the screws; "Not a day passed now but a blow was struck." Alfred is reduced to writing letters in blood with a toothpick on old rims of the *Times*, while his inner torment increases with the addition of jealousy to his other passions: "This corroder was his bitter companion day and night; and perhaps of all the maddeners human cunning could have invented, this was the worst. It made his temples beat, and his blood run boiling poison. Indeed, there were times when he was so distempered by passion that homicide seemed but an act of justice, and suicide a legitimate relief." Outwardly as well, he begins to resemble "a lunatic of the unhappiest class, the melancholiac." The keepers deliberately provoke him to violence so that he can be classified as a dangerous maniac and confined in the "noisy ward." Here Reade cuts loose from all control in order to produce a nightmare vision of the chaos that results from the flight of reason. Alfred is conducted gradually down to the lowest circle of hell and left there among the vile remnants of former humanity and rationality:

As they neared it, strange noises became audible. Faint at first, they got louder and louder. Singing, roaring, howling like wolves. . . . Here he was surrounded by the desperate order of maniacs he at present scarcely knew but by report. Throughout that awful night he could never close his eyes for the horrible, unearthly sounds that assailed him. Singing, swearing, howling like wild beasts! . . . His ears assailed with horrors, of which you have literally no conception, or shadow of a conception, his nose poisoned with ammoniacal vapors, and the peculiar wild-beast smell that marks the true maniac, Alfred ran wildly about his cell, trying to stop his ears, and trembling for his own reason.

As the narrator has remarked elsewhere, à propos of his hero, "Now man is an animal at bottom, and a wild animal at the very bottom."[28] This sequence has a frantic, hallucinatory quality: fundamental distinctions are blurred until it seems to be taking place both outside and inside the protagonist's overwrought brain. A few pages later, the whole madhouse experience culminates and explodes in the grand sensation scene of the asylum fire—a violent orgy of unrestraint:

> Wild, weird forms, with glaring eyes and matted hair, leaped out and ran into the hall, and laughed, and danced, and cursed in the lurid reflection of the fires above. Hell seemed discharging demons. . . . Now the skylight exploded, and the pieces fell tinkling on the marble hall fast as hail. The crowd recoiled and ran, but those awful figures continued their gambols. One picked up the burning glass, and ground it in his hands that bled directly; but he felt neither burn nor cut.

Again there is a sense, at least momentarily, that Reade is not altogether in control, that his extreme materials have gotten away from him, and left him as horror-stricken as his characters or his reader.

After this climactic outburst, as in the earlier novel, the narration returns to the more ordinary sensation entanglements of Alfred's meeting with Julia and the new obstacles to their engagement, the disappearance and rumored death of Captain Dodd, and the lunacy trial. Even in these tamer sections, the threat of madness and anarchy reverberates beyond the bounds of the asylum; nearly every character in the book shows some promise of going insane at one point or another. Captain Dodd leads off by falling down in a fit when Mr. Hardie appropriates his cash, allowing a doctor to intone for what is only the first time, "HE IS A MANIAC."[29] Then there is James Maxley, with his delusions of snakes and dragons, whose derangement causes the brutal murder of Jane Hardie, Alfred's sister. When Alfred fails to appear for the scheduled wedding, Julia's distress is so vehement that, as Jane reports, "they fear for her reason." Mrs. Dodd, in her turn, puts "life and reason . . . at stake" on Edward's attempt to rescue his father from the burning Drayton House; and when her husband disappears after the fire, she begins to sink under the workings of her "distempered brain" and has to be gently prepared for the violent shock of his restoration to health. Dr. Wycherly, pompous director of the most civilized asylum in the novel, suffers an epileptic fit over the theoretical question of Hamlet's madness and reveals himself for a "monomaniac." In the course of the trial, it comes out that Alfred has been signed into the madhouse by his uncle Thomas Hardie, alias "soft Tommy," under the fear that if he does not cooperate with Richard Hardie's schemes he will himself be put away, being "next door to an idiot." And finally, even the villain, Richard Hardie, joins the popular ranks of monomania in the end, cherishing the delusion of bankruptcy in spite of his new wealth and gratefully accepting a guinea a week from his dutiful son. Occasionally Reade is forced to undo some of this madness, for the sake of a happy ending, but that proves no more difficult than creating it in the first place; in the case of Captain Dodd, "a shock had brought back the reason a shock had taken away. But how or why, I know no more than the child unborn." The obvious consequence of all this rampant lunacy is ridiculous rather than horrifying, just another instance of overworked techniques and *reductio ad absurdum*.[30]

For all his faults—and they are sometimes glaring—Charles Reade boldly undertakes what the daily-life novelists purposely avoid; in his perennial search for new "sensations," he conjures up the Terrible as an aspect of human experience—the violent, the mysterious, the irrational, the most disturbing of anxieties and possibilities. This venture is never wholly successful because it is circumscribed by the facile patterns of stage melodrama that Reade so naively admired. In order to express his authentic concerns, he has to go almost berserk, to release his most violent demons; it is only then that he can begin to surmount the conventional histrionics and to free himself from the barren stereotypes of his chosen melodramatic form. Only at the pitch of hysteria, only in unfettering "the genius of the madhouse," does he approach the level of genuine art. Like so many of the Victorians, Reade cannot quite bring himself to confront his own threatening or disreputable subject matter, but neither can he entirely leave it alone. In his best novels, he alternates between pure formula and frenzied outburst; either he has lost touch with the depths of his own psyche or he lets them loose willy-nilly and indiscriminately. There is a wonderful intensity in the prison scenes or the mad scenes, but no adequate artistic structure or encompassing artistic vision. His instinctive attempt to break out of the confinement of his stock techniques produces at times a powerful effect—as crude and chaotic as his subject, but not finally revelatory.

The crux of the problem is that Reade remains generally incapable of uniting the two basic elements of any literary art: authentic, highly-charged experience and appropriate congenerous form. Whenever he succeeds with one, the other is certain to be lacking or insufficient. Reade's is an illuminating case, however, because the reasons for his comparative failure are not narrowly personal but are representative of the difficulties confronted by an entire generation. A fundamental change in attitude had taken place since the heyday of the Romantics, since the time when Sir Walter Scott and the gothic novelists could capture the prevailing spirit of the age. For the Victorians at mid-century, the high deeds and unambiguous emotions of romanticism no longer corresponded to their contemporary experience of life in a bourgeois industrial society and of the new, often unsettling, intellectual and philosophical currents.[31] Realism, with its focus on average humanity and concrete detail, had already become the dominant mode of literary expression. The sensation novel, with its sudden, full-blown appearance in the 1860s, represents both a nostalgic throwback to an earlier era and a more progressive groping for alternative values to those propounded by the realists. The sensational element undoubtedly resurfaced as a counterpoint to the novel of everyday life, offering at the same time, paradoxically, the security of old-fashioned, black-and-white melodrama and the opportunity to explore the less mundane areas of human concern—the intense passions, the daring actions, the extreme situations.

The old form, however, could not be resurrected solely on the old terms. Every one of the major sensation novelists, not excluding Mrs. Henry Wood, was forced to deal with this fact and in the process to come up with innovative approaches to the fiction of crime and adventure. They modernized it, refined it, domesticated it.[32] Reade is significant in this connection because his instincts, however unwittingly, frequently coincided with rising trends. In spite of his avowed sensationalist tenets and his envious paranoia on the subject of George Eliot, in spite of his uneven literary quality, Reade commonly surpasses his friend Wilkie Collins in making his treatment of sex, violence, and insanity—the stock-in-trade of melodrama—something more than just the exciting element of a wild and complex plot.[33] In the "immortal parts" of his work, Reade is always less interested in action for its own sake than in emotional implications and psychological excitement or pathology. His characters are less apt to fit the traditional molds of grandiose villain or fatal temptress than to establish the more modern roles of petty sadist (Mr. Hawes) and sexually aggressive woman (Mrs. Archbold). And sex itself, notably, is no longer totally confined to the opposing stereotypes of sin or happy marriage in the concluding chapter. These changes are typical of the new understanding of human character, as less monolithic and more subconsciously motivated, that was already beginning to appear in literature by the 1860s. Although the twentieth-century reader senses that Reade was not himself entirely aware of his own methods of characterization in these instances, nevertheless his novels indicate the increasingly less submerged conflicts within the stultifying, relentlessly clean-minded attitude that remains the popular conception of Victorianism. Charles Reade is not just a lonely madman. His ultimate artistic failure stems from his inability to invent a new form to contain his unprecedented content. Although his novels are messy, chaotic, the reverse of well-made, Reade at his best comes closer to the deepest imaginative springs of art than the more efficient practitioners of what eventually became known as the "thriller." In *Hard Cash* and *It Is Never Too Late To Mend*, there are at least glimpses of the greater possibilities of a revitalized melodrama.

## IV.

"It *'tis* so dull when everybody is good like mamma."
Rose in Reade's *Griffith Gaunt*

Reade's last readable novel—the last in which he successfully indulges his penchant for forbidden topics—is *Griffith Gaunt* (1866), an outrageous sensation mélange of dueling, murder, bigamy, and mistaken identity that somehow manages to contain a sensitive portrayal of feminine sexual psychology and "the great thirsty heart of woman that married or single, pines for eternal Courtship."[34] The artistic center of the work is the experience of the heroine, Kate Gaunt, a haughty and spirited beauty with complex emotions, if a rather naive conscious understanding of them. After eight or ten years of comfortable marriage to a good-hearted, uninspired country squire, Kate finds the religious fulfillment and exultation her idealistic nature has always yearned for, in the fiery and eloquent sermons of a young, ethereal Italian priest, called Brother Leonard. Her rapture can be justly compared with that of Dorothea Brooke in Eliot's *Middlemarch*, only the object here is a sexually attractive Mr. Casaubon—a fact that disguises and encourages sexuality, rather than submerging it. In the course of Kate's slow-motion near seduction, both parties are late to recognize and reluctant to admit what is happening. With unusual subtlety, Reade employs terms with sexual connotations for ostensibly religious situations. After Leonard's first sermon, Kate avoids trivial chit-chat on the way home, "and by this means she came hot and undiluted to her husband; she laid her white hand on his shoulder, and said, 'Oh, Griffith, I have heard the voice of God.' "[35] Although "every syllable that passed between these two might have been published without scandal," the self-deceiving priest appeals to her "in words of practical good sense, but in tones of love"; "In truth, if Love was really a personage, as the heathens feigned, he must have often perched on a tree, in that quiet grove, and chuckled and mocked, when this man and woman sat and murmured together, in the soft seducing twilight, about the love of God."

For a sensation novelist who has abjured direct analysis of his characters, Reade is surprisingly adept at indicating his heroine's minute changes of feeling and grudging self-awareness. When Leonard is suspected by his housekeeper of harboring a "hussy" in his room, Mrs. Gaunt becomes unaccountably jealous: "A strange feeling traversed her heart for the first time in her life. It was a little chill, it was a little ache, it was a little sense of sickness; none of these violent, yet all distinct. And all about what? After this curious, novel spasm at the heart, she began to be ashamed of herself for having had such a feeling." Later, she is forced to consider an equally unaccountable probability: "She found her mind constantly recurring to one person. . . . Here, in her calm solitude and umbrageous twilight, her mind crept out of its cave, like wild and timid things at dusk, and whispered to her heart that Leonard perhaps admired her more than was safe or prudent. Then this alarmed her, yet caused her a secret complacency: and that, her furtive satisfaction, alarmed her still more." Whatever the other flaws in his novels, it must be conceded that Reade stands nearly alone among the mid-Victorians, for once on a level with his rival George Eliot, in his perceptive creation of women as full, intelligent, sexual beings. Even the conventional heroines, such as Julia Dodd and Jane Hardie in *Hard Cash*, are never in danger of approximating the prim, sexless creatures that Dickens favors. Although Reade treats active female sexuality as an abnormal condition in a character like Mrs. Archbold, he also treats it as a normal, even desirable attribute of his most memorable heroine, Kate Gaunt.

In spite of the cautious hedging and the inevitable disavowals of his own meaning that tend to undermine every one of his novels, Reade still found himself in trouble with the self-appointed guardians of Victorian morality throughout his career. Before the publication of *It Is Never Too Late To Mend*, he minimized the chances of a decided hit in England in a letter to his American distributors, Ticknor and Fields: "In this country it is very doubtful. I shock their prejudices so, poor dear old souls."[36] *Griffith Gaunt*, predictably, touched off a transatlantic melee, into which the injured author plunged with typical abandon, filing suit first against *The Round Table*, a New York weekly, for libelous statements, and then against *The London Review* for repeating the same charges. In an open letter to the American press, entitled "The Prurient Prude," he castigated the editor of *The Round Table* for his "deliberate attempt to assassinate the moral character of an author and a gentleman, and to stab the ladies of his own family to the heart, under the pretense of protecting the women of a nation from the demoralizing influence of his pen."[37] (In this case Reade was eventually awarded six cents in damages.) Although before reading *Griffith Gaunt* Dickens conveyed "everything that is brotherly in art" to the plaintiff, after reading it he unequivocally declined to defend it in court:

If I [had] read to me in court those passages about
Gaunt's going up to his wife's bed drunk and that last
child's being conceived, and was asked whether, as
Editor, I would have passed those passages, . . . I should
be obliged to reply No. . . . I should say that what was
pure to an artist might be impurely suggestive to inferior minds. . . . Asked if I should have passed the passage where Kate and Mercy [Gaunt's bigamous second
wife] have the illegitimate child upon their laps and
look over its little points together? I should be again
obliged to reply No, for the same reason. Asked
whether, as author or Editor, I should have passed
Neville's marriage to Mercy, and should have placed
those four people, Gaunt, his wife, Mercy, and Neville
in those relative situations towards one another, I
should again be obliged to reply No. Hard pressed upon
this point, I must infallibly say that I consider those
relative situations extremely coarse and disagreeable.[38]

Of course, the sales of *Griffith Gaunt* soared after this
kind of publicity, but Reade himself seems to have become increasingly discouraged by Grundyism, in spite of
his spirited defense. The reviews of *A Terrible Temptation*
(1871) were still more vituperative, and this time the
commercial effect was adverse, at least according to a
communication from his Canadian publisher proposing
"an abatement in the rates of payment."[39] Ironically, although the controversy centered on the portrait of Rhoda
Somerset, mistress to a fashionable young baronet who
later marries the heroine, none of the characters or situations has the psychological depth or even pornographic
appeal of his earlier work. By 1876, during the composition of *A Woman-Hater* for serialization in *Blackwood's
Magazine*, Reade was reduced to writing cringing letters,
explaining away the implications of his novel and surrendering the final control over his own words: "If language can be found to convey that guarded meaning more
precisely, you would only have to suggest it, and it should
be employed"; or again, "I have struck out Rhoda's

prayer, and corrected the matter; also, with much pleasure, the word seduction, substituting a vague sentence that will convey no distinct idea to the reader."[40] This is Victorian censorship at its cruelest and most nonsensical; Reade was an old man now and could no longer resist.

Reade's biographer dates his gradual death as a novelist from the period of *A Terrible Temptation* and attributes it to a combination of critical attack and "inner failure of nerve."[41] His last feint at a full-scale novel-with-a-purpose is *Put Yourself in His Place* (1869-70), by all accounts an unmitigated disaster, with no energy left to inform the bizarre and lurid details.[42] In *A Terrible Temptation*, he returns to the madhouse theme but yields to feeble dependence on stock formulas, giving no evidence of conviction, much less doubt or anxiety. The weak-willed hero, Sir Charles Bassett, is again wrongfully confined by a designing relative, but the asylum in question turns out to be that paradoxical thing, a "well-ordered madhouse," presided over by "a pale, thoughtful man, with a remarkably mild eye: is against restraint of lunatics, and against all punishment of them,— Quixotically so; being cross-examined, declares that if a patient gave him a black eye, he would not let a keeper handle him roughly, being irresponsible." This is self-parody of the most humiliating sort. So much for "Mad Charles" and the garish playthings of his previous obsession.

# 4

## The Wickedness of Woman:
## M. E. Braddon and Mrs. Henry Wood

### I.

"My own Edgardo!—and you still love me? You still would
marry me in spite of this dark mystery which surrounds me? In
spite of the fatal history of my race? In spite of the ominous
predictions of my aged nurse?"

"I would, Selina"; and the young man passed his arm around
her yielding waist. The two lovers gazed at each other's faces in
unspeakable bliss. Suddenly Selina started.

"Leave me, Edgardo! leave me! A mysterious something—a
fatal misgiving—a dark ambiguity—an equivocal mistrust op-
presses me. I would be alone!"

"Ah!—what if he should know that I have another husband
living? Dare I reveal to him that I have two legitimate and
three natural children? Dare I repeat to him the history of my
youth? Dare I confess that at the age of seven I poisoned my sister, by putting verdigris in her cream-tarts,—that I threw my
cousin from a swing at the age of twelve? That the lady's-maid
who incurred the displeasure of my girlhood now lies at the bottom of the horse-pond? No! no! he is too pure,—too good,—too
innocent, to hear such improper conversation!" and her whole
body writhed as she rocked to and fro in a paroxysm of grief.

Edgardo galloped rapidly towards Sloperton. . . . "Yet if . . .
she knew that I were a disgraced and ruined man,—a felon and
an outcast. If she knew that at the age of fourteen I murdered
my Latin tutor and forged my uncle's will. If she knew that I
had three wives already, and that the fourth victim of misplaced confidence and my unfortunate peculiarity is expected to
be at Sloperton by to-night's train with her baby. But no; she
must not know it. Constance must not arrive. Burke the Slogger must attend to that."

A nameless terror seemed to have taken possession of
Clarissa, Lady Selina's maid, as she rushed into the presence of
her mistress. . . . "An accident has happened on the railway,
and a man has been killed."

"What—not Edgardo!" almost screamed Selina.

"No, Burke the Slogger! your ladyship."

"My first husband!" said Lady Selina, sinking on her knees.
"Just Heaven, I thank thee."

Bret Harte, *Condensed Novels*

These stirring vignettes from "Selina Sedilia, by Miss M. E. B-dd-n and Mrs. H-n-y W-d"[1] represent a kind of distilled essence of sensationalism, a Platonic ideal of the sensation novel. Bret Harte's composite, unfolded in a dozen pages instead of the usual three volumes, manages to include all of the essential devices in their essential multiplications: passion, secrets, murder, bigamy (not to mention trigamy), dark misgivings, and a family curse. There is the wicked and tortured heroine, a titled lady burdened with an inconvenient lower-class husband, the disgracefully ungrammatical Burke the Slogger; there is her dashing lover, the disguised criminal-hero, practiced in seduction and the forging of wills. There is even a railway accident, a crucial occurrence in such novels as *No Name*, *East Lynne*, and *John Marchmont's Legacy*. On the whole, the parody is inspired, the best of a spirited outpouring, which became "itself a part of the lighter reading of the time."[2] But even "Selina Sedilia" encourages a misleading tendency, common enough in the 1860s and more pronounced since then, to lump the two best-selling authoresses together unceremoniously, without inquiring into any particular differences between them.

Perhaps inevitably, Braddon and Wood were reviewed together, sometimes in the midst of a crowd of the anonymous and forgettable, who busily produced such titles as *Nobly False*, *Recommended to Mercy*, *The Law of Divorce*, *The Weird of the Wentworths*, and *Passages in the Life of a Fast Young Lady*. Because they were women, writing about the sins of women, both of them were subject to reproof in reference to that susceptible organ, "the cheek of the young person." In her extended campaign in *Blackwood's* against the author of *Lady Audley's Secret*, the indefatigable Mrs. Oliphant accords similar, often identical, treatment to the author of *East Lynne*: "This is [a] dangerous and foolish work, as well as false, both to Art and Nature. Nothing can be more wrong and fatal than to represent the flames of vice as a purifying fiery ordeal, through which the penitent is to come elevated and sublimed."[3] As Mrs. Oliphant and other critics point

out, both Miss Braddon and Mrs. Wood demand sympathy
for their fallen heroines, their bigamists or adulteresses,
by making them suffer tremendously at the hands of fate
and their own remorse. Both write about marriage as an
unsatisfactory or illusory state instead of relegating it to
the happy ending. Both rely heavily on "involuntary"
motivation—destiny, insanity, circumstance. The *Christian Remembrancer* brackets their novels under the
single nefarious category of "animalistic" fiction, which is
found to register an alarming "drop from the empire of
reason and self-control, . . . a consistent appeal to the
animal part of our nature." For both Wood and Braddon,
with little to choose between them, it appears to be this
very quality of abandon and unrestraint, this lack of
civilized decorum, that constitutes the irresistible fascination and charm of the ideal heroine.[4] Under the
influence of righteous indignation, these reviewers understandably lose sight of any trivial distinctions in their
effort to counteract the "perverted and vitiated taste"[5] for
sensationalism.

The reviewers who undertake to distinguish between
the leading female sensation novelists, do so on two
grounds: grammar and morals. While a Henry James
may remark of Miss Braddon, with fastidious precision,
that she "writes neither fine English nor slovenly English; not she. She writes what we may call very knowing
English,"[6] even the average hack reviewer is likely to
mention Mrs. Wood's noticeable weakness in the matter
of relative clauses, sentence fragments, use of "like" for
"as," and general vulgarity of expression. These lapses
are accompanied by an incongruous delight in high-sounding phrases and long words as well as a running
commentary on the grammatical practice of her characters. In this case, however, style and morality diverge; for
those moralists who see any difference at all between the
two writers, it is invariably the ungainly prose of Mrs.
Wood that receives the imprimatur. The *Examiner*, which
comes out with the strongest statement of this position,
finds that with the publication of *Verner's Pride* (1863)

Mrs. Wood has already begun to "[fall] behind in the race," precisely because she "bases her fiction on a womanly notion of right, and shows a sense of delicacy that restrains her from the coarser imaginings of the sensation novelist."[7] The rationale for this apparently depends on the fact that in *Verner's Pride* supposed bigamy and murder turn out to have been mere seduction and suicide. *Fraser's*, on the other hand, tries to have it both ways, by castigating the system of literary terrorism patronized by Miss Braddon and at the same time criticizing Mrs. Wood for her "temperance tincture" and her ambition to write with-a-purpose. For *Fraser's*, indeed, her less sensational works, *The Channings* and *Mrs. Halliburton's Troubles*, are *too* tame, "wanting in force, in plot, in love-making, in almost everything which goes to make up a novel."[8]

Behind this diversity of opinion, there are crucial indications of what is happening to popular melodrama during the second half of the nineteenth century. In many ways Braddon and Wood had parallel careers: they were chiefly responsible, together with Wilkie Collins, for initiating the craze for sensationalism; they both achieved their most stunning hits with early novels, *Lady Audley's Secret* and *East Lynne*, published within a year of each other; they proved astonishingly prolific afterwards, Wood living to complete more than fifty novels, Braddon more than eighty, both successfully holding on to their loyal public well after the end of the sensation decade. On the surface, their novels deal with the same concerns, fitting them into the same venerable melodramatic molds and exploiting the same sensational turns of plot. But those critics who saw M. E. Braddon as "coarser," more dangerous, more subversive, were right. Mrs. Henry Wood, for all her dalliance with seduction and unexplained drownings and the dead alive, preserves the conventional meanings of stage melodrama, while herself doing much to foster the "increasing tendency of the heroine to die of sin,"[9] through the numerous dramatized versions of *East Lynne*. M. E. Braddon, however, deliberately undermines the traditional moral assumptions. If Wood's novels show a new emphasis on the repentant sinner within the compass of authentic melodrama, Braddon's show the beginning of a change in substance that will eventually make melodrama itself an empty and outdated form.


## II.

"Nothing disagreeable should ever be looked at. Apart from such a habit standing in the way of that graceful equanimity of surface which is so expressive of good breeding, it hardly seems compatible with refinement of mind. A truly refined mind will seem to be ignorant of the existence of anything that is not perfectly proper, placid, and pleasant."
                                Mrs. General in Dickens' *Little Dorrit*


Mrs. Henry Wood (1814-1887) lived an entirely unremarkable life. She was born Ellen Price, daughter of a Worcester glove manufacturer, and was a semi-invalid from girlhood, suffering from curvature of the spine. At the age of twenty-two, she married *Mr.* Henry Wood, of whom nothing else is known except that he supplied her pen name and himself possessed "a mind a little wanting in ballast."[10] This unfortunate lack finally cost him his job as foreign agent for a banking and shipping firm and sent his family back to England in straitened circumstances after twenty years' affluent residence in France. In this crisis, Ellen Wood hurriedly transformed her hobby of writing short sketches for Harrison Ainsworth's magazines into a paying career. Her first full-length novel was *Danesbury House* (1860), which won her £100 in a contest sponsored by the Scottish Temperance League. Her second—amazingly—was *East Lynne* (1860-61), which took off after a seasonable puff in the *Times* and sold unremittingly for the rest of the century. Widowed in 1866, she continued to grind out popular fiction, both three-volume snifflers and the "Johnny Ludlow" series of short stories, while at the same time taking over as the editor of *Argosy*, which she single-handedly rescued from the debacle caused by its serialization of

*Griffith Gaunt.* She lived quietly and respectably, the only one of the major sensation novelists without scandals and irregularities in private life. She had no literary pretensions and avoided anything like literary circles; Mrs. E. M. Ward found her "a very nice woman, but hopelessly prosaic. Calling upon her one day when she was alone I hoped that perhaps she would reveal some hidden depth yet unseen. But alas! the topics she clung to and thoroughly explored were her servants' shortcomings, and a full account of the cold she had caught."[11] This same quality pervades her fictional world, which is founded on gossip and trivia, much occupied with servants and the lower classes, filled with explicit details of dress, furnishings, and the color schemes of fashionable carriages.

Mrs. Henry Wood seems an unlikely sensation novelist, in her work as well as her life. Her most highly developed talent is for the wringing out of emotion, the calculated and relentless assault on the tear ducts of the average reader. Her books are pure soap opera, loaded down with pathos, disaster, tortures of guilt and repentance, interminable deathbed interviews. One of her favorite situations involves the hero who loves or is loved by two heroines; she focuses, lingeringly, on the anguish of the outsider, forced to contemplate the wedded bliss of her more fortunate rival. All of her novels, in spite of the wild occurrences, have a domestic slant, an air of housekeeping and family relations. It is hardly surprising that the ultimate in ambivalent titles belongs to Mrs. Wood: *The Mystery; A Story of Domestic Life*. Although this touches on the central paradox of the sensation genre, Mrs. Wood remains an extreme case; any of her colleagues would have written "A Romance in Real Life," or "A Matter-of-Fact Romance." The *Saturday Review* describes her novels as a battleground, a scene of competition between two unassimilated modes, sensationalism and domesticity.[12] The sensational incidents exist less for their own sake than for their emotional repercussions, the frequently hysterical encounters between people who have betrayed or persecuted or jilted one another, between people who ought not to reveal their hopeless passions. The murders take place offstage, but the deaths from remorse or consumption are vividly dramatized. What holds it all together is the rule of propriety, in its most rigid and conventional sense. The fact that this rule is continually broken only serves to strengthen it; the offenders are fully aware of the terms of their offenses, either regretting the mad folly that has cut them off from decent society or, if they happen to be villains, striving vainly to keep up appearances. With Mrs. Henry Wood, there is no room for a divergence between morality and propriety. What other novelist could have envisioned this response by an older member of the landed gentry to a possible suicide on his estate? "A well-conducted girl like Rachel Frost throw herself wilfully into a pond for the purpose of drowning! . . . She would be one of the last to do it."[13]

Mrs. Wood's *East Lynne*, having survived an early rejection in manuscript by George Meredith, then a reader for Chapman and Hall, went on to become, with *Lady Audley's Secret*, one of the two top English best sellers of the nineteenth century. If nothing else, it reflects the popular taste of an era. The unbeatable combination of sin and sentiment, the unrestrained emotional wallowing, ultimately depends on an unquestioning acceptance of conventional morality and conventional standards of behavior. It may seem daring, as it was certainly unusual in Victorian fiction, to make the central character an adulteress, and a sympathetic one at that. But the narrator's sympathy, as in stage melodrama, is contingent upon the heroine's remorse, upon the heroine's own total acceptance of the law that she has transgressed. Her greatest punishment, apart from the internal gnawings of shame and guilt, comes from her irrevocable position as a social outcast. From the moment of her elopement with the villain, she has put herself beyond the pale; she may be forgiven, piously and tearfully, by the husband she has wronged, but she can never be taken back. An unmarried and fallen heroine might eventually have made amends by a legal marriage with her repentant seducer, as frequently happened on the nineteenth-century stage.[14] For the adulteress, however, there is only one permissible cure, morally as well as dramatically: an early and contrite death.

The seduction of Lady Isabel Carlyle, scandalous as it might appear in potential, is never permitted to become anything more than an object lesson for erring wives. Like all writers of moral tales, from St. Augustine on, Mrs. Wood is open to the charge of portraying the sin as well as the penance it entails. In *East Lynne*, however, the emphasis actually does fall on the punishment, on the exquisite agony of the penitent adulteress, rather than on the original temptation. Although it is clear enough that Lady Isabel is sexually attracted to Sir Francis Levison, both before and after her marriage to Mr. Carlyle, infatuation alone is not intended to be her "moving motive"; it is not sufficiently powerful to overcome her conventional terror, her sense of duty and propriety. "Oh, reader!" interjects the narrator, "never doubt the principles of poor Lady Isabel, her rectitude of mind, her wish and endeavour to do right, her abhorrence of wrong; her spirit was earnest and true, her intentions were pure."[15] The first time Levison declares his passion, Lady Isabel takes refuge in shocked hauteur and effectively removes herself from his company. But when he reappears at East Lynne, as her husband's guest, he finds an ally in her jealousy of Barbara Hare, a family friend with whom Mr. Carlyle has frequent, unexplained meetings. Apparently Wood cannot bring herself to let her heroine knowingly violate a perfect home and a perfect marriage. In any case, Lady Isabel is given plenty of reason to think that it has already been violated: "She was most assuredly out of her senses that night, or she never would have listened. A jealous woman is mad; an outraged woman is doubly mad; and the ill-fated Lady Isabel truly believed that every sacred feeling which ought to exist between man and wife, was betrayed by Mr. Carlyle."

Following this "moment of wild passion," retribution

sets in promptly. The wretched Lady Isabel is not even permitted to enjoy any "fleeting moments of abandonment" unaccompanied by the "adder stings" of conscience. Indeed, from "the very hour of her departure, . . . a lively remorse, a never-dying anguish, took possession of her soul for ever." This supplies the occasion for another direct homily, courtesy of Mrs. Wood:

> Oh, reader, believe me! Lady—wife—mother! should you ever be tempted to abandon your home, so will you awake. Whatever trials may be the lot of your married life, though they may magnify themselves to your crushed spirit as beyond the endurance of woman to bear, *resolve* to bear them; fall down upon your knees and pray to be enabled to bear them: pray for patience; pray for strength to resist the demon that would urge you so to escape; bear unto death, rather than forfeit your fair name and your good conscience; for be assured that the alternative, if you rush on to it, will be found far worse than death.

Although there are ample doses of conventional religious sentiment administered throughout, it is no accident that "fair name" precedes "good conscience" in this central exhortation to the reader. For Mrs. Wood never really addresses the question of morality, or does so only on the most superficial level; "conscience" is mentioned, certainly, but the social punishments are far more graphic and harrowing. In *East Lynne*, the moral sense is bound up in social status; it is equivalent to breeding, to the "feeling of an English gentlewoman":

> It is possible remorse does not come to all erring wives so immediately as it came to Lady Isabel Carlyle—you need not be reminded that we speak of women in the better positions of life. Lady Isabel was endowed with sensitively refined delicacy, with an innate, lively consciousness of right and wrong: a nature, such as hers, is one of the last that may be expected to err; and but for that most fatal misapprehension regarding her husband, . . . she would never have forgotten herself.

Where moral right is so completely identified with genteel conduct, there is no chance of criticism or subversion
of conventional values. By "forgetting herself," in Wood's
phrase, the adulteress has forfeited her identity as an
English lady, becoming "a poor outcast; one of those
whom men pity, and whom women shrink from," even before she is reported dead in a French railway accident and
assumes the name and occupation of Madame Vine, the
widowed governess.

The unique "sensation" of *East Lynne*, undoubtedly the
source of its enormous popular appeal, is the return of
Lady Isabel, disguised and disfigured, as the hired governess to her own children. For a good third of the novel,
Mrs. Wood indulges her heroine (and readers) in a prolonged, luxurious orgy of self-torture, as the miserable
governess, in going about her humble duties, must watch
the repeated caresses of her former husband showered
upon his second wife, the hated Barbara Hare.[16] At every
turn Lady Isabel is subjected to agonizing torments: she is
reminded, in low tones, of the story of her own disgrace;
she suffers through the death of her son William, unrec-
ognized as his mother; she realizes the depths of her own
shame when Francis Levison is convicted of murder. In
the end it kills her: this is clearly the only proper response for someone in her situation, remorseful but socially irretrievable. If the author admitted any possibility
of her being reinstated as a wife and mother, her plight
would lose its terrible poignancy. As it is, Mrs. Wood
milks the last bitter drops of emotion from the deathbed
scene between Lady Isabel and Mr. Carlyle, in which he
nobly forgives her and they bid each other farewell, "until
eternity." Lady Isabel herself fully expects to go to
heaven. That is evidently much easier to achieve than
any kind of social redemption: "My own sin I have surely
expiated: I cannot expiate the shame I entailed upon you,
and upon our children." The novel leaves her figuratively
in the same place as the popular stage versions, with
their final tableau of Lady Isabel and little Willie en-
throned together on a golden cloud.[17]

The narrow focus on emotional states, while effective in

its way, deprives *East Lynne* of much of the violence and excitement that enliven more typical sensation novels. Although she invokes the darker elements of evil and crime, so that at least her plot outlines look recognizably sensational, Wood makes no attempt to portray them in any depth or to explain her criminal characters. Sir Francis Levison is a convenience for the plot—he gets final credit for everything from the seduction of Lady Isabel to the impulsive murder of George Hallijohn—but he is a colorless and perfunctory villain, distinguished only by the requisite black whiskers. Although Mrs. Wood has her unlimited reserves of ineptness, to which this failure may easily be attributed, it is also apparent that she intends Levison to be commonplace, a coward and a cad, who receives his most fitting punishment when the mob treats him to a ducking in Justice Hare's horse-pond. On a popular level, this is again symptomatic of the banality of evil as the Victorians perceived it—the "decay of murder" in Leslie Stephen's terms. By the 1860s the primitive vitality of the stage villain has receded even in an unsophisticated melodrama like *East Lynne*, leaving behind only his established physical traits.

In *Verner's Pride*, the case of the diminished villain becomes rapidly more acute. Frederick Massingbird, who seduces and abandons a respectable lower-class girl, is singled out from the beginning by a strange black mark on his cheek, "quite as large as a pigeon's egg, with what looked like radii shooting from it on all sides." In spite of this mark (a dead giveaway to the reader), his guilt remains officially unproven until near the final reckoning. What is most remarkable, however, is the fact that Massingbird is killed off before the end of the first of the three volumes. Although the supposed appearance of his ghost casts a shadow over the subsequent action, for most of *Verner's Pride* the villain is irrelevant enough to be safely dead and buried in Australia. He is far removed from the center of dramatic conflict—he is never even introduced to the heroine—and the good characters, oppressed mainly by the results of various misunderstandings and misplaced codicils, are left with nothing very tangible to fight against.

*Verner's Pride*, Mrs. Wood's second attempt at out-and-out sensationalism, lacks the intense urgency of situation that saves *East Lynne* from the cumbersome paraphernalia of its own plot. Here the rule of propriety has tightened its grip, emerging, quite explicitly, as the central issue. What little tension there is results from the spectacle, obviously titillating to Mrs. Wood, of men and women of refined delicacy thrust by circumstance into extremely indelicate positions. The whole plot, reduced to essentials, becomes a series of trials of Lionel Verner's sense of propriety, as he is alternately shunted in and out of his inheritance through the confusion over his uncle's will. The dilemma of his personal life is created by a youthful infatuation with the shallow coquette Sibylla West and failure to recognize his own deeper passion for the heroine, Lucy Tempest. When Sibylla suddenly returns from Australia, already the widow of Fred Massingbird, Lionel proposes to her on impulse, almost immediately regretting it, as he later explains to Lucy's father: "I engaged myself to my first wife in an unguarded moment. . . . I might have retracted: but the retraction would have left a stain on my honour that could never be effaced." For this initial mistake, Lionel condemns himself to "years of penitence" and "expiation" on the principle that "a man who has come to the years I had, should hold his feelings under his own control." Although Sibylla plagues him with her extravagance and her uncertain temper, Lionel resolves never to quarrel with her or complain of her, only reminding her, again and again, "If you have no care for what may be due to me and to yourself, you will do well to bear in mind that something is due to others." Out of chagrin over the loss of Verner's Pride and out of jealousy over Lucy Tempest, Sibylla constantly embarrasses her husband in front of his family, finally accusing him and Lucy of having an affair: "All the courtesies of life were lost sight of—its social usages were as nothing. . . . Sibylla, lost in that moment to all sense of the respect due to herself, to her husband, to Lucy, allowed her wild fancies, her passion, to overmaster everything." All this is unutterably painful to someone of "Lionel's refinement of mind," but even worse is the period of suspense caused by reports of Fred Massingbird's resurrection, which would make Sibylla a bigamist. Although Sibylla herself is indifferent, as long as she remains mistress of Verner's Pride, Lionel stays awake nights pondering his "great anxiety for his wife" in these terms: "To what conflict might she not be about to be exposed! to what unseemly violence of struggle, outwardly and inwardly, might she not expose herself!" In each new instance Mrs. Wood hastens to apply what may be called the "seemliness" test, and the occasions for it become more and more frequent, as though she is in the process of discovering her own true subject in the novel.

Lionel's greatest temptation comes in the stolen interviews with Lucy Tempest, in which he contrives to reveal his passion without gratifying it, generally by patting her on the head "reverently as any old grandfather might have done," for "Lionel Verner was not one to lose his self-control where there was real necessity for his retaining it." Even after Sibylla has conveniently died, he carries on with his romance in the same backhanded way: "There are moments when I am tempted to forget my position, to forget honour, and speak words that—that—I ought not to speak. Even now, as I look down upon you, my heart is throbbing, my veins are tingling; but I must not touch you with my finger, or tell you of my impassioned love. All I can do is to carry it away with me, and battle with it alone." This time the impediment is overwhelming debt, which according to the narrator's solemn pronouncement "placed him beyond the reach of social ties," but which is instantly dissolved by the accidental discovery of the lost codicil. The strained sufferings of the principal characters are based on entirely artificial predicaments, growing out of their own exaggerated notions of honor and delicacy. The minor subplot of Decima Ver-

ner's romance is emblematic of the whole: she is arbitrar-
ily separated from her lover, Edmund Hautley, when his
father disapproves of their engagement for no other reason than "self-will," merely for the sake of opposing his
son's free choice. The lovers are too strictly honorable to
elope, or to correspond secretly during the ten years or so
of their separation, or even to break their promises to
each other. All they can do is wait for the old man's death,
while Decima's youth fades and she is taunted as an old
maid. This same sort of thing happens in *A Life's Secret*
(1867), in which the secret, after ruining a man's life,
turns out to have been a lie, told by the villainess for im-
plausibly oblique motives of revenge.

In *Verner's Pride* Mrs. Wood seems almost desperate to
avoid vulgarity, which is obviously her element; she betrays herself as the outsider, the glove manufacturer's
daughter, imagining the incredible refinement of the
upper-middle and gentry classes to which she does not belong. She plays off propriety and impropriety, weaker
counterparts of the conventional melodramatic principles
of good and evil, but there is no question of which is to be
the ultimate standard. The taste of "kitchen literature,"
though palpable to the discerning reader, is unwitting
and unwilling on the author's part; if she imports lower-
class fantasies and preoccupations into her respectable
drawing rooms, it is out of ignorance, rather than an
impulse toward rebellion or an exposure of nasty middle-
class secrets. Quite simply, she transfers popular melodrama intact into a more exalted setting, none too convincingly, but in total innocence of ulterior designs. In
Mrs. Henry Wood, wicked or unseemly conduct is always
identified as such; it is never excused on the basis of circumstance or given the protection of law—this is why she
consistently avoids bigamy, which is a much more
equivocal proposition than outright adultery. In all
three novels—*East Lynne, Verner's Pride*, and *A Life's
Secret*—she provides apparent bigamy, but ultimate legal
vindication, for her virtuous heroes. With M. E. Braddon,

Mrs. Wood's chief rival and originator of the Bigamy Novel, the lines are never so clearly drawn and the implications are far more revolutionary.

## III.

The Forger, the Murderer, the Upholsterer—where is he?
*Punch*, 1868

Although her son W. B. Maxwell speaks primly of her "entirely sheltered life," Mary Elizabeth Braddon (1835-1915) boldly disregarded, from a very early age, the restrictions and conventionalities that normally shackled Victorian women of her upper-middle-class background. It was her own experience, and not some magical gift of "creative imagination which seems so like the record of reality,"[18] that gave her novels their characteristic flavor of worldliness, or what Henry James would call "the exact local coloring of Bohemia."[19] At the age of twenty-two, determined to support her mother after her father's disappearance, Mary Elizabeth launched her career by taking to the stage under an assumed name,[20] like any typical sensation heroine. By 1860 she was on her own in London, serving her apprenticeship in fiction while turning out blood-thirsty serials for the *Halfpenny Journal* and *Reynolds' Miscellany*. It was around this time that she met John Maxwell, a rising magazine publisher with a wife in a mental institution. For the next fourteen years, the period of her greatest fame, Miss Braddon's well-kept secret was her domestic life with Maxwell, which eventually included five illegitimate children. In spite of the early triumph with *Lady Audley*, she continued to write furiously, even desperately, producing an average of three triple-deckers a year as well as founding the monthly *Belgravia* and keeping up her anonymous connection with the penny dreadfuls. Most of the time she worked under intense pressure, as she explains in more than one letter to Bulwer-Lytton, her literary mentor: "I know that my writing teems with errors, absurdities, contradictions, and inconsistencies; but I have never written a line that has not been written against time—sometimes with the printer waiting outside the door."[21] Incredibly, she came up with the first installment of *Lady Audley* overnight, in a futile attempt to salvage one of Maxwell's publishing ventures, and she later knocked off part of the second and the entire third volume in "less than a fortnight."[22]

For M. E. Braddon, no genteel lady amateur, writing was primarily a way of making money. She lends something of her own experience in the subculture of hack journalism to her young hero in *Birds of Prey* (1867) and its sequel *Charlotte's Inheritance* (1868). His attitude is defined in terms that apply equally to Braddon herself: "He had been brought up among people who treated literature as a trade as well as an art; and what art is not more or less a trade? He knew the state of the market and what kind of goods were likely to go off briskly, and it was for the market he worked. When gray shirtings were in active demand, he set his loom for gray shirtings; and when the buyers clamored for fancy goods, he made haste to produce that class of fabrics." Here, as well as on questions of morality, she had her chronic difficulties with the reviewers: "The critics were not slow to remark that he worked at a white-hot haste, and must needs be a shallow pretender, because he was laborious and indefatigable."[23] For the most part, however, Miss Braddon approaches her craft with zest and good humor, remarkable under the circumstances, maintaining an ironic perspective on her own stock-in-trade, which some of her more solemn critics would have done well to imitate. To her editor at *Temple Bar* she confides:

> The Balzac-morbid-anatomy school is my especial delight, but it seems you want the right-down sensational; floppings at the end of chapters, and bits of paper hidden in secret drawers, bank-notes, and title-deeds under the carpet, and a part of the body putrefying in the coal scuttle. . . . I will give the kaleidoscope . . . another turn, and will do my very best with the old bits of glass and pins and rubbish. . . . the young lady

who has married a burglar, and who does not want to
introduce him to her friends; . . . the two brothers who
are perpetually taken for one another; . . . the high-bred
and conscientious banker, who has made away with
everybody's title-deeds.[24]

The author of *Lady Audley's Secret* obviously enjoys an
inside joke at her own expense. In *Birds of Prey* the hero
collects novels for his half-witted mother-in-law; among
those "adapted to Georgy's capacity" are some "deeply interesting romances of the sensational school, with at least
nine deaths in the three volumes." In *The Doctor's Wife*
(1864) one minor character is actually a sensation
novelist, who thoroughly enjoys his occupation while
slyly admitting that "there's only one objection to the
style—it's apt to give an author a tendency towards
bodies. . . . And when you've once had recourse to the
stimulant of bodies, you're like a man who's accustomed
to strong liquors, and to whose vitiated palate simple
drinks seem flat and wishy-washy."[25] This cheerful detachment, to which even Bulwer-Lytton objected as "flip-
pancy of tone,"[26] colors all of her fiction; where Wood is
mawkish and moralizing, Braddon is jaunty, cynical, and
tough. She knows exactly what she is doing; she has no
exalted opinion of her material or her mission; she is
quite willing and capable of playing around with her chosen conventions and making her own ironic compromises
with the sticklish requirements of Victorian taste.

The critical reactions range from amusement to outrage, sometimes both at once, as in the *Examiner's* intended critique, during the course of which the reviewer
gets carried away with his own sensational tale of "Medea
Blenkinsop, or the Octogamist":

But think of the shifts and perplexities of a wife with
eight husbands, being not only mysteriously married
like Aurora Floyd to her noble husband's horse-trainer,
but . . . also to the Emperor of China, who writes compromising letters by each mail, the more compromising
as she is also secretly married to the postman, who is of

a suspicious temper . . . ; also, under peculiar circumstances, to the giant of a show that is coming to be set
up at a fair in the neighborhood; also to a maniac whom
she keeps in the cellar. . . .[27]

In passing the harshest judgment on "Miss Braddon and
her class," the *Contemporary* brands them as practitioners of "artistic atheism in its lowest phase," a heresy in
which "the existence of any law beyond the caprice of the
individual is implicitly denied" and "savage gratification
of sense and of personal desire is the supreme good." The
*Contemporary* is quite accurate in diagnosing this as a
case of "spirit . . . opposed to form";[28] Braddon and Collins,
in particular, delight in exposing the arbitrary nature of
the letter of the law.

Oddly enough, it is the disapproving critic in the *Christian Remembrancer* who offers the most penetrating
analysis. Miss Braddon, he submits, consistently deals
with "human nature . . . in a scrape. . . . And it is with
people in a scrape, or ready at any moment to fall into
one, that she sympathizes." Her heroines possess what
might be called "expansive natures," impetuous and undisciplined, while their villainous counterparts, from
Lady Audley to Olivia Marchmont, ominously fulfill the
role of "the ordinary feminine ideal." The Braddon ethos
is compared, unfavorably, with that of the long-forgotten
author of *Lost and Saved*, in which a titled murderess is
left in "unabated prosperity" at the end:

If Mrs. Norton attacks apparent and recognized respectability, professes to unmask false pretences, and
shows that the worst people are those most in the
world's good graces, Miss Braddon, the first and, at
present, pre-eminent sensation writer, sets herself to
defy and expose the real thing. Her bad people don't
pretend only to be good: they *are* respectable; they really work, nay slave, in the performance of domestic
duties and the most accredited of all good works. . . .
Her odious females are all remarkable for conformity to
the respectable type.[29]

Here, of course, the *Christian Remembrancer* falls into the same confusion of goodness with respectability, of virtue with domesticity, that Braddon deliberately combats in the best of her fiction. The feminine ideal, as she portrays it, is potentially treacherous, for both the women who conform and the men who worship them; the standard feminine qualities—childishness, self-suppression, the talent for pleasing—inherently contain the seeds of their own destruction. By reversing conventional expectations, within the safe and familiar framework of stage melodrama, Miss Braddon redefines the heroine and relocates the traditional conflict of good and evil firmly within the boundaries of middle-class domesticity. Instead of abandoning the popular conventions, she circumvents them, using them against themselves, investing them with a new ironic significance.

*Lady Audley's Secret* (1862), denounced on all sides as "one of the most noxious books of modern times,"[30] is also credited with the introduction of a new type of villainess—the frail, fair-haired child-woman with murder and bigamy in her heart. Lady Audley's beauty and charm, described without editorial comment at the start of the novel, exactly suits the Victorian style: "The innocence and candor of an infant beamed in Lady Audley's fair face, and shone out of her large and liquid blue eyes. The rosy lips, the delicate nose, the profusion of fair ringlets, all contributed to preserve to her beauty the character of extreme youth and freshness"; "It was so natural to Lucy Audley to be childish, that no one would have wished to see her otherwise."[31] She is irresistibly merry and playful, tripping about the garden, "warbling long cadences for very happiness of heart, and looking as fresh and radiant as the flowers in her hands." Not only that, she is benevolent, in accordance with the persistent Victorian cliché for the truly virtuous heroine: "Wherever she went she seemed to take joy and brightness with her. In the cottages of the poor her fair face shone like a sunbeam. She would sit for a quarter of an hour talking to some old woman, and apparently as pleased with the admiration of a toothless crone as if she had been listening to the compliments of a marquis."

Her general reward is that "everyone loved, admired, and praised her. . . . everybody, high and low, united in declaring that Lucy Graham [her alias] was the sweetest girl that ever lived"; her more particular reward is the "pure" and generous love of Sir Michael Audley, a rich and elderly baronet. After her marriage to Sir Michael, which of course is bigamous, Lady Audley successfully performs all the duties of a conventional well-to-do wife, whether engaged in displaying her domestic graces at the tea table or anxiously nursing her husband, with "the beautiful blue eyes watching Sir Michael's slumbers; the soft, white hands tending on his waking moments; the low musical voice soothing his loneliness, cheering and consoling his declining years." In spite of the initial bigamy, there is not even any question of her chastity, usually all-sufficient for Victorian womanly virtue; she is too cold and calculating to be subject to sexual passion: "The common temptations that assail and shipwreck some women had no terror for me. I would have been your true and pure wife to the end of time, though I had been surrounded by a legion of tempters." She is to all appearances the embodiment of the feminine ideal; no one, not even her husband, can tell the difference under ordinary circumstances. Although her nephew, Robert Audley, comes to think of her as an "arch trickster . . . an all-accomplished deceiver," there is no need for deception in her performance as Sir Michael's wife; as long as she can keep her secrets and her position, she is perfectly happy in the conventional mold. This is what she still clings to after she has finally been unmasked:

I was very happy in the first triumph and grandeur of my new position, very grateful to the hand that had lifted me to it. In the sunshine of my own happiness I felt, for the first time in my life, for the miseries of others. . . . I took pleasure in acts of kindness and benevolence. . . . I dispensed happiness on every side. I

saw myself loved as well as admired, and I think I
might have been a good woman for the rest of my life, if
fate would have allowed me to be so.

In sketching the portrait of her "beautiful fiend," Braddon insists upon all the most impeccable of feminine attributes, which themselves lead to bigamy and murder.
Lucy Audley may claim, with justice, that she is only
doing what is expected of her as a Victorian lady. Like
Rosamond Vincy in Eliot's *Middlemarch*, she has an instinct for pleasing, for "mak[ing] herself agreeable to
everyone," especially men; when her stepdaughter re-
monstrates with her, she answers, "I suppose you mean to
infer by all that, that I'm deceitful. Why, I can't help smil-
ing at people, and speaking prettily to them. I know I'm
no *better* than the rest of the world; but I can't help it if
I'm *pleasanter*. It's constitutional." She traces her crimes,
again with some justice, to the universal and absolute
necessity of finding a husband: "I had learnt that which in
some indefinite manner or other every school-girl learns
sooner or later—I learned that my ultimate fate in life
depended upon my marriage, and I concluded that if I was
indeed prettier than my schoolfellows, I ought to marry
better than any one of them." When the governess Lucy
Graham, apparently deserted by her first husband and
teaching under an assumed name, is offered the dazzling
opportunity of marrying a baronet, her employer, Mrs.
Dawson, impresses on her, in much the same terms, the
advantages of the match; indeed, the Dawsons "would
have thought it something more than madness in a penni-
less girl to reject such an offer." Braddon herself, in the
narrator's voice, charts the beginning of Lady Audley's
history in the "frivolous, feminine sins" of her unthinking
youth, in the "petty cruelties" encouraged by the "right
divine" of her good looks. The underside of the feminine
image, as Braddon exposes it, is anything but pretty: beneath her "innocent frivolity" is shallowness and greed;
beneath her childishness is selfishness; beneath "the virtue of constancy" is "the vice of heartlessness"; beneath
the smiles are deceit and "petty woman's tyranny." Be-

cause people believe in the myth, which she so closely approximates, Lady Audley nearly gets away with her masquerade. When she refuses to heed Robert's final warning, it is because she is still supremely confident of her dominion over her indulgent husband; as she boasts to her stepdaughter: "he will believe anything that I tell him."

In *Lady Audley's Secret*, the threat of crime and insanity has penetrated not only into respectable society, but into the family circle itself and into the heart of that circle, the wifely paragon. Lady Audley is completely natural, completely satisfied, in the feminine role. She is childlike and passionless, in the approved Victorian manner, exploiting her charms efficiently to manipulate others but unencumbered by any active sexuality of her own. She certainly has no objection to the conventional middle-class values of domesticity and respectability; in fact, she commits bigamy in order to get them and murder in order to keep them. Although Lucy Audley is a social climber, originally marrying both husbands for money and position, she embodies an internal threat to the respectable classes because she identifies with them; she wants what they value and brilliantly parodies their ideal. It is the validity of this ideal that Braddon repeatedly calls into question, exploring its latent dangers and possibilities in the character of Lady Audley, this "childish, helpless, babyfied little creature," whom even her accuser pities on that account. The import of Lady Audley's crime of bigamy is that the conventional marriage, which remains at the center of so much of Victorian fiction, becomes an illusion. But it is a persuasive illusion, one that only the special knowledge of the amateur detective is sufficient to dispel. During the progress of his investigation after his friend George Talboys, the inconvenient first husband, has been pushed down a well, Robert Audley begins to view the domestic scene at Audley Court with new insight: "What a pleasant picture it might have been, had he been able to look upon it ignorantly, seeing no more than others saw, looking no further than a stranger could look. But with the black cloud which he saw brooding over it, what an arch mockery, what a diabolical delusion it seemed." After the impostor's secrets have finally been revealed, we are left with the image of Robert Audley "brooding over the desolate hearth" with a "sense of strange bewilderment," wondering at "the change in that old house which, until the day of his friend's disappearance, had been so pleasant a home for all who sheltered beneath its hospitable roof." Sir Michael Audley's domestic idyll is discovered to be founded on lies and crime; the unsettling implication is that it could happen under any such "hospitable roof," that the reality of the middle-class dream is not automatically assured. At the end of the novel, as many marriages have been destroyed as have been newly created.

If Lady Audley represents the feminine ideal as would-be murderer, Aurora Floyd, in the novel of that name, represents the *femme fatale* as heroine. For this second smash hit in a row (1863), Miss Braddon exploits the melodramatic stereotype of the villainess, again slyly reversing its accumulated connotations. Aurora Floyd, the banker's daughter, is an imperious, tempestuous, dark-haired beauty, who exerts a powerful fascination over her unwilling admirer, the fastidious gentleman Talbot Bulstrode: she seems "barbarous, intoxicating, dangerous, and maddening"; "she is like everything that is beautiful, and strange, and wicked, and unwomanly, and bewitching."[32] At the same time, there is "a certain gloomy shade [that] would sometimes steal over her countenance," the sign of a "horrible fatality," a "frightful curse," that pursues her. In spite of his misgivings, Bulstrode proposes marriage and is accepted, only to find out about the scandalous rumors connected with her attendance at a French boarding school, from which she once ran away. When he demands an explanation as a prelude to withdrawing his proposal, she demands that he trust her, while hinting mysteriously at her own guilt: "I am only nineteen; but within the last two years of my life I have done enough to break my father's heart." It turns out that Braddon has impishly duplicated the plot of her previous novel in all its memorable details: Aurora, like Lady Audley, has a secret; she commits bigamy; she attempts to bribe her former husband and ends up suspected of murdering him. The surprise is not that she becomes a bigamist but, as *Temple Bar* observes, "that she is an amiable one."[33] Once again, Braddon mixes up the approved categories, to the reviewers' dismay: "So far as real life sees, or ever has seen anything like this, it is among the Cleopatras and other witch-like charmers who have misled mankind; not among wives and daughters of repute in Christian or even in heathen times."[34]

The essential difference between Aurora Floyd and her lovely predecessor is passion, which Lady Audley lacks and Aurora has in abundance. She is given to sudden rages, of the kind which expend themselves "in sharply cruel words, and convulsive rendings of lace and ribbon, or coroner's juries might have to sit even oftener than they do." On one such occasion, "sublime in her passion," she horse-whips an imbecilic stablehand who has mistreated her dog; on another, she enters into incriminating dialogue, overheard by an eavesdropper, with her legal husband: " 'You'd like to stab me, or shoot me, or strangle me, as I stand here; wouldn't you, now?' asked the trainer mockingly. 'Yes,' cried Aurora, 'I would!' " In the course of the novel, she loves three different men and marries two of them, including her father's groom. The nature of her attraction to this James Conyers is evident: "You give him credit for thoughts to match with his dark, violet-hued eyes, and the exquisite modelling of his mouth and chin; you give him a mind as aesthetically perfect as his face and figure, and you recoil on discovering what a vulgar, every-day sword may lurk under that beautiful scabbard." Even though she elopes with him as a schoolgirl, pays him to leave her alone, and lies to her father about his supposed death, Aurora is excused as a "wretched girl, whose worst sin had been to mistake a bad man for a good one; the ignorant trustfulness of a child who is ready to accept any shabby pilgrim for an exiled nobleman or a prince in disguise!" While the narrator admits that "there

is much need of apology for her," Aurora Floyd is ultimately vindicated and established in the role of heroine.

Like all English sensation novelists, Braddon is ham-
pered by the code of Grundyism, which makes bigamy an
acceptable subterfuge as long as the various ceremonies
are duly performed. It has been argued that her compliance with this code leads to a kind of "thwarted sensationalism which did not at bottom make sense," because "she would falsify her own realism by explaining
everything away."[35] Actually, Braddon takes full advantage of the prevailing hypocrisy to indulge her heroine in
such questionable escapades as running away with a
horse trainer before settling down into conventional
domesticity. Because of the erroneous obituary in the
sporting news, Aurora Floyd is technically in the right;
her worst mistake is in concealing her past instead of
suing for a divorce from the faithless Conyers. Her second, and bigamous, marriage to the Yorkshire squire
John Mellish is ironically more genuine than her legal
one. Although she decamps temporarily after the murder
of Conyers ("Good-bye, dear home, in which I was an impostor and a cheat"), the narrator obviously approves of
the instinct that tells her, "There is no wrong you can do
him so bitter as to desert him. There is no unhappiness
you can bring upon him equal to the unhappiness of los-
ing you." John Mellish, unlike the retired suitor Talbot
Bulstrode, is tolerant of anything that is Aurora's doing
because he is unconditionally in love with her. Not only
does he take her back, privately remarrying her, he is
willing to do so even while he still thinks she is involved
in the murder. The "cruel expiation" for her youthful
folly, which causes her to carry on like Bret Harte's
Selina Sedilia, is certainly moderate by melodramatic
standards. In spite of that unfortunate interlude when
Conyers has reappeared and she offers to send him to
Australia, thus deliberately continuing the bigamy committed in good faith, Aurora Floyd is granted her happy
ending: "So we leave Aurora, a little changed, a shade
less defiantly bright, perhaps, but unspeakably beautiful

and tender, bending over the cradle of her first-born." This would be inconceivable in popular melodrama, or in Mrs. Henry Wood; it subverts the essential meaning of the heroine, whose absolute purity or sacrificial death true melodrama unequivocally demands.

In *John Marchmont's Legacy* (1863), Braddon proposes a curious amalgam of the darkly passionate heroine (Aurora Floyd) and the conventionally respectable villainess (Lady Audley). The character of Olivia Marchmont is wildly overdrawn but interesting in concept. The strained histrionics, borrowed from the axiomatic tragedy queen of the popular stage, are employed in a new way, not to identify the typical sexually threatening villainess, but to approach a study in sexual repression. Endowed with the "raging fire" of a passionate nature, with "the ambition of a Semiramis, the courage of a Boadicea, the resolution of a Lady MacBeth,"[36] Olivia Marchmont might seem cut out to be one of Miss Braddon's favorites, in the tempestuous mold of Aurora Floyd. Her explosive passions, however, are held rigidly in check by her "sense of duty," which her clergyman father describes as "more powerful than any other sentiment." No wonder the *Christian Remembrancer* bridles at the terms in which Braddon introduces her villainess: "Yes, the life of this woman is told in these few words: she did her duty. . . . She was a good woman. The bishop of the diocese had specially complimented her for her active devotion to that holy work which falls somewhat heavily upon the only daughter of a widowed rector." In fact, she is rather too perfect, with "no blemish of mortal weakness upon the good deeds she performed"; and unlike Lady Audley, she is not loved by "the recipients of her bounties," who, "seeing her so far off, grew afraid of her, even by reason of her goodness." She is "Church-of-England charity personified; meting out all mercies by line and rule; doing good with a notebook and a pencil in her hand." At the same time, there is something obsessive and masochistic in her charity. Even in her girlhood, "her life was one perpetual sacrifice to her father's parishioners. There was no natural womanly vanity, no simple girlish fancy, which this woman had not trodden under foot." And later, in her struggle against serious temptation, "she made a routine of penance for herself . . . going long distances on foot to visit her poor, when she might have ridden in her carriage; courting exposure to rain and foul weather; wearing herself out with unnecessary fatigue, and returning footsore to her desolate home to fall fainting into the strong arms of her grim attendant." Religion becomes an indirect outlet for her passion, an instrument of self-suppression and self-torture for this "woman who was for ever fighting against her nature; . . . for ever measuring herself by the standard she had set up for her self-abasement." Whenever she feels particularly restive, she finds relief in writing sermons—"fierce denunciatory protests against the inherent wickedness of the human heart."

Although it is reiterated that she "tried, and tried unceasingly, to do her duty, and to be good," Olivia's secret is that "she was weary of her life," and further, that she is infatuated with the hero, her boyish cousin Edward Arundel. Because of her "narrow," rigorous existence, because she scorns to "fling myself upon my knees at his feet," this unexpressed and unrequited love becomes the single focus of her "volcanic forces," "until that which should have been a sentiment became a madness." As in other Victorian fiction, female sexuality is connected with insanity—here not in itself or in its unbridled state, as in Reade's novels, but in its systematic repression. The evil is in the thwarting of impulse, which causes Olivia's mysterious illness and leads to her mistreatment of her stepdaughter Mary Marchmont, the ill-fated object of Edward Arundel's affection. For Olivia, love is "a dark and terrible passion, a thing to be concealed, as monomaniacs have sometimes contrived to keep the secret of their mania, until it burst forth at last, fatal and irrepressible, in some direful work of wreck and ruin." Impulse, indeed, is the greatest virtue in Braddon's fictional characters; she suggests that in the case of sexual desire, abandonment, like that of Aurora Floyd, is less destructive than obsessive control: "Better to have been sorrowful Magdalene, forgiven for her love and tears, than this cold, haughty, stainless woman, who had never been able to learn the sublime lessons which so many sinners have taken meekly to heart."

In her despairing jealousy, Olivia Marchmont consigns herself to her attendant devils, giving free reign to "the spirit of a murderess raging in her breast." Twice she drives her stepdaughter to flee from home, and afterward participates in the villainous Paul Marchmont's conspiracy to keep Mary and her child hidden away while he usurps the inheritance of Marchmont Towers. Olivia finally reveals the plot on the day of Edward's second marriage, only because she is jealous of his second bride. In spite of the fatal adherence to duty, Braddon seems to admire this strange villainess, who "had all the elements of greatness" and more passionate energy than the pallid hero and heroine; in fact, the author seems to warm to her own creation once Olivia has lost all control. In the end, the childish, weak-minded Mary Marchmont, briefly restored to her husband, is killed off by consumption, and the other good characters are sparingly provided with "that modified happiness which is chastened by the memory of sorrow." Olivia Marchmont, never exposed or punished, simply "burnt out" at last, is left to her everlasting rounds of charity. Although subject to fits of mental abstraction, she is looked upon by the local villagers "with considerable respect, as a heroine by whose exertions Paul Marchmont's villainy had been discovered." This is not quite the sort of poetic justice to which Victorian readers had become accustomed.

With her revolting combination of "nasty sentiments and equivocal heroines,"[37] M. E. Braddon brashly challenges the two most cherished myths of her middle-class Victorian audience: respectability and the feminine ideal. In her novels, the worst sort of criminality—passionless and calculating—is always associated with a concern for appearances and a high standing in the world's estimation. Philip Sheldon, the murderer in *Birds of Prey* and

*Charlotte's Inheritance*, is an "eminently respectable" dentist who later becomes a stockbroker with his ill-gotten gains. These are prosaic occupations, and Mr. Sheldon is a prosaic man, totally absorbed in the business of making money. In the midst of his early financial difficulties, he keeps up a spotless establishment, distinguished by a neat display case of "glistening white teeth and impossibly red gums," causing his neighbors to reflect that "a householder with such a doorstep and such muslin curtains could not be other than the most correct of mankind." The "irreproachable neatness" of his person is complemented by his well-regulated behavior; he gets away with the murder of his wife's first husband, simply because he seems such an unlikely candidate for committing it, even to the servant who has unwittingly helped him to administer the poison: "Day by day she saw the man whom she had suspected, going about the common business of his life, coldly serene of aspect, untroubled of manner, confronting fortune with his head erect, . . . haunted by no dismal shadows, subject to no dark hours of remorse, no sudden access of despair, always equable, business-like, and untroubled; and she told herself that such a man could not be guilty of the unutterable horror she had imagined." This view of him is entirely accurate, except in the conclusion drawn from it; even when he takes the second risk of slowly poisoning his stepdaughter, Sheldon's dreams are troubled only by the mundane images of financial ruin: "a blackboard fixed against the wall of a place of public resort, a blackboard on which appeared his own name"; the sound of the "three deliberate strokes" of the hammer at the Stock Exchange, which precedes the announcement of default. It is the peculiar danger of the modern murderer that he is no different from anyone else, that he inhabits the most ordinary dwellings and executes his crimes in the most scientific and businesslike fashion. "And this is our modern civilization!" exclaims the hero, "Give me the desert or the jungle. The sons of Bowanee are no worse than Mr. Sheldon, and one might be on one's guard against them."

Murder of course has its entertaining aspects, and there is no suggestion that it has the power to dismantle the mechanism of a whole society. That power is reserved to female sexuality, which in the Victorian theory necessarily invites illicit expression. Mrs. Oliphant is not alone in drawing parallels between the sensation novel and the fall of the Roman Empire. "There can be no possible doubt," she fulminates in the pages of *Blackwood's*, "that the wickedness of man is less ruinous, less disastrous to the world in general, than the wickedness of woman. That is the climax of all misfortunes to the race."[38] Within the limits ordained by Mudie's Circulating Library, Braddon endeavors to counteract this most firmly entrenched of Victorian dogmas. In popular melodrama she finds the perfect vehicle: the heroine's purity, under attack by the villain, is already the central issue; she needs only to reverse, or rather to qualify, the final outcome.

According to the *Examiner*, Miss Braddon's "style and matter" are "perfectly well suited" to *Reynolds' Miscellany* but ought not to be given "currency . . . among educated readers."[39] It is true that she supplies a direct link between the sensation novel and the "kitchen literature" of the penny journals, but it is also true that she succeeded in capturing the mainstream market as G.W.M. Reynolds never did. In spite of her slapdash methods of composition, she is a novelist of genuine talent and vitality; even Dean Mansel is forced to admit that "the skill of the builder deserves to be employed on better materials."[40] This "comet of literature,"[41] in the *Contemporary's* hopeful phrase, had remarkable staying power. Although she never quite lived down her reputation as the author of *Lady Audley's Secret*,[42] she later moved on to other genres besides the sensation novel and outlasted the initial opprobrium through sheer longevity. At the end of the century, she receives affectionate tribute in the *Academy* as "part of England; she has woven herself into it; without her it would be different. . . . She is in the encyclopaedias; she ought to be in the dictionaries."[43] It is ironic to find a mellowed Mrs. Oliphant, thirty years after the series of articles in *Blackwood's*, crediting Miss Braddon's novels with "some sense of life as a whole, and some reflection of the honest sentiments of humanity, amid the froth of flirtation and folly which has lately invaded, like a destroying flood, the realms of fiction."[44] By the time of Miss Braddon's death during World War I, her novels seemed old-fashioned and pleasantly cosy, objects of a wistful nostalgia in an uncertain age.

# 5

## Wilkie Collins: The Triumph
## of the Detective

### I.

"Just like me," he said to himself, remorsefully. "Always chok-
ing, or shooting somebody. I must give it up."

*Punch*, 1868

O f all the sensation novelists, it is Wilkie Collins
who most wants to make sense out of the sensational universe—that bizarre and turbulent arena from
which the old world order of romance and melodrama has
already irrevocably receded. In Reade and Braddon, the
dynamics of plot are based on the release of chaos and
irrationality, of incomprehensible forces, internal and external, that are never entirely explained away by the discovery of the secret or the equivocal conclusion. But Collins is not satisfied with this haphazard approach; he is
looking for nothing less than a new design, a grand controlling mechanism to replace the traditional morality of
stage melodrama, which once provided both meaning and
aesthetic structure. Where Braddon and Wood casually
invoke "the hand of Destiny" as a matter of narrative
convenience, Collins explicitly poses the philosophical
questions of fate in opposition to accident, and of character in opposition to both. In orchestrating his labyrin-
thine constructions, Collins is attempting to close the gap
that has developed in the other sensation novelists between form and content. In each of his four major works,
all published during the sensation decade, he tries out
various solutions to this central dilemma, finally achieving an unrivaled perfection of form in *The Moonstone*,
generally hailed as "the first and greatest of English detective novels."[1]

Collins' fundamental literary principle, to which he adheres unswervingly, is "the old-fashioned opinion that the primary object of a work of fiction should be to tell a story."[2] His practical applications of that principle have elicited a remarkable unanimity on the part of the critics, from his own time down to the present. Whether it is applauded or disapproved of, his signal contribution to fiction is in the area of plot; "Take that away," sniffs the *Dublin University Magazine*, "and there is nothing left to examine."[3] For the young Henry James, Collins' books are "not so much works of art as works of science." For Trollope, "the construction is most minute and most wonderful. But I can never lose the taste of the construction. The author seems always to be warning me to remember that something happened at exactly half-past two o'clock on Tuesday morning; or that a woman disappeared from the road just fifteen yards beyond the fourth milestone. One is constrained by mysteries and hemmed in by difficulties."[4] In the face of such universal disdain for his kind of "mechanical talent,"[5] Wilkie becomes understandably defensive: in one preface he contends, "It may be possible, in novel-writing, to present characters successfully without telling a story; but it is not possible to tell a story successfully without presenting characters." In another he admits rather wistfully that, as far as English readers are concerned, "the two qualities in fiction which hold the highest rank in your estimation are: Character and Humour. Incident and dramatic situation only occupy the second place in your favour."[6] Still, it is to incident and situation that he has committed himself; it is through them that he seeks to impose order on the typically chaotic material of the sensation novel and to regain some measure of control, if not for the fictional characters, at least for the author and his readers.

In *The Woman In White* (1860), archetype of the sensation genre, Collins sets up the terms of his philosophical problem and suggests in outline the two possible solutions that he will later pursue in exhaustive detail: the novel in which everything is hinted at beforehand and that in which everything is found out afterward. In the first half of *The Woman in White*, as in *Armadale*, the future impends ominously and is partially foreshadowed by the prophetic dream of Marian Halcombe; in the second half, as in *The Moonstone*, the past is uncovered and the mystery revealed through the detective work of the hero. Throughout the novel, Walter Hartright, its chief narrator, is obsessed with the idea of design and fatality, of some irresistible cosmic force that he calls, among other things, "the Hand that leads men on the dark road to the future." At first, during the episodes at Limmeridge, there seems to be an irreconcilable conflict between "the ordinary rules of evidence" and Walter's admitted "monomania" on the subject of Anne Catherick, the woman in white. By the time he departs on the expedition to Central America, however, he has become convinced, as he writes to Marian, that "these events have a meaning, these events must lead to a result. The mystery of Anne Catherick is *not* cleared up yet."

Both Walter and Marian attach an ultimate and conventionally religious significance to the complex series of occurrences in the novel and to their own part in them. When Walter meets with the fugitive sisters in the churchyard after his return, he attributes the fateful encounter to something more than chance: "I believe in my soul that the Hand of God was pointing their way." Even when he resolves "to act for myself" in exposing the conspiracy, he feels obliged to connect his own assertion of will with the larger scheme of destiny, so that acting for himself means entering into the design: "The End is appointed; the End is drawing us on—and Anne Catherick, dead in her grave, points the way to it still!" Although he freely confesses the "instinct of revenge" that motivates him in the "trial of strength between myself and Sir Percival Glyde," the brutal husband of the woman he loves, Hartright still sees himself as the chosen instrument of fate and of retribution. Although he is twice denied the satisfaction of inflicting direct punishment on his enemies, Sir Percival and Count Fosco, he interprets their deaths, by accidental fire and political assassination, as manifestations of divine justice. Of Sir Percival, whom he sees "for the first and last time" as a corpse, Hartright says, "So the Visitation of God ruled it that he and I should meet"; "How awfully, at the last moment, had the working of the retribution . . . been snatched from my feeble hands!" Of Count Fosco, tracked down by the secret society that he has betrayed, Hartright concludes, "Other vengeance than mine had followed that fated man. . . . Other vengeance than mine had called him to the day of reckoning." Still, by whatever means, the retribution sought by the hero has been effectively fulfilled, and the villains of the piece have paid with their lives. The final design, which is the plot of the novel as narrated by the various eyewitnesses, seems to Walter Hartright to reflect an ultimate world order, bounded by the traditional moral and religious dimensions familiar from stage melodrama.

Although this conventional view dominates, no doubt to the relief of most Victorian readers, there is an ironic counterpoint to it in the form of conflicting opinions advanced by some of the minor narrators and accomplices. There are suggestions, as yet fleeting and indirect, that the same facts or events will bear opposing interpretations, according to the different perspectives from which they are evaluated. Hartright receives disturbing confirmation of this in the anonymous letter directed to him by Mrs. Catherick after Sir Percival's death. Her choice of words parodies his own belief in his role as an agent of retribution: "I was wondering whether the day of his downfall had come at last, and whether you were the chosen instrument for working it. You were—and you *have* worked it." Against his will, Hartright finds that in defeating the villain and vindicating the truth, he has also "served the hatred and wreaked the vengeance of three-and-twenty years." The shameless Mrs. Catherick, to whom Walter ascribes an "atrocious perversity of mind which persistently associated me with a calamity for which I was in no sense answerable," rejoices as heartily as any of the good characters in the results of Sir Perci-val's demise and continues uninterrupted with her campaign to achieve complete respectability by "mak[ing] the clergyman's wife bow to me next."

Of course, the most radical alternative to Hartright's philosophy is proposed by Count Fosco, whose outlook is entirely amoral and relativistic—"glib cynicism" as Marian labels it. During the marvelous conversation by the lake at Blackwater about hypothetical crime, when he claims to "say what other people only think," Fosco points out that moral standards, far from being absolute, may vary considerably from one society to another: "I am a citizen of the world, and I have met, in my time, with so many different sorts of virtue, that I am puzzled, in my old age, to say which is the right sort and which is the wrong." With the observation that "English society . . . is as often the accomplice, as it is the enemy of crime," he proceeds to divide criminals into two categories, based not on morals but on intelligent action: "The fool's crime is the crime that is found out; and the wise man's crime is the crime that is not found out." In spite of his general fatalism—"What are we (I ask) but puppets in a show-box?"—the count never hesitates to act in particular situations, making imaginative use of them, precisely as they already exist, for his own purposes. In this way, as he protests at the end, he has avoided "the odium of committing unnecessary crime" and has only twice, in minor instances, relied on drugging his victims: "To all other emergencies and complications my natural capacity for grappling, single-handed, with circumstances, was invariably equal. I affirm the all-pervading intelligence of that capacity." For Fosco, the life-and-death bargaining with Hartright has no overtones of morality or even personal enmity; it is simply a "skirmish," "hot while it lasted," in which each of the opponents plays out his hand. He takes a similar view of another kind of situation, which Hart-right (and traditional melodrama) would consider to be an obvious example of the fundamental conflict between the forces of good and evil: "The hiding of a crime, or the detection of a crime, what is it? A trial of skill between the police on one side, and the individual on the other."

All of these pronouncements might be dismissed as the "mountebank bravado" appropriate to a grandiose villain, except for the fact that this is exactly how the novel actually works. Divested of its gothic trappings and conventional moralizing, the central action of *The Woman in White* is nothing more nor less than a "trial of skill" between cunning adversaries. The "unseen Design," the "appointed and . . . inevitable End," that looms so awesomely over the first half of the novel, is after all nothing more than an ingenious crime, conceived and perpetrated by an individual criminal. Similarly, the final pattern, into which even the most trifling bits of evidence are neatly dovetailed, has not been supplied by some ultimate power, but by the commission and detection of two such crimes—Sir Percival's forgery and Fosco's conspiracy. In the latter case, Count Fosco is perfectly accurate in identifying society as his accomplice; the "machinery of the Law" places the burden of proof on the victim rather than the conspirators, while popular opinion brands Walter and Marian as "at once the dupes and the agents of a daring imposture."

When Hartright at length begins to make progress, it is not because his claim is just, but because he has learned to act in the manner of Fosco, with increasing success; because he, like Fosco, has become "equal to circumstance." First he attacks Sir Percival in the only "weak place" he knows of, ferretting out Anne Catherick's secret by a methodical process of investigation and deduction. Then he strikes at the count, seizing without hesitation on the "chance-way" offered by his friend Pesca's old association with a group of Italian political terrorists. His weapons, like Fosco's, are chance and accident, skillfully turned against his enemies.

Here, as in any novel by Wilkie Collins, victory belongs to rationality, defeat to the failure of reason, whether through passion or miscalculation. Sir Percival Glyde, for all his viciousness, proves an incompetent villain because of his superfluous and irrational violence. And even Count Fosco, unable to control the timing of Anne Catherick's death, is forced to concede that his "grand scheme" is therefore no longer "unassailable." In his final confession, Fosco credits his downfall to his single lapse from rationality, which is also the cause of his repeated forbearance toward Walter and Marian: "In brief, Fosco, at this serious crisis, was untrue to himself. Deplorable and uncharacteristic fault! Behold the cause, in my Heart—behold, in the image of Marian Halcombe, the first and last weakness of Fosco's life!"

The moral of the story, which Hartright declines to draw from it, is that while individual characters remain subject to the larger play of circumstances, they can nevertheless operate successfully within a limited sphere by using whatever opportunities are given. Although they can achieve nothing more, they can still be "master of the situation," in Hartright's phrase, if only in specific instances. Thus the design of the novel, however intricate and flawless in itself, has only a local rather than an absolute application. It has not been imposed by any divine power, only by Hartright's wishful thinking; it cannot in the end be said to reflect any universal order of morality or justice.

In defiance of Marian's hatred and Hartright's platitudes, Count Fosco retains the distinction of being one of the most delightful villains in literature; even the proper Mrs. Oliphant admits to a sneaking affection for him, going so far as to add that "it is with a certain sensation of sympathetic triumph that we watch him drive away in safety at last, after the final scene with Hartright, in which his own victorious force and cleverness turn discomfiture and confession into a brilliant climax of self-disclosure. So far from any vindictive desire to punish his ill doing, we cannot understand how Hartright . . . finds it in his heart to execute justice upon so hearty, genial, and exhilarating a companion." Although she duly enters the moral objection against this "dangerous" error of Collins' art,[7] it is with much less fervor than usual and only after glowing paragraphs in Fosco's praise. The portrait of Fosco is fertile in such subversive ironies. Not only is the villain more likeable than any of the heroes, he is vanquished as a result of the only morally desirable quality he possesses—his genuine admiration for Marian Halcombe. "The best men are not consistent in good—why should the worst men be consistent in evil?" is Hartright's comment, but he does not scruple to take advantage of the count's "sacrifice." In his last explanation, Fosco alleges an equivalent virtue on the part of his wife, who has assisted him in carrying out his crimes: "I ask, if a woman's marriage-obligations, in this country, provide for her private opinion of her husband's principles? No! They charge her unreservedly, to love, honour, and obey him. That is exactly what my wife has done. I stand, here, on a supreme moral elevation; and I loftily assert her accurate performance of her conjugal duties. . . . Your sympathy, Wives of England, for Madame Fosco!" This, from the pen of a consummate scoundrel, aims directly at the foundation of Victorian social dogma, which makes England, as Fosco calls it, "the land of domestic happiness." A few lines more and Fosco's eloquence is silenced, but Collins himself has barely warmed to his subject.

In an article entitled "The Counterworld of Victorian Fiction and *The Woman in White*," U. C. Knoepflmacher suggests that beneath the orthodox morality of Victorian fiction as a whole there "lurks a vital 'counterworld' that is asocial and amoral, unbound by the restraints of the socialized superego." He argues that Collins in particular "has given a fuller hearing than any of his English predecessors to the antisocial voice of the Rebel" in his portrait of Fosco, and of the unconventional heroine Marian Halcombe as well.[8] Application of this insight can be profitably extended to the entire genre of the sensation novel, which typically explores forbidden territories and releases hidden sources of energy. In his reassessment of the nineteenth-century realist novel, George Levine finds that "the tradition of realism is incoherent with ambiguities and self-contradictions, forcing the novelist to deal with excess—which inevitably becomes the most exciting part of his work—in order to reject it. . . . There is a Frankenstein in every great realistic fiction struggling to get out."[9] One of the major reasons for the outcry against the sensation novel was its undeniable tendency to disturb the accepted balance between restraint and excess. Where realism evokes the extraordinary only to reject it in the end, sensationalism embraces it and revels in it wholeheartedly, all the while neglecting to append the traditional apologies for doing so. In Wilkie Collins' next two novels, *No Name* and *Armadale*, the "counterworld," or the Frankenstein's monster, actually begins to take over, threatening, infiltrating, and at times replacing the established moral and social order normally taken for granted by Victorian novelists and their readers.

With *No Name* (1862) the primitive moral scheme of stage melodrama, generally under assault in the sensation novel, has broken down altogether, leaving behind only pallid abstractions of the vital principles that were once personified in hero and villain. In the preface, belligerent as ever, Collins creates a diversion for the critics, by throwing in a little moral elevation of his own, on the plan perfected by Fosco: "Here is one more book that depicts the struggle of a human creature, under those opposing influences of Good and Evil, which we have all felt, which we have all known."[10] The fact is, however, that the "terrible fight for [the heroine's] soul," while it may disrupt her night's sleep, never seriously affects the realm of action, either her own or anyone else's. The real conflict in the novel is not between good and evil, as in authentic melodrama, but between two sets of more or less unscrupulous characters led by Mrs. Lecount, the "sharp practitioner in petticoats," and Captain Wragge, the professional swindler. The real challenge is not to the heroine's virtue, but to her intelligence and daring, with which she is much more liberally endowed than the typical female lead in Victorian literature, even at its most sensational.

At the outset Collins announces a complete reversal of

narrative strategy, coolly abandoning the tactics that produced the staggering popular success of *The Woman in White*: "The only Secret contained in this book is revealed midway in the first volume. From that point, all the main events of my story are purposely foreshadowed, before they take place—my present design being to rouse the reader's interest in following the train of circumstances by which these foreseen events are brought about." Without secrets, without mysteries—simply through the intellectual fascinations of chicanery, through the practical exercise of the faculty of reason—Collins still contrives to grip the reader's attention and screw it to the pitch of excitement. In the absence of secrets, the focus is shifted from past to present, from characters engaged in hiding crimes or detecting them to active plotters, currently embroiled in the trammels of circumstance. Because of this shift, the protagonists can no longer be merely victims, foreboding unknown disasters or exposing them after their occurrence. In *No Name* the heroine is no longer the object of conspiracy, as in *The Woman in White*, but the instigator, herself the "arch-contriver of incident."[11]

This time the conspiracy, as it is openly designated, is directed by Magdalen Vanstone, illegitimate and disinherited, against her sickly, miserly cousin Noel Vanstone, who has legally robbed her of her father's fortune. When she finds him immune to the ordinary temptations of speculation or misplaced confidence, Magdalen chooses "the short way and the vile way" to the achievement of her own purpose, proposing nothing less than to marry him under an assumed name. While she herself undertakes to charm the susceptible Noel, she employs Captain Wragge to impersonate her respectable uncle and to hoodwink the victim's sharp-eyed housekeeper, Mrs. Lecount. The entire interest, which Collins brilliantly sustains, is dependent on plot and counterplot, move and countermove, as the opponents match wits with each other on the battleground of Noel Vanstone's credulity.

The mental processes of Wragge and Lecount, each in turn, are recorded in minute detail, as they draw their

logical conclusions, interpret motives, anticipate re-
sponses and consider specific alternatives for future pro-
ceedings. When the captain first encounters the runaway
Magdalen, he uses his powers of deduction against her:
" 'One of two things,' thought Wragge to himself, in his
logical way. 'She's worth more than fifty pounds to me in
her present situation, or she isn't. If she is, her friends
may whistle for her. If she isn't, I have only to keep her
till the bills are posted.' " Later, for a price, he gives her
the full benefit of those same powers, never more trium-
phantly than on the occasion when he paints out her
birthmark:

> There was no time to think; the whole enterprise was
> threatened with irrevocable overthrow. The one re-
> source in Captain Wragge's present situation was to act
> instantly on the first impulse of his own audacity. Line
> by line he read on, and still the ready inventiveness
> which had never deserted him yet failed to answer the
> call made on it now. He came to the closing sentence . . .
> which mentioned the two little moles on Magdalen's
> neck. At that crowning point of the description, an idea
> crossed his mind; . . . Wragge was himself again.

Captain Wragge's essential quality is his "inexhaustible
fertility of resource," which operates in particular con-
texts and grapples with particular options. In the conduct
of his own profession, he is supreme, finally earning the
appropriate compliment from the still unsuspecting dupe
of his stratagems: "You're the most extraordinary man I
ever met with. One would think you had done nothing all
your life but take people in." Nevertheless Wragge is only
a specialist in crime, incapable of anything more daring
than a confidence trick: "A man of boundless audacity and
resource, within his own mean limits; beyond those
limits, the captain was as deferentially submissive to the
majesty of the law as the most harmless man in existence."
The world of the novel, with its limited scope and
equally shady groups of antagonists, is aptly described in

a passage from the *Spectator* review of *Armadale*, which may be applied even more pointedly to *No Name*:

> Is it, then, the whole truth about the world in which we live that it is peopled by a set of scoundrels qualified by a set of fools, and watched by retributive providence in the shape of attornies and spies? Is it the object of half the world to cheat the other half, and the object of the other half to put itself in the way of being cheated?[12]

In *No Name*, neither side in the main contest has any pretensions to honesty or rectitude; at the same time, neither commits any actual crimes. The conventional categories of good and evil are simply irrelevant to the action that takes place and even to the motives of the participants. For Magdalen, those categories are often reversed, while for the other characters the game is everything in itself, without reference to absolute standards. Captain Wragge, who delights in the exercise of his talents and embodies the carefree spirit of the novel, not only protests against the inclination of society to pass moral judgments but also denies the unqualified validity of them: "Narrow-minded mediocrity, envious of my success in my profession, calls me a Swindler. What of that? The same low tone of mind assails men in other professions in a similar manner—calls great writers scribblers—great generals, butchers—and so on. It entirely depends on the point of view."

The final stance of the novel, echoing the captain, is blatantly amoral and relativistic, mired in contingency. It is hardly surprising that contemporary reviewers were appalled at this tendency in Collins; in fact, it is still troublesome to the critics of a century later. According to one of these, "the lines are less clearly drawn between good and evil with the result that the reader's sympathies are less vitally engaged. There really is no villain in *No Name* and no foul conspiracy, the foiling of which is demanded by the reader's sense of justice."[13] The point, of course, is exactly the opposite: in *No Name* Collins proves that the reader's interest may be thoroughly aroused apart from any considerations of morality and that his "sense of justice" is somewhat less vital than he may have supposed. In any case, as a consequence of this authorial sleight of hand, the reader finds himself sympathizing with the conspirators rather than their victims and supporting the deception rather than the discovery of the truth.

In spite of the appeal to capitalized abstractions, not even Magdalen herself is confronted with any clear alternatives that can be neatly labeled as good and evil. The "Purpose to which she had vowed herself," which has seemed "sacred to her at her father's grave," has grown out of a sense of injustice, an instinctive rebellion against the legal technicality that prevents Magdalen and her sister from inheriting the fortune that their father has plainly intended to leave them. Although she struggles with herself privately at each new stage of the conspiracy, particularly at the "revolting" prospect of marriage to Noel Vanstone, her public statements, in letters to her old governess or explanations to Captain Wragge, are uncompromising: "Any conspiracy, any deception, is justified to my conscience by the vile law which has left us helpless." Although he later comes to think of his client's daughter as "one of the most reckless, desperate, and perverted women living," even the lawyer Mr. Pendril regards the English law concerning illegitimate offspring as "a disgrace to the nation. . . . The accident of their father having been married, when he first met with their mother, has made them the outcasts of the whole social community: it has placed them out of the pale of the Civil Law of Europe."

Deprived of her name and her social position through no fault of her own, Magdalen determines at least to recover the money from the heir at law who has consented to her ruin—"Not for the sake of the fortune—mind that! For the sake of the right." Abandoned by the law and respectable society, Magdalen has no other recourse but to

turn against them. At first, she causes scandal by running away and performing on the stage, but she soon
learns to exploit the social rules for her own ends:

> I am no longer the poor outcast girl, the vagabond pub-
> lic performer. . . . I have made the general sense of
> propriety my accomplice this time. . . . I have got a place
> in the world, and a name in the world, at last. Even the
> law, which is the friend of all you respectable people,
> has recognized my existence, and has become *my* friend
> too! The Archbishop of Canterbury gave me his license
> to be married, and the vicar of Aldborough performed
> the service. . . . You forget what wonders my wicked-
> ness has done for me. It has made Nobody's Child
> Somebody's Wife.

By marrying her cousin under false pretenses, Magdalen
has acquired a legal right to her own name of Vanstone;
with her husband's early death, that right becomes indis-
putable, even if the deception should be discovered. Magdalen's loveless marriage, which she shrinks from as a
"profanation of myself," is condoned by custom as well as
law: "Thousands of women marry for money. . . . Why
shouldn't I?" Conversely, her parents' union, conventional in every way except in the omission of the marriage
service, is based on love and mutual trust; her mother has
saved her father from despair and depravity, freely offering him "the love and fidelity, the suffering and the
sacrifice, of her whole life." In the terms of the novel, "respectability" becomes the closest thing to evil. Behind the
portrait of Magdalen Vanstone lies Collins' scathing de-
piction of a hypocritical and venal society, in which the
traditional moral categories have utterly lost their meaning. Magdalen's choices are not defined solely on the basis
of good and evil; all of them present ambiguous implications. As Collins' editor, Dickens noted his propensity for
"sweeping" declarations, of a sort "unnecessarily offensive to the middle class."[14] If the Victorian middle class
was not offended by *No Name*, it certainly ought to have
been.

The key to Magdalen's character is her "exuberant vitality"; in enterprise and resilience she is a match even for her irrepressible partner in fraud, Captain Wragge. The contrast with her sister Norah is striking; the conventional "good" heroine, who patiently goes out as a governess after the loss of her fortune, is described as both less beautiful and more reserved than her mother, who has long ago defied convention: "If we dare to look closely enough, may we not observe that the moral force of character and the higher intellectual capacities in parents seem often to wear out mysteriously in the course of transmission to children? In these days of insidious nervous exhaustion and subtly-spreading nervous malady, is it not possible that the same rule may apply, less rarely than we are willing to admit, to the bodily gifts as well?" This is a strange way of introducing the supposed heroine; and in fact, Norah remains a shadowy figure throughout—weak, passive, devoid of energy. It is telling that Magdalen's final conversion, or at least reclamation from her life of deceit, is preceded by an ebbing of vitality and near-fatal illness. When she finds herself disinherited for the second time by her husband's will, Magdalen poses as a servant in the executor's house with the intention of stealing the so-called Secret Trust. She fails because her plan has originated in despair rather than logic and audacity; in the end, she is reduced to trying random "chances," such as collecting rusty keys in the woodshed and applying them to cabinets and cupboards in the house. When she is caught in the act of burglary, she submits abjectly: "Her energy was gone; her powers of resistance were crushed." Before she can be readmitted to the conventional world of her sister, Magdalen must pass through debilitating illness, until her health and spirit are completely broken.

Aside from the fever, however, there is nothing to fear from Collins' version of poetic justice. When Magdalen is about to be removed from her squalid lodgings "to the hospital, if they will have her. . . . And to the work-house, if they won't," she is rescued by the timely interference of

Captain Kirke, commander of the merchantman *Deliver-ance*, who has no other function in the novel. When the doctor on the case learns of his patient's "very, very sad story," he offers sympathy rather than condemnation: "I am bound to say that I, for one, make great allowances for the poor girl down stairs." When Kirke himself learns of it, from Magdalen's letters, he recognizes "the priceless value, the all-ennobling virtue, of a woman who speaks the truth"—and asks her to marry him. The hardest part of Magdalen's new life comes with the revelation that her sister has honorably married the latest possessor of the disputed fortune. At that moment, "the old strife was re-newed; and Good and Evil struggled once more which should win her—but with added forces this time . . . fight-ing on the better side." The final triumph of good, as Col-lins recounts it, means that "she had victoriously tram-pled down all little jealousies and all mean regrets; she could say in her heart of hearts, 'Norah has deserved it!' " Once Magdalen has torn up the Secret Trust, which con-stitutes her only claim on her husband's estate, she con-sents to receive her share of the money as a gift from Norah: "I will take from *you* what I would never have taken if that letter had given it to me. The end I dreamed of has come. Nothing is changed but the position I once thought we might hold toward each other. Better as it is, my love—far, far better as it is!" So Magdalen gets exactly what she wants, in spite of this "last sacrifice of the old perversity and the old pride."

In the proposal scene with her future husband, a naive sea captain who has "never breathed" the "artificial social atmosphere," Magdalen passes the final judgment upon herself: "Do I deserve my happiness? . . . Oh, I know how the poor narrow people who have never felt and never suf-fered would answer me if I asked them what I ask you. If *they* knew my story, they would forget all the provocation, and only remember the offense; they would fasten on my sin, and pass all my suffering by. But you are not one of them!" Here, as later in *The New Magdalen* (1873), Col-lins indulges his favorite fantasy of rescuing a beautiful woman in unconventional distress, something he apparently did in reality on behalf of his mistress Caroline Graves, the original woman in white.[15]

Interestingly enough, M. E. Braddon, the creator of another equally unconventional heroine in Aurora Floyd, disapproved of Collins' Magdalen and even went to the length of appropriating the plot of *No Name* in *Eleanor's Victory* (1863) for the purpose of rewriting it to her own satisfaction. In Braddon's rendition, the heroine's father, a decayed Regency buck, has killed himself after being cheated at cards, but not without leaving behind an incoherent suicide note which requires his daughter to avenge his death on the cheater. Eleanor's solemn vow of vengeance is expressed in exactly the same terms as Magdalen's: "I don't know whether it is womanly or Christian-like, . . . but I know that it is henceforward the purpose of my life, and that it is stronger than myself."[16] Like Magdalen, she is forced to operate outside the protection of the law; and again like Magdalen, she marries to further her scheme, although her husband is merely a convenient bystander rather than the villain himself (who, by the way, has also proposed to her). The difference is that Eleanor Vane "was not a good schemer. Transparent, ingenuous, and impulsive, she had the will and the courage which would have prompted her to denounce Launcelot Darrell as a traitor and a cheat" but no talent at all for the kind of "humiliating falsehoods, the pitiful deceptions, the studied basenesses" practiced so skillfully by Magdalen Vanstone. A friend warns her that she will "unsex" herself if she assumes the role of an amateur detective, and Braddon obviously agrees. Passion, weakness, impulse, even sexual desire may excuse a faulty Braddon heroine; cold calculation and systematic imposture, such as Magdalen's or Lady Audley's, always puts her beyond the pale. Here Eleanor's decision to sacrifice her purpose and to forgive her father's foe when she has him at her mercy constitutes her ultimate victory.

At the conclusion of *No Name*, the unregenerate schemers, far from being punished, rejoice in the

achievement of unprecedented solvency and respectability, without the inconvenience of even a token change of
heart. Magdalen's old enemy, Mrs. Lecount, living in
"honorable and prosperous retirement" on her legacy
from Noel Vanstone's will, turns philanthropist in her
native country: "Zurich was congratulated on the possession of a Paragon of public virtue; and William Tell, in
the character of benefactor to Switzerland, was compared
disadvantageously with Mrs. Lecount." Captain Wragge,
when he reappears at Magdalen's bedside, is provided
with "an income, at last," derived from his recent invest-
ment in quack medicine: "I have been occupied," he tells
her, ". . . in slightly modifying my old professional habits.
. . . Formerly I preyed on the public sympathy, now I prey
on the public stomach." There is no suggestion that this
new business is any more legitimate than the previous
one; he is certainly guilty of fraudulent advertising in the
handbills decorated with the portrait of his gigantic and
imbecile wife over the legend, "Before she took the Pill
you might have blown this patient away with a feather.
Look at her now!" Unlike Dickens, who would have chastened the swindler with retribution or reform, Collins
leaves him undiminished in jauntiness and knavery:
"There he was in his own evergreen reality . . . more au-
dacious, more persuasive, more respectable than ever, in
a suit of glossy black, with a speckless white cravat, and a
rampant shirt-frill—the unblushing, the invincible, un-
changeable Wragge!" This similarly unblushing account
of ill-gotten gains slyly parodies the typical Dickensian
ending, with its liberal allotments of philanthropy and
financial success.

In *No Name* Collins has finally done away with the old
melodramatic superstructure—the traditional conflict between elemental forces—which has become increasingly
problematic but lingers on in obsolescent form in the
other sensation novelists. The upshot is flagrant relativism—a welter of individual characters, unencumbered
by moral affiliations, busily working in opposition to each
other, doing their own plotting and constructing their

own designs on a limited scale. The total design of the
novel transcends the scheming of any one character,
which is likely to be inconclusive or temporary at best.
Mrs. Lecount fails to prevent Magdalen's marriage, succeeds in altering Noel Vanstone's will, then fails again in
the intended application of the Secret Trust. Magdalen,
on the other hand, seems utterly defeated, but in the end
her purpose is achieved by circumstances outside her control. The author brings it all together with the help of
coincidence, but on the whole the structure is remarkably
loose for a Wilkie Collins production. In *No Name* Collins
has rejected the pattern of melodrama, but not pattern itself as an aesthetic device; in subsequent novels he tries
out new justifications for it.

## II.

Find me some material, though it is no bigger than a fly's foot,
give me but a clew no thicker than a spider's web, and I'll follow
it through the whole labyrinth.

                    The Detective in *Foul Play*

Collins' obsession with plotting—his own and his
characters'—reaches a climax in *Armadale* (1866), surely
one of the most over-plotted novels in English literature.
Here, in default of the old melodramatic order, a new
framework is imposed in the form of a prophetic dream in
seventeen segments, followed by its inexorable fulfillment. A "rational" theory of the dream is supplied as a
professional exercise by a certain Dr. Hawbury, who
traces the "reproduction, in the sleeping state of the
brain, of images and impressions produced on it in the
waking state."[17] A "supernatural" theory is supplied not
by conventional moral values or religious beliefs, as in
*The Woman in White*, but by the "heathen" superstition of
a murderer, transmitted to his son by means of a
deathbed confession. It is the murderer who proposes the
theme of the novel by expressing "the doubt whether we
are, or are not, the masters of our own destinies. It may be
that mortal free-will can conquer mortal fate; and that

going, as we all do, inevitably to death, we go inevitably to nothing that is before death." It is the murderer who turns prophet, warning his own son against the son of the man he has murdered: "Again, in the second generation, there are two Allan Armadales as there were in the first. After working its deadly mischief with the fathers, the fatal resemblance of names has descended to work its deadly mischief with the sons. . . . I see danger in the future, begotten of the danger in the past—treachery that is the offspring of *his* treachery, and crime that is the child of *my* crime." Although there is a peripheral clergyman who interjects the "Christian's point of view," the novel is dominated by the vision of a murderer, which defines fatality in terms of a curse.

The murderer's son, who goes by the alias of Ozias Midwinter, struggles against his "hereditary superstition" on the advice of the clergyman, but it happens that each "victory over his own fatalism . . . actually favored the fulfillment" of the dream; his determination to ignore the deathbed warning actually opens the way for the threat of more crime initiated by a woman involved in the original murder. In the author's appendix, Collins professes to leave his readers "in the position which they would occupy in the case of a dream in real life: they are free to interpret it by the natural or the supernatural theory, as the bent of their own minds may incline them." At the same time, he takes care to have every detail of the dream precisely reenacted on the narrative level. By carrying out this devious policy, Collins manages at once to confirm the operation of something that looks like fatality and to avoid endorsing any particular interpretation of it. In spite of the uncanny coincidences, most of the characters in *Armadale* maintain their prosiac outlook, one of them calling Midwinter a "mystic" with all the condescension of a practical man. In any case, the "supernatural" element is no longer inherently connected with conventional morality; the search for ultimate meaning, begun by Walter Hartright and continued here by Midwinter, leads only to the occult—to dreams, portents, curses, and crime. Once again, the plot reflects a single amazing series of events, spawned by a long-ago murder, rather than a transcendent world view.

Without the distorting medium of Midwinter's superstition, the world of *Armadale* looks much like that of *No Name*, with its aimless collisions of knaves and fools, but here the stakes are higher; the conspiracy threatens murder as well as deception. Through the daring imposture of Lydia Gwilt, the respectable society in the novel intersects with the criminal underworld, unflinchingly portrayed in all its sordidness and degradation. Instead of the swashbuckling foreign agent (Count Fosco) or the engaging confidence man (Captain Wragge), in *Armadale* Collins offers for the reader's consideration Miss Gwilt, a forger, thief, adulteress, and convicted murderer who has served time in prison; Mother Oldershaw, a procuress and restorer of decayed beauty who operates the Ladies' Toilet Repository in Pimlico; and her associate Dr. Downward, abortionist and medical practitioner for the same clients.[18]

The chief activity of all the characters is not so much plotting against one another as spying on one another, whether in amateur or professional capacities. It is the occupation of spying, "so essentially base in itself," that brings the two societies together, as each engages in it in order to find out about the other. At the heart of the whole society, both respectable and disreputable, like a spider at the center of his web, is "the Confidential Spy of modern times. . . . the necessary Detective attendant on the progress of our national civilization . . . a man professionally ready on the merest suspicion (if the merest suspicion paid him) to get under our beds, and to look through gimlet-holes in our doors; a man . . . who would have deservedly forfeited his situation if, under any circumstances whatever, he had been personally accessible to a sense of pity or a sense of shame." This particular private detective, Jemmy Bashwood by name, hires himself out on both sides of the case at different times, first making inquiries about the Armadale estate for Mrs. Oldershaw and then uncovering Miss Gwilt's past history, for a fee, at the request of his ancient and miserable father, who has developed a senile passion for the beautiful adventuress. As much as they claim to despise Bashwood and his ilk, the good characters do likewise in self-defense; even old Mr. Brock finds himself shadowing Miss Gwilt and keeping watch on her apartment, although "all my feelings, as a gentleman and a clergyman, revolt from such an occupation." More than any other sensation novel, *Armadale* depicts an entire populace down on its knees before its neighbors' keyholes, prying into their unsavory secrets. Such knowledge brings a certain amount of power, for purposes of blackmail if nothing else, but in spite of the unbridled curiosity, no single character ever finds out the entire story.

The centerpiece of the novel, the character around whom all these complications revolve, is Lydia Gwilt, universally denounced in the reviews as "one of the most hardened female villains whose devices and desires have ever blackened fiction."[19] At the age of thirty-five, already convicted and pardoned in the poisoning of her first husband, Miss Gwilt is an older and unredeemable Magdalen Vanstone, who plots to marry Allan Armadale or, failing that, to kill him and establish a claim as his widow. Like her counterparts in *No Name*, Miss Gwilt is stimulated by the excitements of plotting: "Curious! . . . here I am, running headlong into a frightful risk—and I never was in better spirits in my life!" But her enjoyment is more ferocious and less exuberant than theirs. If it is somewhat difficult to believe in her strange, unwilling affection for Midwinter, which takes the place of her lost conscience in her inner debates, Collins very nearly succeeds in dramatizing her degraded sexuality, which has survived the abuse of her husband and lover as well as her own deliberate exploitation. The conspiracy against Armadale turns on the practical use of her charms, first to enslave Allan himself, then Midwinter, and finally old Mr. Bashwood, who serves as her infatuated instrument. Her private distaste for this expedient is not the result of inexperience, as in Magdalen's case, but of the horrors through which she has already passed—the brutality of the husband she has murdered and the desertion of her bigamous lover. As she tells Mother Oldershaw, "the bare idea of marrying again (after what I have gone through) is an idea that makes my flesh creep." Still, she is involuntarily attracted to Midwinter, idly dreaming of him over her looking-glass: "The color returned to her cheeks, the delicious languor began to suffuse her eyes again. Her lips parted gently, and her quickening breath began to dim the surface of the glass. She drew back from it, after a moment's absorption in her own thoughts, with a start of terror. 'What am I doing? . . . Am I mad enough to be thinking of him in *that* way?' " Miss Gwilt represents the extreme form of the species of sensation heroine, at once passionate and cold-blooded, resolute and capable of murder. Beneath the impeccable facade of the Victorian lady, she conceals a jealousy and hatred of her victim that spurs her on in the direction charted during her moments of more detached calculation: "If so lady-like a person as I am could feel a tigerish tingling all over her to the very tips of her fingers, I should suspect myself of being in that condition. . . . But, with *my* manners and accomplishments, the thing is, of course, out of the question. We all know that a lady has no passions."

With the ending of *Armadale*, Collins escalates the subversive tendencies of *No Name*, taking his leave on a note that has become more savage than humorous. Although Miss Gwilt finally commits suicide and Allan marries her insignificant rival Miss Milroy, this is by no means to be confused with a general or permanent victory of good over evil, as is affirmed in genuine melodrama. The cynical voice of the lawyer Mr. Pedgift, who is permitted almost the last word, describes the successful transformation of Mother Oldershaw into an evangelical preacher in the penitential style and of Dr. Downward into a fashionable psychiatrist. As Miss Gwilt has already observed of Oldershaw's reformation, "it was . . . plain that she had found it to her advantage—everybody in

England finds it to their advantage in some way—to cover the outer side of her character carefully with a smooth varnish of Cant." As Pedgift observes of the reconstituted "Dr. Le Doux," who has forced Miss Gwilt into her final attempt at murder:

> As to evidence against him, there is not a jot; and as to Retribution overtaking him, I can only say I heartily hope Retribution may prove, in the long run, to be the more cunning customer of the two. There is not much prospect of it at present. The doctor's friends and admirers are, I understand, about to present him with a Testimonial, "expressive of . . . their undiminished confidence in his integrity and ability as a medical man." We live . . . in an age eminently favorable to the growth of all roguery which is careful enough to keep up appearances. In this enlightened nineteenth century, I look upon the doctor as one of our rising men.

In *Armadale* the respectable classes are not merely threatened or infiltrated from below; their respectable position is squarely founded on the seething underworld of vice and crime. If the occult agencies of dream and prophesy favor the dubious artistic practice of "mak[ing] one's audience uncomfortable without letting them know why,"[20] the realistic exposé of the foundations of Victorian society gives them ample reason for their discomfort.

The comparative failure of *Armadale* results from the unresolved tension between Collins' desire for pattern in art and his perception of the lack of it in contemporary life. In all three novels—*The Woman in White, No Name*, and *Armadale*—Collins seems to feel a need for some larger explanation of his particular sets of circumstances, some all-encompassing world order to which they can be ultimately attributed. Narrators as well as characters raise the issue periodically, very often in the form of a question: "Providence? . . . Or Chance?"; "Fate or Chance?"; "*Is* there a fatality that follows men in the dark?"[21] As in the notorious case of Armadale's dream, Collins hedges whenever possible, taking full advantage of the sinister atmosphere of fatality, then leaving his readers at the end to puzzle out its significance for themselves. This causes all sorts of difficulties about the premises of fiction and the author's responsibility for his fictional creations; the appendix to *Armadale*, with its choice of "natural" or "supernatural" theories for the marvelous dream, reminds the *Saturday Review* of the nonsense metaphysical problem, "If you had a brother, do you think he would like cheese?"[22] Collins' own uneasiness—the fact that he keeps asking the question and ducking the answer—proves that fate or providence, no longer bolstered by the melodramatic world view, has already lost its effectiveness as the controlling mechanism of an ordered and predictable universe. The rigid pattern of the dream and its fulfillment disconcertingly contradicts the evidence of the rest of the novel, in which "Retribution," like everything else, has to take its chances. Unlike the melodramatists of the popular stage, Collins no longer equates plot with moral content or with the ultimate meaning of human destiny.

In *The Moonstone* (1868), Collins finds the pattern he has been looking for by narrowing the scope of his fiction: instead of solving the general problem of human destiny, the detective novel solves the particular problem of a single crime. By restricting himself in this way, Collins eliminates the strained quality of his previous narratives while preserving the elaborate construction. The central action—here, the theft of the moonstone—is essentially a past event. What this means is that the pattern is already there, in the specific form of what happened and "whodunit"; the detective is presented with concrete results rather than vague suspicions, and his object is simply "to trace [those] results back, by rational means, to natural causes."[23] There is no longer any need to invoke "the fatal force of circumstance" or "the hidden Influence that works in darkness"[24] in order to impress the reader; events receive significance not from their ultimate sources, but from their practical bearing on a criminal case. The reviewer's complaint that "every trifling incident is charged with an oppressive importance,"[25] while accurate enough for the three earlier novels, loses its force when applied to *The Moonstone*. In detective fiction, even the most minute details achieve the legitimate status of clues. When Sergeant Cuff asserts that "in all my experience along the dirtiest ways of this dirty little world, I have never met with such a thing as a trifle yet," he is speaking precisely in terms of his own line of work. It is still true in *The Moonstone* that "if a tea-cup is broken, it has a meaning, it is a link in a chain; you are certain to hear of it afterwards,"[26] but the weight of that meaning is no longer intolerable. In the detection of crime, Collins has found a situation in life, entirely dependent on plausible human agencies, that will yield the same sort of pattern as one of his own ingenious plots. It is the task of the detective, unlike Walter Hartright or Ozias Midwinter, to reconstruct facts and motives, while strictly avoiding any approach to moral or mystical evaluations.

The enclosed world of the detective novel contrasts strangely with the uncertainties and excesses of the original sensation genre. Since Collins, popular developments have tended in the direction of an increasingly comfortable order and stability:

> The whodunit assumes a benevolent and knowable universe. . . . that can be interpreted by human reason, embodied in the superior intellect of the detective. His penetration of facts and clues shows his power to apprehend particular reality and attach significance to the trivial residue of any human action. Finding a meaning in the tiniest clue enables the detective to know the truth; thus, his universe seems explainable, the typical cosmos of English fiction.[27]

It is sufficiently ironic to find this tidy, complacent literary product as the only direct descendant of a genre that attempted to deal with the grotesque and the irrational in a modern framework. The link between the two visions, between the sensation novel and the detective thriller, is

Wilkie Collins himself and *The Moonstone* in particular. Although the mystery of the Indian diamond may be amenable to explanations and solutions, Collins makes no suggestion that the detective has access to absolute truth. On the contrary, Sergeant Cuff's interpretations are frankly limited, his universe only partly explainable. The almost eerie serenity of *The Moonstone* cannot be said to correspond to Collins' world view as much as to an escape from it, a deliberate narrowing of concern.

Although the action of the novel takes place within a restricted sphere, there are numerous hints of dimensions beyond it. The social unrest that provides the mainspring of *No Name* recurs here at a comfortable remove in the sad history of Rosanna Spearman and the angry commentary of her friend Limping Lucy: "the day is not far off when the poor will rise against the rich." The personal torment of Ezra Jennings, another version of Midwinter, bears no relation to the principal inquiry; he is schooled in self-repression and never reveals the details of his mysterious calamity. The strain of bitterness and rebellion that marks such novels as *No Name* and *Armadale* here acquires a curiously epigrammatic quality, an air of detachment and resignation. When Sergeant Cuff remarks that "human life . . . is a sort of target—misfortune is always firing at it, and always hitting the mark," or Gabriel Betteredge observes that "we are all of us more or less unwilling to be brought into the world. And we are all of us right," the effect is not unlike the ideal of Frederick Fairlie in *The Woman in White*, who objects to tears, "except when the refining process of Art judiciously removes from them all resemblance to Nature." What happens in *The Moonstone* is that the professional viewpoint begins to take over—the dispassionate, almost clinical perspective on human sin and human suffering expressed by the various doctors, lawyers, and police detectives who play a larger and larger role in sensational fiction. As M. E. Braddon puts it, "physicians and lawyers are the confessors of this prosaic nineteenth century."[28] This modern phenomenon, alarming to the sensation writer, ultimately becomes consoling to the full-fledged detective novelist. And the detective himself, a figure of opprobrium and marginal social position in the sensation novel, gradually becomes the hero as well as the guardian of conventional values.

The Collins universe, even in *The Moonstone*, is at once more complex and less subject to individual control than the paler imitations of it in the popular detective mode. The totality of the design, as in his earlier novels, remains beyond any one criminal's power of executing or any one detective's power of unraveling. The moonstone passes through a number of hands, both innocent and guilty, in the course of its journey from the drawer of the Indian cabinet in Rachel Verinder's sitting room to the headdress of the four-armed deity of the night in the remote province of Kattiawar. The stages of that journey are traced only through the cooperation of various authorities and detectives, both official and unofficial, who gradually piece together all the logical deductions of their partial information or expertise. Mr. Murthwaite, the Indian traveler, penetrates the disguise of the itinerant jugglers and the motive of the Hindu conspiracy; Ezra Jennings, the doctor's assistant, discovers Mr. Candy's part in the aftermath of the birthday dinner and conducts the crucial test of the opium. Even the great Cuff, while operating alone, makes a mess of it, "Not the first mess . . . which has distinguished my professional career!" The individual characters, on both sides of the law, are essentially functionaries and specialists, who are prevented from dominating in either the realm of action or the realm of knowledge. In the end, the moonstone is not recovered and the murderers are not punished, at least not according to European standards. The prologue and epilogue, set in the wilds of India and infused with the spirit of the Hindu religion, confirm the existence of realities beyond the reach of the detective, the appropriate emissary of modern rationality and legal sanctions.

Denied the reassurance of melodrama—the black-and-white simplicity, the moral certainty—Wilkie Collins takes refuge in logic and aesthetic form. Solving crimes and conundrums is one way of making order out of one's world. The novel as riddle, which met with uniform objections from the critics of the 1860s, offers the not inconsiderable satisfaction of fitting things neatly into place; as old Betteredge explains it, while in the process of harnessing a pony, "in the infernal network of mysteries and uncertainties that now surrounded us, I declare it was a relief to observe how well the buckles and straps understood each other!" In *The Moonstone*, knowledge is a substitute for action. Sergeant Cuff is always just a little too late in arriving on the scene; at the climax, instead of tracking down Godfrey Ablewhite or preventing his murder or capturing his murderers, Cuff performs an astonishing demonstration with a sealed envelope, a towel, and a basin of water. And even if knowledge itself is incomplete, it doesn't matter; Cuff's final report to Franklin Blake relies heavily on "such inferences and conclusions as we are justified (according to my opinion) in drawing from the facts." Although plot, as a device of fiction, no longer guarantees poetic justice, it becomes even more prominent, even more crucial, for its own sake, as the old order of heroine and villain gives way to the new order of criminal and detective. In *The Moonstone*, the frame tale of the Hindu legend and the guardian priests—the very element that transcends the practical sphere of the detective—completes the aesthetic design. The final consolation of *The Moonstone*, for the reader as well as the self-conscious narrators, most of all for Collins himself, is the triumph of form.

# 6

## Influences of the Sensation Novel

### I.

What was he doing with that pen, and that black, black ink, which seemed to grow blacker and blacker under the hands of Piel Dornton?

*Punch*, 1868

**T**he wrathful cry of sensationalism, "that Cry of cries" for the 1860s,[1] made the rounds of the critical journals and became established in their lexicon as a fashionable slogan, with automatic, if somewhat vague, connotations. The word itself, with its aura of patronizing disapproval, became an instrument of the status quo, in world view as well as fictional practice. In fact, according to *All the Year Round*, it took on the quality of an "orthodox stone," convenient for the "flinging at any heretic author who is bold enough to think that life has its tremendous passes of anguish and crime, as well as its little joys and little sorrows."[2] By 1864, M. E. Braddon had already begun to feel its effect as a "bitter term of reproach ... invented for the terror of romancers."[3] One reviewer in *Belgravia*, Miss Braddon's publication, objected to the slogan as a "hollow, windy, worthless ululation,"[4] and it is certainly true that both sides used the term loosely, stretching its original application to a specific genre for their own polemical purposes. For the critics, sensationalism was apt to include the lower reaches of *Reynolds' Miscellany* and the Newgate Calendar, yellow journalism, Coburg melodrama, and spasmodic poetry—anything, in short, from "mere trash" to "something worse."[5] For the apologists, with their loftier conception, it encompassed Shakespeare and Sophocles as well as the Poet Laureate, whose popular verse "Enoch Arden" turns on the heroine's unintentional bigamy.[6] Both sides pointed to Dickens, in triumph or in accusation. *Belgravia* claimed him as the "founder" of the sensation school,[7] while *Blackwood's* reviewed *Great Expectations* along with all the other current sensation novels, judging it much inferior to *The Woman in White* as a specimen of the genre: "With the most fantastic exaggeration of means, here is no result at all achieved, and no sensation produced upon the composed intelligence of the reader. . . . In every way, Mr. Dickens's performance must yield precedence to the companion work of his disciple and assistant."[8]

During the 1860s, both readers and reviewers were on the lookout for sensation, whether to devour it in shilling numbers or to denounce it from literary pulpits. For some, like Charles Reade, it is the constitutive element of fiction: "Without sensation there can be no interest."[9] For others, like the worthy Dean Mansel in the *Quarterly*, the only sensation provoked is a distinctly unpleasant one, as certain popular novels "with or without the intention of the writer, are strongly provocative of that sensation in the palate and throat which is a premonitory symptom of nausea."[10] In any event, sensation was in the air, a part of the temper of the times.

As a separate genre, the sensation novel now looks irretrievably minor in the context of literary history. It became a genre in its own right through the process of revising the ancient verities of romance and melodrama, and through the same process, abolished itself as a viable and relevant means of expression. Still, there are remnants of its brief popular reign even in the major realist works of the sensation decade. One obvious way for its influence to surface is in the form of parody, to which the sensation novel was particularly susceptible because of its transitional status. As early as 1864, the *Edinburgh Review* was reporting that "two or three years ago nobody would have known what was meant by a Sensation Novel; yet now the term has already passed through the stage of jocular use . . . and has been adopted as the regular commercial name for a particular product of industry for which there is just now a brisk demand."[11] The jocular meaning seems to have coexisted quite comfortably with the serious one, diminishing neither the sales nor the impact of the sensation genre. In fact, the irreverent imitations in *Punch* appear to have attracted a following of their own; at one point, the *Examiner* ironically recommended that Mrs. Henry Wood, to keep up her standing in the public favor, ought to read "the thrilling romance of 'Mokeanna,' and write something like that."[12] And of course, M. E. Braddon, who sometimes wrote for *Punch*, enjoyed poking fun at the very conventions she had done so much to establish in the first place.

Although Trollope, as the quintessential novelist of everyday life, had his reservations about the sensational mode, even he dabbled in it towards the end of the decade with a serial that "did much to repair the injury which I felt had come to my reputation in the novel-market by the works of the last few years."[13] That novel was *The Eustace Diamonds*, which has been identified as a close parody of *The Moonstone*.[14] Here Trollope takes up the idea of a young lady's stealing her own jewels, erroneously suggested by Collins' detective Sergeant Cuff, and works it out in the story of Lizzie Eustace, the grasping, deceitful social climber who gets in over her head by lying to the police. The two robberies in the novel provide the occasion for the comical activities of Major Mackintosh and his cohorts, who weave complicated theories and work at cross-purposes to each other, prompting the narrator to remark that, even for a detective, "perhaps, on the whole, more power is lost than gained by habits of secrecy."[15] The narrator himself has no such habits, as he delights to inform his audience, against all sensationalist tenets:

> He who recounts these details has scorned to have a secret between himself and his readers. The diamonds were at this moment locked up within Lizzie's desk.

> In the meantime, the Eustace diamonds were locked up in a small safe fixed into the wall at the back of a small cellar beneath the establishment of Messrs. Harter and

Benjamin, in Minto Lane, in the City. . . . The chroni-
cler states this at once, as he scorns to keep from his
reader any secret that is known to himself.

Among the characters, however, the little mystery causes
quite a sensation, helping to keep the old Duke of Om-
nium alive and entertained over a period of several
months. As in *The Moonstone*, the diamonds are never recovered; they are last seen, not in the headdress of a
Hindu deity, but "adorning the bosom of a certain enor-
mously rich Russian princess. From the grasp of the Russian princess it was found impossible to rescue them."

Along with his parody of specific elements from *The
Moonstone*, Trollope puts the sensation conventions to
practical use in his characterization of Lizzie Eustace.
One of her flaws is a falsely inflated romanticism, which
sets her dreaming over Shelley's "Queen Mab" and imagining a Byronic Corsair of her own to fall in love with.
She watches herself acting out scenes with her various
suitors, calculating the effect as though she is on stage in
a romantic drama. In his most penetrating stroke, Trollope understands that "she liked lies, thinking them to be
more beautiful than truth." Although in her perplexity
over the diamonds, "her mind reverted to all the stories
she had ever heard of mysterious villainies," Lizzie Eustace is not really equal to the role of a Lady Audley, but
harbors "a morbid desire on her own part to tell the
secret"—and does tell it, to the wrong person. When she is
questioned by Major Mackintosh after the second robbery, she outdoes any sensational heroine by deciding to
fall in love with the detective: "such a handsome man as
he was, . . . a powerful, fine fellow, who would know what
to do with swords and pistols as well as any Corsair;—and
one, too, no doubt, who would understand poetry! Any
such dream, however, was altogether unavailing, as the
major had a wife at home and seven children." Given the
dubious social status of detectives in the sensation novels
of the time, this is another high-comic signal of Lizzie's
vulgarity. It is Trollope's final irony that Lizzie Eustace
triumphs over the lawyers, not being liable to prosecution

and leaving town with the parting shot, "I ain't a bit
ashamed of anything." Shortly afterwards, she marries
the insinuating Mr. Emilius and thus becomes a partner
in bigamy, since "he has a wife in Prague and probably
two or three elsewhere."

It should also be pointed out that melodrama functions
on a more straightforward level in the subplot of Lucinda
Roanoke and Sir Griffin Tewett. At Lucinda's first appearance in the novel, she is summed up in a rather sensational epigram: "She's a heroine, and would shoot a fellow as soon as look at him." Lucinda is a portionless
beauty, introduced into fashionable society by her aunt
for the express purpose of being auctioned off to the highest bidder. In compliance with this grim necessity, she ac-
cepts the proposal of the brutal Sir Griffin Tewett, without mitigating the savagery of her tongue and without
pretending to do otherwise than hate him. Their courtship is ferocious and even physically violent; Sir Griffin
forces her to kiss him and on one occasion she strikes him.
After their first kiss, she stands looking at herself in the
mirror: "Never before had she been thus polluted. The
embrace had disgusted her. It made her odious to herself.
And if this, the beginning of it, were so bad, how was she
to drink the cup to the bitter dregs?" As the wedding
draws near, she warns her friends that "I sometimes
think I shall—murder him"; "I really think that I
should—kill him, if he really were—were my husband."
On the appointed morning, Lucinda refuses to leave her
room and threatens the best man with a poker from the
fireplace, saying of Sir Griffin, "he shall never touch me
again;—not alive; he shall never touch me again alive."
Later, her mind gone "astray," she promises to "give him
a kiss with a vengeance" if he ever returns to claim her.
Significantly, Trollope resorts to this melodramatic
mode—everything from brandished pokers to female
insanity—for dealing with the question of sexual repug-
nance, described here with unusual directness and in
explicitly physical terms. This kind of subject matter
seems to have been instinctively associated with this kind

of treatment, even for Trollope, the mild-mannered realist. Nor should it be forgotten that *The Eustace Diamonds* is one of the so-called "dark novels," which date from the 1860s and reflect the same currents of uneasiness that once stimulated the sensation vogue.

So inevitable was this association of subject matter and treatment that it recurs in George Eliot's novel of the mid-sixties, *Felix Holt*, with the haunting, tormented presence of Mrs. Transome. Although Eliot was generally the darling of the critics, at least one eager opponent of sensationalism and moral laxity finds evidence of both in her portrait of the suffering adulteress, on whose behalf she endeavors to "extort" the reader's sympathy. The objection in the *Contemporary* centers on the identification of a new form of tragedy, in which weakness, rather than overweening strength, plays the definitive part: "Practically, the result of such books is to reverse the grand old idea of what constitutes heroic behaviour, by cunningly eliciting our sympathy for individuals placed in doubtful circumstances, who fall into falsely tragical positions because of their weakness, and their want of that will in which lies the very root of heroic action. And here, we regret to say, Miss Braddon and George Eliot join hands, Lady Audley and Mrs. Transome being true twin-sisters of fiction." This linking of Braddon and Eliot, strange as it looks on the whole, is more than just a wild accusation in the specific case of *Felix Holt*. For the reviewer himself, the emphasis is moral; Eliot, like Braddon, is "setting herself in conscious and declared revolt against the common beliefs, thoughts, and aspirations of her time."[16] But the parallel cuts deeper than this: both writers, however ill-assorted in talent and fictional method, are faced with the same restrictions of modernity, and both are tempted by the doubtful prospect of reconstructing tragedy in modern terms.

Eliot's handling of the material of illicit sex, which she shares with the sensation novelists, shows more than a trace of their influence. Mrs. Transome is endowed with all the approved qualities of a sensational heroine: imperiousness, repressed passion, "bitter discontent," even a private taste for certain "dangerous French authors."[17] She paces restlessly through the moldering grandeur of Transome Court, like a quieter and more decorous Olivia Marchmont; she is frequently caught in static tableaux, in which her outward aspect—her manner of sitting, or "her cheek upon her hand"—corresponds with the inner drama of memory and fear. The opening chapter, in recounting the momentous arrival of her son Harold, introduces the repeated motifs of her "sin" and her "secret," both of them somehow connected with this "loved child of her passionate youth." The plot, one of Eliot's least effective, is worthy of a sensation novel, with its complicated legal technicalities, its discoveries of natural parents. Interestingly enough, Mrs. Transome's secret functions in much the same way as it would in the sensation tradition: it undermines the respectable classes and puts them in the power of their social inferiors. Mrs. Transome has not married her father's horse trainer, like Aurora Floyd, but she has taken the "low-bred" foundling Mr. Jermyn as her lover, with the consequence that the current heir to the Transome estates is illegitimate. Eliot chooses these melodramatic conventions, which had been given currency and new applications by the sensation novel, to express the sterility of the world of Transome Court. The vitality in the novel comes from the working class, the happy ending from the young heroine's renunciation of her grand inheritance.

## II.

"Whatever may be the truth on't I trust Providence will settle it all for the best, as He always do."
"Ay, ay, Elizabeth, . . . good people like you may say so, but I have always found Providence a different sort of feller."
Conversation in Hardy's *Desperate Remedies*

In 1871, when the sensation novel was still selling, it touched a new generation of novelists in the person of Thomas Hardy, whose first published venture into fiction is an extreme example of the genre. With *Desperate Remedies*, which appeared anonymously, the sensation novel finally runs amuck, as it has continually threatened to do amid the wilder extravaganzas of Reade and Braddon. In the process of unraveling his "long and intricately inwrought chain of circumstance,"[18] Hardy trots out all the familiar devices, including murder, blackmail, illegitimacy, impersonation, eavesdropping, multiple secrets, a suggestion of bigamy, amateur and professional detectives. The overworked sensational machinery begins to creak and groan, even more audibly than usual. The plot is modeled after Collins but developed without any of Wilkie's plausibility or concern for precision of detail; the young Hardy spends most of his time painting himself in and out of corners, often with astonishing results. Fairly early in the action, an old housekeeper named Mrs. Crickett discovers a long brown hair on the villain's pillow and wraps it up in a bit of paper with all the instinct of a police detective: the hair later reappears as a means of identifying the corpse. Again, when Hardy wishes to hint at the secret relationship between Miss Aldclyffe and her steward Manston, who is actually her illegitimate son, he adopts the awkward and artificial method of comparing them in the voice of the narrator: "It may be remarked that a lady, a year and a quarter before this time, had, under the same condition—an unrestricted mental absorption—shown nearly the same peculiarities as this man evinced now. The lady was Miss Aldclyffe." At the climax, when Manston reburies the body of his murdered wife in the dead of night, he fails to notice that he is being followed by a procession of no less than three hidden watchers; at one point, "the four persons proceeded across the glade, and into the park plantation, at equidistances of about seventy yards." The effect, of course, is more ludicrous than gruesome, but it does carry out certain preoccupations of the sensation novel to their logical conclusion.

What occasional success Hardy manages in this staggeringly uneven work comes not from the clumsy apparatus of clues and detection, but from the loves and trials of Cytherea Graye, the first in a long line of charming, irresolute, and persecuted heroines. All the complications of the remarkably complicated, not to say chaotic, plot spring from thwarted passion, whether licit or illicit; as always Hardy is drawn to the plight of characters who have become involved with more than one lover, and to the intrusion of the past into a present love affair. Cytherea is pursued by two lovers, who represent constant types in Hardy: Edward Springrove is an incipient Angel Clare, while Aeneas Manston is an early Alec d'Urberville. A series of misunderstandings between Cytherea and Edward leads to her reluctant marriage with Manston, whom she regards as she would "some fascinating panther or leopard." The scene of belated explanation between the parted lovers, who clasp hands tremblingly across a flowing river on the afternoon of the wedding, is one of the best in the novel; the note of despair, the sense that it is too late, foreshadows the similar encounter between Angel and Tess Durbeyfield after she has returned to Alec. For Manston—who actually leaps upon the heroine with the cry, "At last! my Cytherea!"—Hardy simply appropriates the stock villain of the Adelphi theater. Although he himself admitted that his villain is "just about as human as the giants slain by Jack, and capable of corrupting to the same degree,"[19] Hardy needed seducers for a number of his later plots and he never seemed to understand them; even in his mature work they rarely drop the Adelphi accent. Here, Manston transcends the stereotype only at the end in his formal confession, which begins, "Having found man's life to be a wretchedly conceived scheme, I renounce it . . . ," and concludes, "I am now about to enter on my normal condition. For people are almost always in their graves. When we survey the long race of men, it is strange and still more strange to find that they are mainly dead men, who have scarcely ever been otherwise." In *Desperate Remedies* this outlook is restricted to the villain; later it will become increasingly pervasive.

Hardy's primary motive in concocting this strange imitation of the Collins formula was a desire to break into print; in fact, he was acting rather literally upon the advice of George Meredith, then a reader for Chapman and Hall, who had rejected an earlier manuscript with a general recommendation for attempting "a more complicated 'plot.' " In later years the author of *Desperate Remedies* tried to disown this troublesome first novel by dismissing its style as "quite against his natural grain."[20] But sensation melodrama was congenial to Hardy, and he never entirely abandoned it. From it he inherited both a theme and a method—a central concern with the experience of the irrational, of the strange or the excessive, and a means of dealing with that experience aesthetically through the use of exaggeration and heightened intensity. Hardy wrote in his notebook for 1890:

> Art is a disproportioning—(i.e. distorting, throwing out of proportion)—of realities, to show more clearly the features that matter in those realities, which, if merely copied or reported inventorially, might possibly be observed, but would more probably be overlooked. Hence "realism" is not Art.[21]

In practice Hardy staged a conscious revolt against the strictures of the conventional realistic novel. His vision of reality, his whole fictional universe, is founded on radically different premises, which undermine the realist formulations and make them finally irrelevant. For Hardy, as for the sensation novelists who preceded him, the patterns of melodrama offered a potentially rich alternative. If in the end his reliance on melodrama is the source of his most glaring flaws, as the critics never tire of pointing out, it is also the source of his greatest artistic power.

Classic nineteenth-century melodrama, as we have seen, boldly confronts the most basic of human anxieties—the sense of an enemy, the loss of control, the apparent triumph of anarchy and misfortune. Even the crudest popular versions on the stage and in the penny

dreadful or shilling shocker derive their compelling vitality from the deliberate evocation of the psychological condition of nightmare, the violent if temporary overthrow of
rational order and moral stability. Although the ending
can always be counted on to dispel any lingering remnants of the nightmare, the fact is that even in conventional melodrama most of the action takes place under its
uncomfortable sway. For the better part of three acts or
three volumes, the melodramatic hero or heroine is at the
mercy of villains, shipwrecks, and avalanches—mis-
judged, disinherited, seduced, threatened with physical
harm. In a study primarily concerned with French melodrama, Peter Brooks has argued that even the earliest
nineteenth-century prototypes express "the anxiety
brought by a frightening new world in which the traditional patterns of moral order no longer provide the
necessary social glue"; that melodrama, by definition, attempts "to find, to articulate, to demonstrate, to 'prove'
the existence of a moral universe which, though put into
question, masked by villainy and perversions of judgment, does exist and can be made to assert its presence."[22]
Although these typically modern anxieties tended to surface later across the Channel, English melodrama in its
purest form can profitably be seen as an effort to hold on,
to identify unequivocally the forces of good and evil and
their operation in the world, to affirm a transcendent
order based on poetic justice. This kind of melodrama
provides a context for nightmare; its readers or theatrical
audience could abandon themselves to its ecstasies of horror and violation in the full confidence of a guaranteed
awakening.

By the 1860s, with the rise of the sensation novel,
the melodramatic nightmare—that state of anarchy un-
leashed when the benevolent order of providence is
eclipsed or called into question—had already begun to
take over as the traditional consolations became increasingly problematic. In novels like *Aurora Floyd, No Name*,
and *Griffith Gaunt*, the recognition of virtue and the absolute distinction between good and evil, essential to the

melodramatic vision, had become exceedingly difficult if not impossible. The vindication of the hero or heroine at the end of such novels was no longer a vindication of childlike innocence or unmitigated goodness according to conventional standards. The "signs of virtue," to use Brooks' term,[23] had now been expanded to include such vagaries as elopement with horse trainers, bigamy, and marriage under false pretenses. The sensation novelists had shown themselves to be dissatisfied with the narrower definitions of virtue and vice, particularly in their application to women. Hardy, of course, later escalated this controversy, invoking the old melodramatic formula only to subvert it, when he gave *Tess of the d'Urbervilles* the subtitle *A Pure Woman*. The loss or confusion of moral bearings originally fostered by the sensation novel meant that the *Sturm und Drang* of melodrama—the disasters, the wild coincidences, the hysterical flights of passion— were no longer bounded and controlled by a just and coherent plan of the universe, faithfully reflected in the defeat of villainy and the happy ending. The hostile forces that rage temporarily before burning themselves out in classic melodrama had begun to pose a more ultimate menace to both fictional victims and readers.

With Hardy's major novels melodrama has come full circle; he completes the process set in motion by the sensation novelists. What has happened is that the old benevolent world order of melodrama, the existence of which is already doubtful in the sensation novel, can no longer be asserted even as wishful thinking. Yet the nightmare remains—the experience of anxiety and suffering, the rule of accident, the feeling of victimization and paranoia. The question that Hardy faced was a distinctively modern one: how is it possible to comprehend a world in which there are melodramatic occurrences— seduction, betrayal, murder—but no clearly acceptable standards of morality and no guiding principle, no assurance or even likelihood of a happy ending? In traditional melodrama the mechanism of accident and coincidence typically functions either as a passing hindrance to the proper order of things or as an agent of retribution and rectification. The evil forces that make the protagonist's world seem hostile and threatening are personified in the thoroughly recognizable figure of the villain and purged with his final defeat. In Hardy's novels, in the absence of divine providence or poetic justice, accident and coincidence themselves become the world order; there is nothing beyond them. The very unwieldiness and grotesqueness of coincidence, which Hardy never discards, comes to symbolize the meaning of his universe. Under these conditions the source of hostility is no longer so easily identifiable; both author and characters are tempted to locate their enemy in the world order itself, which now appears sinister and malevolent, rather than in the villain's perversion of it. Hardy, unlike many of his twentieth-century successors, still painfully misses the old order that has been lost. The cry of Angel Clare at his parting from Tess echoes throughout Hardy's work: "God's *not* in his heaven: all's *wrong* with the world!"[24]

Much of Hardy's attention is focused on his characters' response to this predicament, to their experience of suffering and misfortune without the benefit of any reassuring philosophical or religious framework. What the characters do, more often than not, is create their own personal melodramas, casting themselves as hero or heroine, and thus as victim, while attempting to single out and identify their antagonist. Eustacia Vye in *The Return of the Native* (1878) is a case in point: not only does Hardy borrow her trappings as "Queen of Night"[25] from popular melodrama, but Eustacia herself consciously plays the role. The narrator's initial description of her returns to the same stereotypes of the darkly passionate heroine/villainess exploited previously by M. E. Braddon in such characters as Aurora Floyd, Olivia Marchmont, and Isabel Sleaford (in *The Doctor's Wife* [1864]), which may very likely have suggested elements of Hardy's plot.[26] Readers of Braddon must have recognized Eustacia's black tresses, into which "her nerves extended," and her "pagan eyes, full of nocturnal mysteries." From Isabel she

also inherits a hunger for romance and a private dissatisfaction with her own prosaic lot as the wife of a man without worldly ambition. Isabel, we are told, "wanted her life
to be like her books; she wanted to be a heroine—unhappy
perhaps, and dying early"; "A dull despair crept over this
foolish girl as she thought that perhaps her life was to be
only a commonplace kind of existence after all; a blank
flat level, along which she was to creep to a nameless
grave. She was so eager to be something."[27]

Eustacia, too, longs "to be a splendid woman." Ban-
ished to her grandfather's lonely cottage on Egdon Heath,
she directs her reproaches "less against human beings
than against certain creatures of her mind, the chief of
these being Destiny," her ideas of which may easily have
been derived from popular fiction. By the end of the novel,
as her position becomes more and more desperate and intolerable, she succumbs to the melodramatic delusion of
paranoia, feeling that everything is against her and finding her enemy in the "cruel obstructiveness of all about
her." Following the basic impulse behind the literary
form of melodrama, Eustacia projects all the wrong away
from herself and into the external universe: "O, the
cruelty of putting me into this ill-conceived world! I was
capable of much; but I have been injured and blighted and
crushed by things beyond my control! O, how hard it is of
Heaven to devise such tortures for me, who have done no
harm to Heaven at all!" Although she has "burdened herself with a secret" in the proper manner of a sensation
heroine, she instinctively refuses to take the blame for
her misfortunes, instead personifying her antagonist in
the figure of "some indistinct, colossal Prince of the
World, who had framed her situation and ruled her lot."
In Hardy's novels, characters like Eustacia Vye are continually subjected to all the extremity of melodrama, the
passion, torment, and threat of violence, without any
prospect of ultimate rescue.

Eustacia is not alone in her reaction. Even so sophisticated a heroine as Sue Bridehead in *Jude the Obscure*
(1895) eventually gives in to a subtler and more guilt-

ridden version of the same melodramatic world view. Early in the novel, Sue has shocked her cousin Jude with her advanced views on the scriptures, but before the end she reverts to a narrow, self-punishing Christianity. After the catastrophic deaths of their children by murder and suicide, both of them feel like the helpless victims of some "ancient wrath":

> They would sit silent, more bodeful of the direct antagonism of things than of their insensate and stolid obstructiveness. Vague and quaint imaginings had haunted Sue in the days when her intellect scintillated like a star, that the world resembled a stanza or melody composed in a dream; it was wonderfully excellent to the half-aroused intelligence, but hopelessly absurd at the full waking; that the First Cause worked automatically like a somnambulist, and not reflectively like a sage. . . . But affliction makes opposing forces loom anthropomorphous; and those ideas were now exchanged for a sense of Jude and herself fleeing from a persecutor.[28]

The feeling of persecution, of victimization, that lies at the heart of all melodrama is also central to Hardy's fictional rendering of human experience. His analysis of Sue's regression points to the same psychological processes that make melodrama so perennially attractive. Speaking here in the voice of the narrator, Hardy recognizes the fundamental human need for a specific and fully conscious enemy, one clearly defined in anthropomorphic terms, who can be identified as the source of evil and suffering, who can be grappled with and at least hated if not destroyed. But the primitive satisfaction of unmasking the stage villain is no longer possible for such "supersensitive" moderns as Sue and Jude. Indeed, the general decline of the villain is a striking phenomenon of later nineteenth-century melodrama, including the sensation novel. The stage villains of Hardy's previous works—the Sergeant Troys, the Wildeves, the Alec d'Urbervilles— are merely vestigial survivors of a simpler age, going through the familiar motions of seduction and betrayal in a vacillating and perfunctory manner. They are certainly not the prime movers of plot, nor can they be considered entirely at fault. In *Jude the Obscure*, Hardy's last and bleakest novel, there is no villain figure at all. At one point, poor Jude identifies himself as one of "the men called seducers," but it is obvious that he has nothing in common with the swashbuckling fraternity of the black cape and the handlebar moustache.

Deprived of the villain, deprived of the old certainties, Hardy's characters frequently turn on God, or whatever they call the first cause, for the perverse gratification of at least dealing with an intelligent foe rather than suffering at the hands of arbitrary chance or coincidence. Hardy gives expression to this mood in a very early poem entitled "Hap," which dates from 1866, his twenty-sixth year:

> If but some vengeful god would call to me
> From up the sky, and laugh: "Thou suffering thing,
> Know that thy sorrow is my ecstasy,
> That thy love's loss is my hate's profiting!"
>
> Then would I bear it, clench myself, and die,
> Steeled by the sense of ire unmerited;
> Half-eased in that a Powerfuller than I
> Had willed and meted me the tears I shed.[29]

From the human point of view even malevolence is preferable to utter cosmic indifference, to the rule of "senseless circumstance," as Jude puts it. Hardy, like Jude, sturdily rejects this bitter consolation on the level of theory, but his novels are pervaded by the anguished realization that cosmic indifference *is* cruelty, the worst imaginable cruelty, to the highly developed human sense of justice and order and morality. Hardy, like Sue, is all too painfully aware of the gulf between evolving human consciousness and the unconscious workings of the universe, the sense that "at the framing of the terrestrial conditions there seemed never to have been contemplated such a development of emotional perceptiveness among the creatures subject to those conditions as that reached by thinking and educated humanity." As the narrator remarks in the final pages of *The Return of the Native*, "Human beings . . . have always hesitated to conceive a dominant power of lower moral quality than their own"; or, more difficult still, of no moral quality at all. It is Hardy's insight to dramatize this crisis through his refurbishing of the creaky old melodramatic devices, his evocation of the experience of nightmare, his refusal to dismiss the nightmare with platitudes and *dei ex machina*.

Like all melodramatists, Hardy is fascinated by the grotesque and the improbable, by the operation of accident and coincidence and their collision with human aspirations. Since he can no longer believe in the conventional pattern of the happy ending or in the world view it represents, he looks for other meanings behind the melodramatic experience. Hardy's novels add a new dimension to the old formula, a dimension that suggests possibilities for the future. In his hands melodrama becomes the expression of an arbitrary universe; as Albert Guerard contends, "his symbolic use of mischance and coincidence carry us no small distance toward the symbolic use of the absurd in our own time."[30] At the same time, Hardy recognizes that the sources of the irrational are internal as well as external; frequently, as Irving Howe has pointed out, "Hardy is trying to say through the workings of chance what later writers will try to say through the vocabulary of the unconscious."[31] The sensation novelists, as we have seen, were already groping in this direction with their portrayals of uncontrollable passion and fits of insanity. Reade makes the closest approach to this kind of artistic breakthrough, particularly in *Griffith Gaunt*, with such symbolic events as Kate Gaunt's accident on the stairs, which temporarily and conveniently prevents her from sharing her husband's bed while she is infatuated with another man. Accidents of this sort, subconsciously willed or subconsciously seized on, abound in Hardy, complicating and counterpointing, even to some extent determining, the larger mechanism of blind circumstance. The familiar melodramatic expedients of undelivered letters, unreliable messengers, fatal misunderstandings, interrupted weddings, sudden reappearances of lost husbands or wives, come to correspond, more or less successfully, to the psychic condition of the characters involved, whether they are aware of it or not. In a passage from *Tess* that explains the fallen heroine's interpretation of such natural processes as wind and rain in terms of grief and moral reproach, Hardy says that "the world is only a psychological phenomenon," meaning that its actual impassivity must inevitably be animated by human perception. What the novels show is not that the world is only a psychological phenomenon, but that it is partly so, that character interacts with circumstance, will with accident, to create the tangled web of human experience.

Sooner or later in the course of his novels, Hardy's major characters are certain to form an alliance with chance, whether by accepting it placidly, turning it to their advantage, or surrendering to it in despair. An early and simple case is the initially comic episode of Bathsheba's valentine to Farmer Boldwood in *Far from the Madding Crowd* (1874). The original idea is Liddy's and her mistress falls in with it in a spirit of idle mischief. Not caring to make it a matter of direct decision, Bathsheba leaves it to chance by tossing a hymn book; even the seal, with its taunting and provocative message of "Marry Me," which ultimately leads to murder, is chosen blindly and then simply not rescinded. It never occurs to Boldwood to account for the incident in the light of a practical joke, because he fails utterly to see "the difference between approving of what circumstances suggest, and originating what they do not suggest."[32] The two courses of action, as Bathsheba discovers, may converge, looking "the same in the result." Momentary impulse or carelessness may set in motion a chain of events very far removed from anything desired or imagined by the participants.

One of the surest ways for Hardy's protagonists to get into trouble is by not resisting circumstance when it seems to force them into certain positions against their will. Cytherea Graye's dilemma in *Desperate Remedies* is one to which Hardy will return, particularly in *Tess of the d'Urbervilles* (1891). After her true love Edward Springrove has apparently deserted her, Cytherea finds herself involuntarily attracted to Miss Aldclyffe's dashing young steward, Aeneas Manston. They first meet in a thunderstorm: Cytherea takes refuge in Manston's cottage and he plays the organ for her with mesmeric power, in a scene more than a little reminiscent of Jasper's fierce courtship of Rosa Budd in *The Mystery of Edwin Drood*. Her feeling for Manston is clearly sexual, a disturbing mixture of fascination, fear, and a sense of unwilling subjugation: "She was swayed into emotional opinions concerning the strange man before her; new impulses of thought came with new harmonies, and entered into her with a gnawing thrill. . . . 'O, how is it that man has so fascinated me?' was all she could think." She consistently repels his advances until the period of her brother's serious illness, when Manston's unexpected kindness and offers of financial aid begin to weaken her defenses. At a crucial juncture—the first time he takes her hand— Cytherea pauses irresolutely, trying to make up her mind whether to withdraw it, until she realizes that "it was too late, the act would not imply refusal. She felt as one in a boat without oars, drifting with closed eyes down a river—she knew not whither." A little later, when she has resolved to say something definite, she is checked by a commonplace interruption: "The remonstrance was now on her tongue, but as accident would have it, before the word could be spoken, Mrs. Leat was stepping from the last stair to the floor, and no remonstrance came." Thus, gradually, indecision becomes acquiescence, and she finds herself, under the influence of a "wilful indifference to the future," first engaged to Manston and then married to him. Her failure to resist is similar to Tess Durbeyfield's later "confused surrender," but here, in Hardy's first novel, the heroine is artificially rescued from her disastrous situation and the marriage is never consummated.

Although Hardy himself disparaged the stereotyped cast of *Desperate Remedies* as "mere puppets or pegs to weave the work upon—without reality or character enough in them to warrant their being denounced for want of moral attributes,"[33] nevertheless he continued to maneuver the more fully developed protagonists of his major novels into similar predicaments, exploring the psychological reality behind the stock formulas of melodrama. In the process of recombining the key plot motifs of the sensation novels, including his own, Hardy shifts the focus from startling event to human response, from circumstance for its own sake to its complex relationship with character. It is not simply the author behind the scenes but the characters themselves who rely on chance. Eustacia Vye at the climax of the novel—cornered, suffocating, desperate for a way out—is yet ambivalent about her chosen course of action. She does not herself light the bonfire that summons Wildeve on the final Fifth of November; it is an accident, a surprise planned by the faithful Charley. At the same time, Charley is unwittingly externalizing a motive that is still within her, and the accidental bonfire leads to her agreement to elope with Wildeve. On the day of the elopement, she remains divided against herself: "Having resolved on flight Eustacia at times seemed anxious that something should happen to thwart her own intention"; that same night, while crossing the heath in a drenching rain, she is still debating the necessity of becoming Wildeve's mistress. The outcome reflects her psychological state; her death is ambiguous, both accident and suicide, just as the closed door earlier in the novel is both accident and willed rejection of Mrs. Yeobright.

Tess Durbeyfield, too, gives herself up to circumstance or to outside pressure when she is unable to resolve her own conflicting impulses. Tess is certainly capable of decisive action—leaving Alec, telling Angel about her past, committing murder—but only after her previous waverings have made her situation somehow intolerable. She shows "that reckless acquiescence in chance too apparent in the whole d'Urberville family" on occasions when deliberate choice is so difficult or painful as to be impossible. Her recklessness, however, is quite different from that of her irresponsible mother, who deals with Tess's original pregnancy or her broken marriage "as she would have taken a wet holiday or failure in the potato-crop; as a thing which had come upon them irrespective of desert or folly; a chance external impingement to be borne with; not a lesson." Tess's own kind of fatalism takes into account the possibility that events may be at once both chance and something more than chance. Even the notorious letter under the carpet, for example, is partly sheer accident, partly an external reflection of her indecisiveness: by choosing this form of communication, rather than a direct confrontation, she leaves open the improbable mishap that actually occurs. So too the fateful reappearance of Alec d'Urberville, who materializes exactly when Tess is most susceptible, at the low point in her struggle for subsistence, on the very day when she has turned away from the door of Angel's parents, almost as if her doubt and despair have called him up.

It is amusing, in view of the *Spectator's* treatment of the sensation novel, to read R. H. Hutton's review of *Tess*, published in that same periodical a quarter-century later. Here Hutton concedes, with the predictable qualification, that Hardy has indeed drawn "pictures of almost unrivalled power, though they evidently proceed from the pantheistic conception that impulse is the law of the universe, and that will, properly so called, is a non-existent fiction."[34] This, of course, is the major complaint against the sensation novelists, especially Braddon, couched in exactly the same terms; "impulse" is the familiar negative, "will" the familiar positive, in the critical formulations of the 1860s. This notion of "will, properly so called"—will as a conscious, consistent element of human character—dies hard in nineteenth-century English criticism, and in the novel as well. It is the Novel of Incident, identified by E. S. Dallas in its mid-century costume of the sensation novel, that first envisions "the mass of men as endowed with faint characters, and as tossed hither and thither by the accidents of life, which we sometimes call fate and sometimes fortune."[35] It is the Novel of Incident, paradoxically, that first suggests a new view of character as an unstable process rather than a finished entity. For Hardy, unlike Hutton, will is not such a clear-cut issue; it is complex and problematic. In his portrayal of characters assailed by accident or accident corresponding to subconscious motive, Hardy is developing the potential of the best sensation fiction, following up on the hints of Reade, Braddon, and to a lesser extent, Collins. His work realizes what they have fleetingly intuited. With Hardy, and after Hardy, the whole range of passion and motivation included under the single heading of "impulse" becomes the domain of the modern novel.

The sensation novel as a distinct genre was frankly and genuinely popular, with all the characteristic strengths and weaknesses of popular literature: the boldness and dash, the spectacular effect, the vitality, the raw edges, the lack of subtlety and depth, the impatience with detail. There is an unfinished quality about it in both content and form, an explosiveness, a suggestiveness. For Hardy sensation melodrama was fertile ground in spite of its obvious dangers, some of which he failed to elude. His fiction offers a fascinating illustration of the ways in which the imagination of a major novelist can work upon and transform the materials of a popular tradition. A novel like *Tess of the d'Urbervilles* could not be what it is, for both better and worse, without the profusion of minor sensationalist literature that lies behind it. In *Tess* there remain palpable traces of the Braddon style: Hardy speaks early on of "her life's battle," a favorite Braddon phrase, and he describes his heroine's eyes repeatedly as "neither black nor blue nor gray nor violet; rather all those shades together, and a hundred others, which could be seen if one looked into their irises—shade behind shade—tint beyond tint—around pupils that had no bottom."

The plot of *Tess* particularly recalls that of *Aurora*

*Floyd*, as Hardy takes up and works out Braddon's essential themes, carrying the implications further, actualizing the possibilities that Braddon suggests and then withdraws. Both Tess and Aurora are seduced at a tender age, although the social classes of seducer and victim are reversed. Braddon, as originator of the bigamy novel, protects her heroine by furnishing the obligatory legal ceremony, vestiges of which survive in the pretended marriage arranged by Alec d'Urberville for Hardy's bowdlerized serial version. Hardy refuses to romanticize the situation; his victim is unmarried, she never loves her seducer (something that Braddon would not allow) and she bears an illegitimate child, although it conveniently dies as illegitimate children tended to do at all levels of Victorian fiction. Both Tess and Aurora, haunted by the secret of their past, marry in spite of it and face the problem of how much to tell their subsequent lover or lovers. Both come to feel like "a species of impostor"[36] as the wife, nominal or supposed, of a good man. Neither author supports this conventional view, although Braddon pleads extenuating circumstances and impulsive warmheartedness in this one particular case while Hardy presents a more systematic critique of the "accepted social law" that his heroine has been made to transgress. When Aurora's first husband, the horse trainer, returns from the dead to threaten her happy though bigamous union with Squire Mellish, she passionately expresses the desire to kill him, an impulse on which Tess acts. Braddon gives her heroine murderous promptings and teases the reader by having the horse trainer shot offstage at the end of their midnight encounter, but she ultimately draws back from such a conclusion, after having put her characters through all the hysterical scenes a suspected murder entails. Angel Clare's reaction to the wedding-night revelation and then to the murder combines the reactions of Aurora's two suitors—the fastidious Talbot Bulstrode, who breaks off their engagement on account of the secret, and the adoring Mellish, who tries to shield his wife from the consequences of a police investigation into the groom's death, all the while believing her guilty. Hardy's motifs are there, actually or potentially, in the popular melodramatic tradition out of which Braddon writes. In Braddon's own work, and that of the sensation novelists generally, there are clear foreshadowings of Hardy's attitude as well—his rejection of the old moral absolutes and conventional verities.

When the young Thomas Hardy began writing novels, melodrama was the accepted literary mode for approaching his chosen subject matter, and the sensation novel was the most recent attempt to extend the frontiers of melodrama beyond the safe limits established earlier in the century. In taking over the sensation novelists' controversial treatment of that subject matter, Hardy also renewed their battle with the self-appointed censors, now on the whole more sophisticated than their counterparts of the 1860s but no less outraged by the violation of their own equally cherished values. *Tess* and *Jude*, while recognized as masterpieces by all but the least discerning critics, still provoked an outpouring of shocked reviews, some with such titles as "A Novel of Lubricity," "Jude the Obscene," "Hardy the Degenerate," and so forth.[37] Following the uproar over *Jude* in the mid-nineties, Hardy himself pointed out the continuity between that novel and the sensation tradition, as represented in *Desperate Remedies*: "certain characteristics which provoked most discussion in my latest story were present in this my first—published in 1871, when there was no French name for them."[38]

### III.

Well before the end of the century, the "black, black ink"[39] of the sensation novelists was already fading into permanent oblivion; what had scandalized the mid-Victorians merely looked quaint to their successors. Even during the height of the vogue, there were offshoots in the ghost stories of Sheridan LeFanu as well as the society adventures of Ouida, in which the melodramatic impulse degenerated into boredom and ennervation.[40] The direct line of the sensation novel, under the predominate influence of Wilkie Collins, eventually narrowed into the specialized forms of the thriller and detective fiction. The matter-of-fact sensationalism of the 1860s was finished as a subversive force when the mainstream English novel began to accommodate the more troublesome elements denounced by its original reviewers. The pioneering forays of Collins, Reade, and Braddon into forbidden territory served to open the way for the later development of naturalism, one logical extension of the Novel of Incident, as defined by E. S. Dallas. In the area of fictional technique, the sensation novel helped to kill off the tyrannical triple-decker by introducing narrative economy and tight construction in place of the rambling, discursive mode of Thackeray and Trollope. Un-Jamesian as the sensation novel is, the proliferation of secrets and the values of suspense tended to limit the role of the omniscient narrator, already considered old-fashioned by most Victorian critics.[41] The experiments with point of view in novels like *The Moonstone* or *The Woman in White* encouraged a new relativism by offering conflicting perspectives on the same empirical evidence. In the long-forgotten efforts of the sensation novelists, "that much-admired and much-abused class,"[42] we can now recognize the first stirrings of those attitudes and concerns that we are accustomed to associate with the literature of our own century.

The final import of the sensation novel is that things are not what they seem, even—in fact, especially—in the respectable classes and their respectable institutions. At the climax of the Victorian era, the sensation novels portray a society in which secrets are the rule rather than the exception, in which passion and crime fester beneath the surface of the official ideal. Behind this mood of disillusion, this yet indefinite anxiety, is a general loss of confidence, a somewhat confused retreat from the whole-hearted orgy of national "self-admiration"[43] that had accompanied the Crystal Palace Exhibition of the previous decade. In sketching the background of the sensation genre, Mrs. Oliphant connects it with the failure of scientific invention and progressive theory to eliminate the darker elements of human experience and to secure control over world events. As she confesses in *Blackwood's*, while fitting the sensation novel into the context of the Crimean War, "We who once did, and made, and declared ourselves masters of all things, have relapsed into the natural size of humanity before the great events which have given a new character to the age."[44] The same Victorians who were finding themselves still vulnerable to the shocks of war and social unrest, also found themselves subject to the dimly perceived inner forces of passion and irrationality. The mid-Victorian period has been characterized in many ways, by both contemporary and later observers; it was one of the former, writing in *Argosy Magazine*, who called it "an age of sensation."[45]

# Notes

## Notes to Chapter 1

1. "Prospectus of a New Journal," *Punch* XLIV (May 9, 1863), p. 193.
2. "The Popular Novels of the Year," *Fraser's* LXVIII (August 1863), p. 262.
3. "Belles Lettres," *Westminster* LXXXVI (July 1866), p. 126.
4. [Margaret Oliphant], "Novels," *Blackwood's* CII (September 1867), p. 275.
5. These four rate top billing for the early 1860s in Kathleen Tillotson, "The Lighter Reading of the Eighteen-Sixties," Introduction to Wilkie Collins, *The Woman in White* (Boston: Houghton Mifflin, 1969), p. ix.
6. The phrase is from Walter C. Phillips, *Dickens, Reade, and Collins, Sensation Novelists* (New York: Columbia University Press, 1919), p. 108.
7. Here Tillotson, "Lighter Reading," p. xi, is in agreement with earlier commentators, such as the anonymous author of "Our Novels. The Sensational School," *Temple Bar* XXIX (July 1870), p. 412.
8. Henry James, "Miss Braddon," in *Notes and Reviews* (Cambridge, Mass.: Dunster House, 1921), p. 110.
9. H. P. Sucksmith, "The Secret of Immediacy: Dickens's Debt to the Tale of Terror in *Blackwood's*," *NCF* (September 1971), p. 146.
10. Keith Hollingsworth, *The Newgate Novel* (Detroit: Wayne State University Press, 1963), pp. 222-23.
11. Henry James, "Miss Braddon," p. 110; Louis James, *Fiction for the Working Man* (London: Oxford University Press, 1963), pp. 81-82.
12. Louis James, *Fiction for the Working Man*, p. 88.
13. Sucksmith, "Secret of Immediacy," p. 146. Note also the opinion that Phillips "is mistaken, I believe, in trying to trace the development of Dickens exclusively from the Gothic tale through Byron and Bulwer-Lytton" (p. 146).
14. For a detailed discussion of *Eugene Aram*, from which my facts are taken, see Hollingsworth, *The Newgate Novel*, pp. 82-98.
15. Wilkie Collins, "The Unknown Public," in *My Miscellanies* (New York: Harper, 1874), p. 138.
16. Robert Lee Wolff, "Devoted Disciple: The Letters of Mary Elizabeth Braddon to Sir Edward Bulwer-Lytton, 1862-1873," *Harvard Library Bulletin* XXII (January 1974), p. 11.
17. Charles Dickens, "Two Views of a Cheap Theater," in *The Uncommercial Traveller* (London: Chapman and Hall, n.d.), p. 32.
18. Michael R. Booth, Introduction to vol. I, *English Plays of the Nineteenth Century* (Oxford: Clarendon, 1969), p. 28.
19. Ibid., p. 6.

20. See Michael R. Booth, *English Melodrama* (London: Herbert Jenkins, 1965), pp. 61, 136; Booth, Introduction to *English Plays*, p. 24.

21. Booth, Introduction to *English Plays*, p. 24.

22. Frank Rahill, *The World of Melodrama* (University Park and London: Pennsylvania State University Press, 1967), p. 209.

23. Booth, *English Melodrama*, p. 120.

24. David Grimsted, *Melodrama Unveiled* (Chicago: Chicago University Press, 1968), p. 234.

25. Augustin Daly's *Under the Gaslight*, in Booth, *English Melodrama*, pp. 169-70.

26. Quoted in Robert B. Heilman, *The Iceman, the Arsonist, and the Troubled Agent* (Seattle: University of Washington Press, 1973), p. 23.

27. Discussed in Ibid., ch. 2. See also Robert B. Heilman's *Tragedy and Melodrama* (Seattle: University of Washington Press, 1968).

28. See Eric Bentley, "Melodrama," in Robert W. Corrigan, ed., *Tragedy: Vision and Form* (San Francisco: Chandler, 1965), p. 221.

29. Robert B. Heilman, "Tragedy and Melodrama: Speculations on Generic Form," in Corrigan, *Tragedy*, p. 257.

30. Heilman, *Tragedy and Melodrama*, p. 78.

31. Bentley, "Melodrama," pp. 223, 222.

32. Ibid., p. 229.

33. T. S. Eliot, "Wilkie Collins and Dickens," in Ian Watt, ed., *The Victorian Novel* (London: Oxford University Press, 1971), p. 133.

34. Wylie Sypher, "Aesthetic of Revolution: The Marxist Melodrama," in Corrigan, *Tragedy*, p. 262.

35. See Booth, *English Melodrama*, p. 145; and Tillotson, "Lighter Reading," p. xii.

36. For these and other background details, see Booth, *English Melodrama*, ch. 6, pp. 145-76.

37. Wilkie Collins, Preface to *Basil* (New York: Harper, 1873), p. iv.

38. "The Sensational Williams," *All the Year Round* xi (February 13, 1864), p. 14.

39. See Northrop Frye, *Anatomy of Criticism* (Princeton: Princeton University Press, 1957), pp. 303-7; George Levine, "Realism Reconsidered," in John Halperin, ed., *The Theory of the Novel* (New York: Oxford University Press, 1974), p. 244.

40. Dickens' summary of Collins' *The Moonstone*, quoted in Bradford A. Booth, "Wilkie Collins and the Art of Fiction," *NCF* (September 1951), p. 137.

41. Charles Dickens, *Bleak House* (Boston: Houghton Mifflin, 1956), p. xxxii.

42. Charles Reade, *A Terrible Temptation* (Boston: Brainard, circa 1910), pp. 221-22; Reade, Preface to "The Autobiography of a Thief," quoted in Wayne Burns, *Charles Reade: A Study in Victorian Authorship* (New York: Bookman, 1961), p. 159.

43. Collins, Preface to *Basil*, pp. iii, iv.

44. Walter de la Mare, "The Early Novels of Wilkie Collins," in John Drinkwater, ed., *The Eighteen-Sixties* (Cambridge: Cambridge University Press, 1932), p. 88.

45. "Belles Lettres," *Westminster*, p. 127; [H. L. Mansel], "Sensation Novels," *Quarterly* cxiii (April 1863), pp. 488-89, 501.

46. Wilkie Collins, *No Name* (New York: Harper, 1873), p. 69.

47. Article by Charles Reade for *Once a Week* (1872), reprinted in "Charles Reade's Opinion of Himself and His Opinion of George Eliot," *Bookman* XVIII (November 1903), p. 257.

48. Charles Reade, *The Cloister and the Hearth*, quoted in Emerson Grant Sutcliffe, "Plotting in Reade's Novels," *PMLA* (September 1932), p. 850.

49. Sutcliffe, "Plotting in Reade's Novels," p. 855.

50. *"Aurora Floyd," Spectator* XXXVI (January 31, 1863), p. 1586.

51. Laurence Hutton, ed., *Letters of Charles Dickens to Wilkie Collins* (New York: Harper, 1892), p. 109.

52. Tillotson, "Lighter Reading," p. xv; "Sensational School," *Temple Bar*, p. 418.

53. "Sensational School," *Temple Bar*, p. 415.

54. [Mansel], "Sensation Novels," p. 490.

55. In Charles Reade, *Good Stories* (New York: Harper, n.d.), pp. 247-57.

56. "Sensational School," *Temple Bar*, p. 419.

57. "Novels of the Day: Their Writers and Readers," *Fraser's* LXII (August 1860), p. 214.

58. [Mansel], "Sensation Novels," p. 486.

59. "Sensational School," *Temple Bar*, p. 418; "Our Survey of Literature and Science," *Cornhill* VII ( January 1863), p. 136.

60. *Punch*, Preface to vol. XLIV (1863), p. iii.

61. *Punch* XLIV (February 27-March 21, 1863), p. 104.

62. George Henry Lewes, "Farewell Causerie," *Fortnightly* VI (December 1, 1866), p. 894; *Spectator* (February 22, 1862), quoted in Robert A. Colby, "The *Spectator* as Critic," *NCF* (December 1956), p. 186.

63. The subtitle to Reade's *Christie Johnstone* is *A Dramatic Story*. See Phillips, *Sensation Novelists*, p. 128.

64. Collins, Preface to *Basil*, p. iv; see Richard Stang, *The Theory of the Novel in England 1850-1870* (New York: Columbia University Press, 1959), pp. 114-27.

65. Charles Dickens, letter, quoted in Phillips, *Sensation Novelists*, p. 131.

66. Charles Reade, *Foul Play* (Boston: Dana Estes, n.d.), p. 52; Reade, *Griffith Gaunt* (London: Chatto and Windus, 1903), p. 164; Reade, *Bible Characters*, quoted in Burns, *Charles Reade*, p. 75.

67. "Sensational School," *Temple Bar*, p. 419; Henry James, "Miss Braddon," p. 113.

68. Henry James, "Miss Braddon," p. 113; [Oliphant], "Novels" (1867), p. 269. See also "Sensation Novelists: Miss Braddon," *North British Review* XLIII (September 1865), pp. 98-99.

69. Wilkie Collins, *The Moonstone* (Harmondsworth, England: Penguin, 1966), pp. 160-61.

70. [Fitzjames Stephen], "The License of Modern Novelists," *Edinburgh* CVI (July 1857), pp. 125-26.

71. Reade's phrase, quoted in Burns, *Charles Reade*, p. 159.

72. Collins, Preface to *Basil*, p. iv.

73. "The Sensational Williams," *All the Year Round*, pp. 14-15.

74. Ibid., pp. 15-16. See also [Henry Morley], "Something That Shakespeare Lost," *Household Words* (January 17, 1857), pp. 49-52.

75. See Stang, *Theory of the Novel in England*, p. 37.

76. [Oliphant], "Novels" (1867), p. 259.

77. [Margaret Oliphant], "Novels," *Blackwood's* xciv (August 1863), p. 170; [Mansel], "Sensation Novels," p. 492.

78. [Oliphant], "Novels" (1867), p. 263.

79. "Popular Novels," *Fraser's*, p. 256.

80. "Crime in Fiction," *Blackwood's* cxlviii (August 1890), p. 172.

81. Thomas De Quincey, "On Murder Considered as One of the Fine Arts," *Collected Writings* xiii (Edinburgh: Adam and Charles Black, 1890), pp. 72-73; p. 71.

82. [Oliphant], "Novels" (1863), p. 169.

83. J. Herbert Stack, "Some Recent English Novels," *Fortnightly* xv (June 1, 1871), p. 739.

84. Quoted in Burns, *Charles Reade*, p. 286; Burns, p. 224.

85. "Crime in Fiction," *Blackwood's*, pp. 173, 183.

86. Leslie Stephen, "The Decay of Murder," *Cornhill* xx (December 1869), pp. 725-26, 733.

87. Henry James, "Miss Braddon," p. 111.

88. Leslie Stephen, "Decay of Murder," p. 726.

89. [Fitzjames Stephen], "License of Modern Novelists," p. 125; [Mansel], "Sensation Novels," p. 488.

90. See Phillips, *Sensation Novelists*, pp. 96ff.; Lionel Stevenson, *The English Novel* (Boston: Houghton Mifflin, 1960), p. 357.

91. [Mansel], "Sensation Novels," p. 483.

92. E. S. Dallas, *The Gay Science* (London: Chapman and Hall, 1866), ii, 299-300.

93. John Ruskin, "Fiction, Fair and Foul," in *Works* xvi (Boston: Dana Estes, n.d.), pp. 156-58; p. 159; pp. 166, 163.

94. [Mansel], "Sensation Novels," p. 502.

95. "Novels with a Purpose," *Westminster* lxxxii (July 1864), p. 49.

96. Mario Praz, *The Hero in Eclipse in Victorian Fiction* (London: Oxford University Press, 1969), p. 153.

97. "Belles Lettres," *Westminster* (1866), p. 126.

98. M. E. Braddon, *Eleanor's Victory* (New York: Harper, 1863), p. 187.

99. [Margaret Oliphant], "Sensation Novels," *Blackwood's* xci (May 1862), p. 565.

100. *Athenaeum* (September 25, 1841), quoted in Stang, *Theory of the Novel in England*, p. 146.

## Notes to Chapter 2

1. "The Popular Novels of the Year," *Fraser's* lxviii (August 1863), p. 265; "Belles Lettres," *Westminster* lxxxvi (July 1866), p. 126.

2. Anthony Trollope, *Autobiography* (Edinburgh and London: Blackwood, 1883), ii, 41.

3. "Novels with a Purpose," *Westminster* lxxxii (July 1864), p. 27.

4. See Richard Stang, *The Theory of the Novel in England 1850-1870* (New York: Columbia University Press, 1959), p. 58.

5. [Margaret Oliphant], "Novels," *Blackwood's* cii (September 1867), pp. 258, 257.

6. Frances Power Cobbe, "The Morals of Literature," *Fraser's* LXX (July 1864), pp. 131, 129.

7. [H. F. Chorley], "New Novels," *Athenaeum* XXIX (June 2, 1866), pp. 732-33. The target here is Collins' *Armadale*.

8. "Sensation Novelists: Miss Braddon," *North British* XLIII (September 1865), pp. 98, 101, 104.

9. "Crime in Fiction," *Blackwood's* CXLVIII (August 1890), p. 172.

10. [Oliphant], "Novels" (1867), p. 280.

11. "Art and Morality," *Cornhill* XXXII (July 1875), p. 92; "False Morality of Lady Novelists," *National Review* XV (January 1859), pp. 144-45.

12. Wilkie Collins, Preface to *Armadale* (New York: Harper, 1893).

13. Wilkie Collins, "A Petition to the Novel-Writers," in *My Miscellanies* (New York: Harper, 1874), p. 62.

14. [H. L. Mansel], "Sensation Novels," *Quarterly* CXIII (April 1863), pp. 505-6; "Belles Lettres," *Westminster*, p. 126.

15. "Our Novels. The Sensational School," *Temple Bar* XXIX (July 1870), p. 421.

16. "Miss Braddon," *North British*, p. 105; "Sensational School," *Temple Bar*, p. 424.

17. "Sensational School," *Temple Bar*, p. 414.

18. "Miss Braddon," *North British*, p. 98.

19. [Chorley], "New Novels," p. 732.

20. "Sensational School," *Temple Bar*, p. 422.

21. "Our Female Sensation Novelists," from *Christian Remembrancer*, reprinted in Littell's *Living Age* LXXVIII (August 22, 1863), p. 364.

22. E. S. Dallas, *The Gay Science* (London: Chapman and Hall, 1866), II, 297, 298. See also [Oliphant], "Novels" (1867), p. 274.

23. Henry James, "Miss Braddon," in *Notes and Reviews* (Cambridge, Mass.: Dunster House, 1921), pp. 115-16. See also "Miss Braddon," *North British*, pp. 102-3.

24. [Oliphant], "Novels" (1867), pp. 275, 280.

25. Walter C. Phillips, *Dickens, Reade, and Collins, Sensation Novelists* (New York: Columbia University Press, 1919), pp. 109, 91.

26. Ibid., p. 91.

27. See David Masson, *British Novelists and their Styles* (Boston: Willard Small, 1889), pp. 253-54. (Originally published in 1859.)

28. George Henry Lewes, "Realism in Art: Recent German Fiction" (1858), reprinted in Alice R. Kaminsky, ed., *Literary Criticism of George Henry Lewes* (Lincoln, Nebraska: University of Nebraska Press, 1964), p. 87.

29. See Masson, *British Novelists*, pp. 253-56; and George Henry Lewes, *The Principles of Success in Literature* (Boston: Allyn and Bacon, 1891), pp. 82-84. (Originally published in 1865.)

30. Masson, *British Novelists*, pp. 254, 256.

31. See ibid., p. 312: "No more than our metrical Poetry must [the novel] be permitted to degenerate into a ceaseless variation of the speech of Mephistopheles, that men are as miserable as ever, and that the world is all in a mess. . . . accordingly, those occasional prose fictions are to be welcomed which deal with characters of heroic imaginary mould, and which remove us from cities and the crowded haunts of

men." See also [Edward Bulwer-Lytton], "Caxtoniana: A Series of Essays on Life, Literature, and Manners," part XIV, *Blackwood's* XCIII (May 1863), p. 550: "When we come to [the] realm of fiction . . . it is with a desire to escape, for the moment, out of this hard and narrow positive world in which we live. . . . We do not want to see that real life, but its ideal image, in the fable land of art."

32. Masson, *British Novelists*, p. 254; and [Bulwer-Lytton], "Caxtoniana," pp. 552, 556.

33. Lewes, *Principles of Success*, pp. 83, 84; Lewes, "Realism in Art," p. 87.

34. Wilkie Collins, Preface to *Heart and Science* (London: Chatto and Windus, 1890), p. viii.

35. "Popular Novels of the Year," *Fraser's*, p. 266. For more examples of this critical principle, see Kenneth Graham, *English Criticism of the Novel 1865-1900* (Oxford: Clarendon Press, 1965), pp. 21-25.

36. "Miss Braddon," *North British*, p. 100; "Popular Novels of the Year," *Fraser's*, p. 259.

37. "Miss Braddon," *North British*, p. 100; "Popular Novels of the Year," *Fraser's*, p. 261.

38. Lewes, *Principles of Success*, p. 40.

39. G. H. Lewes, "Dickens in Relation to Criticism" (1872), reprinted in Kaminsky, *Literary Criticism*, pp. 97, 98. For a thorough treatment of Dickens and his contemporary critics, see George H. Ford, *Dickens and His Readers* (New York: Norton, 1965), esp. ch. 7, "The Poet and the Critics of Probability."

40. Richard Holt Hutton, *Brief Literary Criticisms* (London: Macmillan, 1906), pp. 53, 56.

41. J. Herbert Stack, "Some Recent English Novels," *Fortnightly* XV (June 1871), p. 743.

42. [Margaret Oliphant], "Charles Reade's Novels," *Blackwood's* CVI (October 1869), p. 510; [Margaret Oliphant], "Novels," *Blackwood's* XCIV (August 1863), p. 170.

43. For a stimulating discussion of this and related matters, see George Levine, "Realism Reconsidered," in John Halperin, ed., *The Theory of the Novel* (New York: Oxford University Press, 1974), esp. p. 252.

44. [Oliphant], "Novels" (1863), p. 170. The target here is Wood's *East Lynne*.

45. "Sensational School," *Temple Bar*, p. 424.

46. [Richard Holt Hutton], "Sensational Novels," *Spectator* XLI (August 8, 1868), pp. 931-32.

47. "Sensational School," *Temple Bar*, p. 424.

48. Charles Reade, *Hard Cash* (Boston and New York: Brainard, n.d.), II, 229-30.

49. Gordon N. Ray, ed., *The Letters and Private Papers of William Makepeace Thackeray* (Cambridge, Mass.: Harvard University Press, 1945), II, 773.

50. *Edinburgh Review* (1850), quoted in Stang, *Theory of the Novel in England*, p. 184.

51. "Sensational School," *Temple Bar*, pp. 412-13, 421.

52. [Hutton], "Sensational Novels," p. 932.

53. Ibid., pp. 931-32.

54. "Sensational School," *Temple Bar*, pp. 416, 421.

55. "Our Female Sensation Novelists," *Living Age*, p. 353.

56. Trollope, *Autobiography* II, 49.

57. See Stang, *Theory of the Novel in England*, pp. 128-30.

58. Dallas, *Gay Science* II, 292-94.

59. Ibid., pp. 294-95.

60. "Our Female Sensation Novelists," *Living Age*, p. 365.

61. Margaret Dalziel, *Popular Fiction 100 Years Ago* (London: Cohen and West, 1957), pp. 168, 169.

62. Dallas, *Gay Science* II, 292.

63. M. E. Braddon, *Lady Audley's Secret* (New York: Dover, 1974), pp. 264-65.

64. See "Popular Novels of the Year," *Fraser's*, p. 258; "Miss Braddon," *North British*, p. 98.

65. Charles Reade, *Griffith Gaunt; or, Jealousy* (London: Chatto and Windus, 1903), p. 228. All quotations from this edition.

66. George Eliot, *Scenes of Clerical Life* (Harmondsworth, England: Penguin, 1973), p. 85. All quotations from this edition.

67. Masson, *British Novelists*, p. 312.

68. Levine, "Realism Reconsidered," p. 252.

69. Dallas, *Gay Science* II, 308.

70. Phillips, *Sensation Novelists*, p. 13.

71. Northrop Frye, "Dickens and the Comedy of Humors," in Ian Watt, ed., *The Victorian Novel* (New York: Oxford University Press, 1971), pp. 49, 57, 68.

72. Stang, *Theory of the Novel in England*, p. 37.

73. George Henry Lewes, "Criticism in Relation to Novels," *Fortnightly* III (December 15, 1865), p. 355.

74. [Hutton], "Sensational Novels," p. 931.

75. Masson, *British Novelists*, p. 255.

76. [Oliphant], "Novels" (1867), p. 265.

77. [Mansel], "Sensation Novels," p. 514; "Popular Novels of the Year," *Fraser's*, p. 263; "Crime in Fiction," *Blackwood's*, p. 189.

78. "Novels with a Purpose," *Westminster*, p. 27.

79. Letter quoted in Malcolm Elwin, *Thackeray* (London: J. Cape, 1932), p. 185.

80. Quoted in Gordon N. Ray, *Thackeray: The Age of Wisdom* (New York: McGraw-Hill, 1958), p. 272.

81. Printed in "Charles Reade's Opinion of Himself and His Opinion of George Eliot," *Bookman* XVIII (November 1903), p. 253.

82. Reprinted in its entirety in ibid., pp. 254-60.

83. Graham, *English Criticism*, p. 19. For him, however, the dialectic is essentially realism vs. idealism.

84. "Sensational School," *Temple Bar*, p. 422.

85. See Laurence Hutton, ed., *Letters of Charles Dickens to Wilkie Collins* (New York: Harper, 1892), p. 27.

86. Michael R. Booth, *English Melodrama* (London: Herbert Jenkins, 1965), pp. 181, 184. On popular fiction, see Dalziel, *Popular Fiction*, p. 172.

87. "Our Female Sensation Novelists," *Living Age*, p. 352.

## Notes to Chapter 3

1. For details, see Malcolm Elwin, *Charles Reade* (London: J. Cape, 1934); and Wayne Burns, *Charles Reade: A Study in Victorian Authorship* (New York: Bookman, 1962).

2. Anthony Trollope, *Autobiography* (Edinburgh and London: Blackwood, 1883), ii, 77.

3. Charles Reade, *Readiana* (Leipzig: Tauchnitz, 1882), p. 144.

4. Burns, *Charles Reade*, p. 202.

5. Quoted in ibid., pp. 187, 186, 58.

6. Charles Reade, *A Terrible Temptation* (Boston and New York: Brainard, circa 1910), p. 221. All quotations from this edition.

7. Burns, *Charles Reade*, p. 192. See also Burns, "More Reade Notebooks," *SP* (October 1945); Emerson Grant Sutcliffe, "Charles Reade's Notebooks," *SP* (January 1930); and Sutcliffe, "Foemina Vera in Charles Reade's Novels," *PMLA* (December 1931).

8. Quoted in Burns, "More Reade Notebooks," p. 834; Sutcliffe, "Foemina Vera," p. 1270; Sutcliffe, "Charles Reade's Notebooks," p. 80.

9. Burns, "More Reade Notebooks," p. 829.

10. Charles Reade, Preface to *A Simpleton* (Boston and New York: Brainard, circa 1910), p. 3; Reade, *Trade Malice*, quoted in Emerson Grant Sutcliffe, "Fact, Realism, and Morality in Reade's Fiction," *SP* (October 1944), p. 585; Reade, Preface to *Hard Cash* (Boston and New York: Brainard, circa 1910).

11. Quoted in Burns, *Charles Reade*, p. 130.

12. Ibid., p. 20.

13. Sutcliffe, "Fact, Realism, and Morality," p. 583.

14. Charles Reade, *It Is Never Too Late To Mend* (Leipzig: Tauchnitz, 1856), ii, 165. All quotations from this edition.

15. Quoted in Burns, *Charles Reade*, p. 155.

16. See Sheila M. Smith, "Propaganda and Hard Facts in Charles Reade's Didactic Novels," *Renaissance and Modern Studies* iv (1960), pp. 135-49.

17. Charles Reade, letter, quoted in Elwin, *Charles Reade*, pp. 112-13.

18. See Smith, "Propaganda and Hard Facts," p. 140.

19. Ibid., p. 139.

20. Burns, *Charles Reade*, p. 168.

21. See ibid., p. 170; and Elwin, *Charles Reade*, pp. 182-83.

22. See Elwin, *Charles Reade*, pp. 166ff.; and Burns, *Charles Reade*, pp. 203-4.

23. Reade, *Readiana*, p. 149.

24. All quotations from the Brainard edition of Reade's *Hard Cash*, unless indicated otherwise.

25. Burns, *Charles Reade*, p. 228.

26. See Charles Reade, *Very Hard Cash*, in *All the Year Round* x (October 3, 1863), pp. 123-24.

27. Burns, *Charles Reade*, p. 217.

28. Reade, *Very Hard Cash*, in *All the Year Round* x, p. 124. This line was edited out of the later versions.

29. Reade, *Very Hard Cash*, in *All the Year Round* IX (August 1, 1863), p. 536. Brainard prudently edits out the capitals.

30. See Walter C. Phillips, *Dickens, Reade, and Collins, Sensation Novelists* (New York: Columbia University Press, 1919), p. 218.

31. See Walter E. Houghton, Introduction to *The Victorian Frame of Mind* (New Haven and London: Yale University Press, 1957).

32. See Kathleen Tillotson, "The Lighter Reading of the Eighteen-Sixties," Introduction to Wilkie Collins, *The Woman in White* (Boston: Houghton Mifflin, 1969), pp. xvi-xx.

33. Compare the treatment of the lunatic asylum in *The Woman in White* with that in *Hard Cash*.

34. Notecard for *Griffith Gaunt*, reproduced in Burns, *Charles Reade*, p. 239.

35. Charles Reade, *Griffith Gaunt; or, Jealousy* (London: Chatto and Windus, 1903), p. 116. All quotations from this edition.

36. Quoted in Elwin, *Charles Reade*, p. 112.

37. Quoted in Burns, *Charles Reade*, p. 269.

38. Laurence Hutton, ed., *Letters of Charles Dickens to Wilkie Collins* (New York: Harper, 1892), pp. 137, 139-40.

39. Quoted in Burns, *Charles Reade*, p. 289.

40. Quoted in ibid., p. 292.

41. Burns, *Charles Reade*, p. 294.

42. See Burns, "The Sheffield Flood: A Critical Study of Charles Reade's Fiction," *PMLA* (June 1948), pp. 686-95.

## Notes to Chapter 4

1. Bret Harte, *Condensed Novels* (Boston: Osgood, 1871), pp. 61-62; pp. 64-65; p. 68.

2. Kathleen Tillotson, "The Lighter Reading of the Eighteen-Sixties," Introduction to Wilkie Collins, *The Woman In White* (Boston: Houghton Mifflin, 1969), p. xiii.

3. [Margaret Oliphant], "Sensation Novels," *Blackwood's* XCI (May 1862), p. 567.

4. "Our Female Sensation Novelists," from *Christian Remembrancer*, reprinted in Littell's *Living Age* LXXVIII (August 22, 1863), p. 354.

5. "The Popular Novels of the Year," *Fraser's* LXVIII (August 1863), p. 262.

6. Henry James, "Miss Braddon," in *Notes and Reviews* (Cambridge, Mass.: Dunster House, 1921), p. 115.

7. "Mrs. Wood and Miss Braddon," from *Examiner*, reprinted in Littell's *Living Age* LXXVII (April 18, 1863), p. 99.

8. "Popular Novels," *Fraser's*, pp. 255-56, 255.

9. Michael R. Booth, *English Melodrama* (London: Herbert Jenkins, 1965), p. 153.

10. The tactful description of his son, Charles W. Wood, in *Memorials of Mrs. Henry Wood*, quoted in Malcolm Elwin, *Victorian Wallflowers* (London: J. Cape, 1934), p. 235. Elwin is the only readily available source of biographical data.

11. Quoted in ibid., p. 245.

12. J. D. Jump, "Weekly Reviewing in the Eighteen-Sixties," *Review of English Studies* III (July 1952), p. 261.

13. Mrs. Henry Wood, *Verner's Pride* (Leipzig: Tauchnitz, 1863), I, 68. All quotations from this edition.

14. See Booth, *English Melodrama*, pp. 153-54.

15. Mrs. Henry Wood, *East Lynne* (London and Glasgow: Collins, n.d.), pp. 291, 225. All quotations from this edition.

16. For the connections between *East Lynne* and the Divorce Law of 1857, which provided "legal punishment" for the adulteress in the form of a second wife, see Margaret M. Maison, "Adulteresses in Agony," *Listener* LXV (January 19, 1961), pp. 133-34. In the novel, Mr. Carlyle sues for divorce but does not think it right to remarry until after the reported death of his former wife. Because of the divorce, however, he is not legally a bigamist.

17. See Booth, *English Melodrama*, p. 79.

18. W. B. Maxwell, *Time Gathered* (New York and London: Appleton-Century, 1938), p. 269.

19. Henry James, "Miss Braddon," p. 116.

20. For biographical details, see Michael Sadleir, *Things Past* (London: Constable, 1944); Norman Donaldson, Introduction to M. E. Braddon, *Lady Audley's Secret* (New York: Dover, 1974); and Robert Lee Wolff, *Sensational Victorian: The Life and Fiction of Mary Elizabeth Braddon* (New York: Garland, 1979).

21. Letter to Bulwer-Lytton, in Robert Lee Wolff, "Devoted Disciple: The Letters of Mary Elizabeth Braddon to Sir Edward Bulwer-Lytton, 1862-1873," *Harvard Library Bulletin* XXII (January and April, 1974), p. 10.

22. Letter to Bulwer-Lytton, in ibid., p. 12.

23. M. E. Braddon, *Birds of Prey* (New York: Harper, 1867), p. 139; *Charlotte's Inheritance* (New York: Harper, 1868), p. 84. All quotations from these editions.

24. Quoted in Edmund Yates, *Fifty Years of London Life* (New York: Harper, 1885), pp. 336-37.

25. M. E. Braddon, *The Doctor's Wife* (London: Simpkin, 1890), p. 42.

26. See Sadleir, *Things Past*, p. 70.

27. "Mrs. Wood and Miss Braddon," *Living Age*, p. 100.

28. H. A. Page [A. H. Japp], "The Morality of Literary Art," *Contemporary* V (June 1867), p. 178.

29. "Our Female Sensation Novelists," *Living Age*, pp. 367, 366, 364-66.

30. "Sensation Novelists: Miss Braddon," *North British Review* XLIII (September 1865), p. 96. For a feminist interpretation of *Lady Audley* and other sensation novels, see Elaine Showalter, *A Literature of Their Own* (Princeton: Princeton University Press, 1977), pp. 153-81.

31. M. E. Braddon, *Lady Audley's Secret*, pp. 35, 186. All quotations from the Dover edition.

32. M. E. Braddon, *Aurora Floyd* (New York: Frank Leslie, n.d.), pp. 25, 36. All quotations from this edition.

33. "Our Novels. The Sensational School," *Temple Bar* XXIX (July 1870), p. 415.

34. "Our Female Sensation Novelists," *Living Age*, p. 368.

35. Sadleir, *Things Past*, p. 79.

36. M. E. Braddon, *John Marchmont's Legacy* (Leipzig: Tauchnitz, 1864), I, 176, 181. All quotations from this edition.

37. [Margaret Oliphant], "Novels," *Blackwood's* CII (September 1867), p. 280.

38. Ibid., p. 275.

39. "Mrs. Wood and Miss Braddon," *Living Age*, p. 99.

40. [H. L. Mansel], "Sensation Novels," *Quarterly* CXIII (April 1863), p. 491.

41. Page, *Contemporary*, p. 178.

42. Sadleir in *Things Past* offers the opinion that "for forty years at least it [*Lady Audley's Secret*] so dominated its author's life that she had persistently to write more or less to its pattern" (p. 74); the opposite opinion—that she deserted the sensation novel after 1873—is argued in Benjamin M. Nyberg, "The Novels of Mary Elizabeth Braddon: A Reappraisal of the Author of *Lady Audley's Secret*" (unpublished doctoral dissertation, University of Colorado, 1965).

43. "Miss Braddon: An Enquiry," *Academy* LVIII (October 14, 1899), p. 431.

44. Margaret Oliphant, *The Victorian Age of English Literature* (New York: Tait, 1892), pp. 494-95. Although Mrs. Oliphant has mellowed, her style has not improved.

## Notes to Chapter 5

1. T. S. Eliot, "Wilkie Collins and Charles Dickens," in Ian Watt, ed., *The Victorian Novel* (London: Oxford University Press, 1971), p. 136.

2. Preface (1861), reprinted as an appendix to Wilkie Collins, *The Woman in White* (Boston: Houghton Mifflin, 1969), p. 501. All quotations from this edition.

3. Unsigned review (1861), reprinted in Norman Page, ed., *Wilkie Collins: The Critical Heritage* (London and Boston: Routledge and Kegan Paul, 1974), p. 105.

4. Henry James, "Miss Braddon," in *Notes and Reviews* (Cambridge, Mass.: Dunster House, 1921), p. 112; Anthony Trollope, *Autobiography* (Edinburgh and London: Blackwood, 1883), II, 81-82.

5. *Saturday Review* (1860), reprinted in Page, *Critical Heritage*, p. 84.

6. Wilkie Collins, *Woman in White*, p. 501; Preface (added in 1883) to *Heart and Science* (London: Chatto and Windus, 1890), p. vii.

7. [Margaret Oliphant], "Sensation Novels," *Blackwood's* XCI (May 1862), pp. 567-68.

8. U. C. Knoepflmacher, "The Counterworld of Victorian Fiction and *The Woman in White*," in Jerome H. Buckley, ed., *The Worlds of Victorian Fiction* (Cambridge, Mass., and London: Harvard University Press, 1975), pp. 352, 366-67.

9. George Levine, "Realism Reconsidered," in John Halperin, ed., *The Theory of the Novel* (New York: Oxford University Press, 1974), pp. 248-49.

10. Wilkie Collins, *No Name* (New York: Harper, 1873), p. 9. All quotations from this edition.

11. Geoffrey Tillotson, *Criticism and the Nineteenth Century* (London: Athlone, 1951), p. 243.

12. Unsigned review (1866), reprinted in Page, *Critical Heritage*, p. 149.

13. Robert Ashley, *Wilkie Collins* (London: A. Barker, 1952), p. 81. See also Geoffrey Tillotson, *Criticism*, pp. 241-42.

14. Quoted in Richard Stang, *The Theory of the Novel in England, 1850-1870* (New York: Columbia University Press, 1959), p. 200.

15. See Kenneth Robinson, *Wilkie Collins* (London: Bodley Head, 1951), pp. 128-36.

16. M. E. Braddon, *Eleanor's Victory* (New York: Harper, 1863), p. 44. All quotations from this edition.

17. Wilkie Collins, *Armadale* (New York: Harper, 1893), p. 146. All quotations from this edition.

18. See S. M. Ellis, *Wilkie Collins, LeFanu and Others* (New York: Richard Smith, 1931), p. 37, for the original of Mrs. Oldershaw.

19. [H. F. Chorley], "New Novels," *Athenaeum* xxxix (June 2, 1866), p. 732.

20. *Saturday Review* (1866), reprinted in Page, *Critical Heritage*, p. 151.

21. Collins, *No Name*, p. 418; *Armadale*, pp. 256, 107.

22. Page, *Critical Heritage*, p. 154. The metaphysical problem is from the play *Our American Cousin* by Tom Taylor.

23. Wilkie Collins, *The Moonstone* (Harmondsworth, England: Penguin, 1966), p. 333. All quotations from this edition.

24. Collins, *No Name*, p. 346; *Armadale*, p. 232.

25. [Alexander Smith], "Novels and Novelists of the Day," *North British* xxxviii (February 1863), p. 98.

26. Ibid., p. 98.

27. George Grella, "Murder and Manners: The Formal Detective Novel," *Novel* (Fall, 1970), p. 47.

28. M. E. Braddon, *Lady Audley's Secret* (New York: Dover, 1974), p. 246.

**Notes to Chapter 6**

1. George Augustus Sala, "On the 'Sensational' in Literature and Art," *Belgravia* iv (1868), p. 453.

2. "The Sensational Williams," *All the Year Round* xi (February 13, 1864), p. 14.

3. M. E. Braddon, *The Doctor's Wife* (London: Simpkin, 1890), p. 10.

4. Sala, "On the 'Sensational'," p. 453.

5. [H. L. Mansel], "Sensation Novels," *Quarterly* cxiii (April 1863), p. 488. Mansel thoroughly covers the dregs of sensationalism.

6. See Sala, "On the 'Sensational'," p. 458.

7. Ibid., p. 455.

8. [Margaret Oliphant], "Sensation Novels," *Blackwood's* xci (May 1862), pp. 577, 580.

9. Charles Reade, Preface to *Hard Cash* (Boston and New York: Brainard, circa 1910), I, 3.

10. [Mansel], "Sensation Novels," p. 487.

11. Review of *The Queen's English, Edinburgh* CXX (July 1864), p. 53. For more examples of parody, see Kathleen Tillotson, "The Lighter Reading of the Eighteen-Sixties," Introduction to Wilkie Collins, *The Woman in White* (Boston: Houghton Mifflin, 1969), pp. xii-xv.

12. "Mrs. Wood and Miss Braddon," from *Examiner*, reprinted in Littell's *Living Age* LXXVII (April 18, 1863), p. 100.

13. Anthony Trollope, *Autobiography* (Edinburgh and London: Blackwood, 1883), II, 197.

14. H.J.W. Milley, "*The Eustace Diamonds* and *The Moonstone*," SP XXXVI (October 1939), pp. 651-63.

15. Anthony Trollope, *The Eustace Diamonds* (Harmondsworth, England: Penguin, 1969), p. 555. All quotations from this edition.

16. H. A. Page [A. H. Japp], "The Morality of Literary Art," *Contemporary* V (June 1867), pp. 179, 178, 179.

17. George Eliot, *Felix Holt* (Harmondsworth, England: Penguin, 1972), pp. 97, 104. All quotations from this edition.

18. Thomas Hardy, *Desperate Remedies* (New York and London: Harper, 1905), p. 1. All quotations from this edition.

19. Letter from Hardy to Macmillan (August 7, 1871) accompanying the manuscript of *Under the Greenwood Tree*, reprinted in Laurence Lerner and John Holmstrom, eds., *Thomas Hardy and His Readers* (New York: Barnes and Noble, 1968), p. 17.

20. Florence Emily Hardy, *The Life of Thomas Hardy* (London: Macmillan, 1962), pp. 62, 85.

21. Ibid., p. 229.

22. Peter Brooks, *The Melodramatic Imagination* (New Haven: Yale University Press, 1976), p. 20.

23. Ibid., pp. 24ff.

24. Thomas Hardy, *Tess of the d'Urbervilles* (New York: Norton, 1965), p. 213. All quotations from this edition.

25. Thomas Hardy, *The Return of the Native* (New York: Signet, 1959), p. 71. All quotations from this edition.

26. Charles Heywood, "*The Return of the Native* and Miss Braddon's *The Doctor's Wife*: A Probable Source," NCF XVIII (June 1963), pp. 91-94.

27. Braddon, *Doctor's Wife*, pp. 26, 65.

28. Thomas Hardy, *Jude the Obscure* (Boston: Houghton Mifflin, 1965), pp. 270-71. All quotations from this edition.

29. Thomas Hardy, *Collected Poems* (London: Macmillan, 1920), p. 7.

30. Albert J. Guerard, *Thomas Hardy* (London: Oxford University Press, 1949), p. ix.

31. Irving Howe, *Thomas Hardy* (New York: Macmillan, 1967), p. 66.

32. Thomas Hardy, *Far from the Madding Crowd* (Greenwich, Conn.: Fawcett, 1960), p. 114. All quotations from this edition.

33. Lerner and Holmstrom, *Hardy and His Readers*, p. 17.

34. *Spectator* (January 23, 1892), reprinted in ibid., p. 71.

35. E. S. Dallas, *The Gay Science* (London: Chapman and Hall, 1866), II, 294.

36. Hardy, *Tess*, p. 192.

37. Lerner and Holmstrom, *Hardy and His Readers*, pp. 132, 109, 113.

38. Hardy, Prefatory Note to *Desperate Remedies*, added in 1896, p. vi.

39. "Chikkin Hazard," *Punch* LIV (March 7-June 27, 1868), p. 133. The title refers to Reade's *Foul Play*.

40. On Ouida, see Walter C. Phillips, *Dickens, Reade, and Collins, Sensation Novelists* (New York: Columbia University Press, 1919), pp. 30-34.

41. See Richard Stang, *The Theory of the Novel in England, 1850-1870* (New York: Columbia University Press, 1959), pp. 91-97.

42. "Novels with a Purpose," *Westminster* LXXXII (July 1864), p. 27.

43. [Oliphant], "Sensation Novels" (1862), p. 564.

44. Ibid., p. 564.

45. "The Sensation Novel," *Argosy* XVIII (1874), p. 142.

# Index

**Library of Congress Cataloging in Publication Data**

Hughes, Winifred, 1948-
   The maniac in the cellar.

   Includes index.
   1. English fiction—19th century—History and
criticism.    2. Sensationalism in literature.
3. Popular literature—Great Britain—History and
criticism.    I. Title.
PR878.S44H8      823'.8'0916      80-7530
ISBN 0-691-06441-5